THE
TOY
STORY

THE
TOY
STORY

The Life and Times of Inventor
FRANK HORNBY

Anthony McReavy

EBURY
PRESS

First published in the UK in 2002

© Anthony McReavy 2002

1 3 5 7 9 10 8 6 4 2

Anthony McReavy has asserted his right to be identified as author of this
work under the Copyright, Designs and Patents Act 1988

Ebury Press
Random House, 20 Vauxhall Bridge Road, London SW1V 2SA

Random House Australia Pty Limited
20 Alfred Street, Milsons Point, Sydney, New South Wales 2061, Australia

Random House New Zealand Limited
18 Poland Road, Glenfield, Auckland 10, New Zealand

Random House (Pty) Limited
Endulini, 5A Jubilee Road, Parktown 2193, South Africa

The Random House Group Limited Reg. No. 954009

A CIP catalogue record for this book is available from the British Library

ISBN 0 09 188117 X

Jacket design by the Senate
Typeset by Andrea Purdie
Printed and bound in Great Britain by Mackays of Chatham plc
Papers used by Ebury Press are natural, recyclable products made from wood grown in
sustainable forests.

Contents

Acknowledgements

Perhaps appropriately, this book about toys is dedicated to two little boys, Sam and Will. The least of their gifts to me has been the opportunity to get down on my hands and knees and play with toys once more. With this, as with so many things, my partner Karen has been as patient as she is supportive - thank you.

Almost as patient have been Thomas and Hannah at Ebury Press. Thanks also to Peter & Susi Williams for their help, kindness and support, without which I would have struggled even more than usual. Many Meccano, Dinky and Hornby enthusiasts at home and abroad have patiently guided me and directed me to sources and material, and they are sadly too numerous to mention, but not to remember. Also thanks to Pauline Greeves for her recollections of Uncle Frank, Matthew Parker for his encouragement, Suzanne & Ivor for being so accommodating, and to Clare Tunstall at the National Galleries on Merseyside Business Archive. Finally, a special mention to Lydia, whose contribution was simply immeasurable.

Introduction

The Empire of Meccanoland

The favourite toys of my two small boys are small German-made play figures about two inches high. They are cleverly made, with a large amount of detail for little hands, lots of accessories and clothing that can be used to create whole worlds of adventure. They are well designed, with nicely observed and often charming features, and they clearly appeal to my children's imaginations.

I like them too. At times I linger too long over them when I'm supposed to be putting them away, fastidiously reuniting different figures with their equipment and accessories while trying to imagine what small boys' game had demanded that they wear each other's clothes. They come in all the incarnations a boy could want – fireman, pirate, cowboy, redskin, knight, construction worker . . . These are the figures which populate the sunny uplands of boys' imaginations. At least they did mine, because, if I'm honest, what I like most about these tiny plastic men and women is not their design, their quality or their appeal to children; what I like most about them is that I used to play with them myself. I can relate to these little toys in a way that I find hard to do with Pokémon or mutant space rangers. When I see my boys playing with them I am suddenly reminded of games I used to play, and that were so important to me, and yet treacherously I haven't thought of them for thirty years. It's one of the times when being a parent makes you feel young rather than old.

Shared memories like this probably owe as much to my fear for the loss of innocence in my children as to my delight at seeing them enjoy toys that I played with in what surely *was* a more innocent time. For one thing, there was nothing like the range of toys that are available now. Those that we did have were pretty much the same as our parents' – dolls, soldiers, guns and swords, bats, balls, train sets and tea-sets. Even those toys that were 'new' had prewar roots. Action Man was just a small doll or a large toy soldier, and Scalextric was a train set with cars. By the 1970s, however, the toy shop was already a very different world from that of my parents' generation. Women's groups had been campaigning about the ludicrous proportions of Barbie's figure that appeared to promote both a sexist ideal of femininity, and unhealthy images of women's bodies to young girls. Similarly, in the wake of the Vietnam War Action Man or its American ally GI Joe had been the target of campaigns to promote 'affirmative toys' that did not encourage militarism or violence.

Other concerns centred on the increasing commercialisation of childhood, and the ways in which children were being targeted by advertising – particularly at Christmas. The friendly toy shops carrying 'traditional' toys were already on the road that would lead to the stacked-high, priced-low toy warehouses of the 1990s.

By the 1960s the playroom had already become a commercial battleground. One of the main charges was that toys were no longer promoting the kind of values our parents wanted, or recognised and valued from their own upbringing. The other was that the world of toys had become too real, and that this was threatening the innocence of childhood itself.

Such loss of innocence coincided with the decline of those toys that bridged the generations, and that parents remembered from their own childhoods. Hornby's three greatest brands – Meccano, the Hornby train sets, and Dinky Toys – were three examples. They won for themselves a special place in the toy shops of the world, becoming some of the most successful toys in the history of the industry. Their success spanned generations from grandfather to father to son (since they were aimed almost exclusively at boys) across the world. Many never lost the love of model-making, engineering or trains that these toys fostered. As they grew older their interests in Meccano or model-making matured. When some became scientists or engineers in later life they took with them the skills they had learned playing with their toys. Many even took the toys themselves. Meccano in particular was a feature of many research laboratories and workshops, used to make models and prototypes of everything from computers to cars. It was a testament to the success of Meccano's inventor in producing a system which taught children the principles of mechanics and engineering in a realistic and accurate way. It was also an indication of the affection and gratitude many of these children felt for their teacher. Yet within thirty years of the death of the man behind Meccano, Hornby trains and Dinky Toys, their futures were far from certain.

As the 1960s progressed, many of the toys which had specifically been designed and marketed to develop, promote and inculcate values and skills that adults wanted their children to have in both childhood and later life were struggling to hold their own in the market. Well-crafted wooden construction sets or educational toys were gradually moving out of shop windows in favour of more modern, futuristic or glamorous toys. Sometimes they were evicted from the shop altogether, ending up as refugees in craft shops or specialist hobby shops. Then the companies themselves were sold, restructured or disappeared. By the early 1960s Meccano, makers of the eponymous construction sets, the toy trains and the Dinky range, was in serious financial trouble. In part this was due to a worldwide recession, but it was also due to poor management at Meccano's famous Binns Road headquarters. In 1964 with a huge overdraft and estimated trading losses of nearly a quarter of a million pounds the directors voted to accept the takeover bid of the company's famous competitor Lines Brothers, owners of the Triang range of toy trains. The takeover, for £781,000, was agreed to at a meeting on 14 February 1964. Frank Hornby's son Roland and his sister-in-law Una were removed from the board as the Hornby inheritance crashed down around them.

The situation was no better across the Atlantic. In 1967 A. C. Gilbert, the American manufacturer of Meccano's US counterpart the Erector Set, died. His company was sold shortly afterwards. Both Hornby and Gilbert had produced toys to educate and amuse children, while giving them skills which would equip them for adult life in science or industry. Toys for girls that offered a similar grounding – kitchen playsets or dolls that would prepare them for motherhood – were also losing ground in the marketplace. Partly they were the victims of the trend that would see educational toy makers like Playskool and Fisher-Price bought up by giants such as Hasbro and Mattel, and the broadly educational toy become increasingly out of favour. There were changes afoot that seemed to threaten the values that such toys and their makers had appealed to. Companies were changing hands and the map of the toy world was being redrawn. The toy industry was no longer insulated from the realities of the wider business world. Nor were its customers, the children.

Yet these toys were falling foul of more than just the economics of the industry and the consequent takeovers. For one thing they were competing for space on increasingly over-populated toy shelves. Changes in ideas about play, childhood and children's development had led to increasingly child-centred approaches to a whole range of issues from education and leisure to material culture and manufactures. This child-centred approach had been gathering pace for well over a century – a product of and a stimulus to many of the reforms of public health, employment law and education of the nineteenth century. Manufacturers had been quick to recognise that children constituted a growing market, and one which they could engage with more directly. As living standards rose and the twentieth century gathered pace, children came to exercise more control over how they spent their growing leisure time, what they occupied themselves with and even what they spent their new-found pocket money on.

This autonomy was itself new. For well over half a century manufacturers like Hornby had produced and marketed toys that appealed to parents as much as children. They reflected adult life and promised parents that playing with them would prepare their children for it, while at the same time letting them enjoy a familiar, protected childhood. Moreover it was parents who bought the toys, usually at Christmas. It was important, therefore, that these toys appealed to parents, and that they felt good about giving them to their children. Naturally, parents responded most to those toys with which they were familiar and comfortable, and which embodied acceptable values.

Trains, dolls, soldiers, kitchen sets, construction kits all reflected nineteenth- and early-twentieth-century ideas about childhood, child rearing and the values that children should acquire to equip them for adulthood. But many of these toys were no more timeless than the values they promoted or that created them, and their decline reflects the changes in society which underpinned their invention, manufacture and successful promotion. Dolls and tea-sets prepared girls for the role of mother and homemaker at a time when any other future for adult women was, if not unimaginable, certainly not expected. Similarly, boys' toys encouraged male values of strength, competition and even aggression. Yet a succession of increasingly bloody wars and growing fears about crime and violence in society led to questions about whether toy soldiers and weapons were appropriate for young boys.

Construction sets had promised to prepare boys to become scientists and engineers at a time when the great successes of

Victorian science and industry had opened up a modern world of seemingly endless technological progress, and one in which adults still had great faith. These toys allowed parents to communicate directly with their children, and to share some of their beliefs, their opinions on what was good, and their cherished memories of what was enjoyable, amusing and positive. Adults were still in control of the free time of their children.

In the 1950s, however, things began to change. In 1951 Hasbro ran the first advert for a toy on US television: Mr Potato Head. Manufacturers were now looking to appeal to the children themselves through television, sidestepping their parents. Mattel took advertising on the *Mickey Mouse Club* in 1955, setting in motion a trend that would culminate in the successful TV and movie tie-ins of the 1980s and 1990s. By then adults would increasingly be relegated to the role of providers of funds, rather than selectors of purchases, as children sought the latest must-have item.

Moreover, the current generation of adults were questioning the roles prescribed for them by their own parents. The women's movement was far from convinced that domestic values and skills were the only ones that young girls needed to be happy and fulfilled in adult life and rapid technological change meant that skills learned in childhood would soon become redundant. As one historian has put it, 'The erector sets and baby dolls that had trained children to assume adult roles made no sense to parents who no longer knew what to train their children to become.'[1]

In the space of less than forty years things had changed radically. By the 1930s Frank Hornby's Meccano had swept the world. It had become one of the world's most popular toys selling hundreds of thousands of kits in its own right, but also spawning hundreds of imitators, keen to cash in on the huge popularity in construction toys which Meccano was spearheading. Over one-third of its sales were abroad, averaging £137,000 per annum, almost a third of total British toy exports.[2] The company had an empire on which the sun never set, with agents in Africa, Australia, North and South America, the Indies, the Middle East and Europe.

In promoting his toy Hornby had developed a highly effective and innovative business style. His Binns Road factory produced three household names, each toy a classic: Meccano, the train sets with which his name is still closely associated, particularly in Britain, and Dinky Toys. Meccano in particular had become so successful that it was a byword for construction toys. In litigation for infringement of copyright in 1953 the defendant had claimed that the use of the word 'Meccano' could not be a breach of copyright since

> 'Meccano' is given as the Italian word for metal
> constructional kits in the authoritative Italian dictionary
> by Palazzi (Milan, 1939), and since moreover according
> to our translator – whose knowledge of the Italian
> language is outstanding – the expression has become
> completely common usage in the language, it seems to us
> your request goes too far.[3]

The company's uncompromising response was in itself illustrative of just how big Meccano had become as a product, and a brand.

> Your translator's argument that the Italian language has
> no other expression than Meccano for metal building
> outfits overlooks the fact that there were no
> constructional outfits of this kind until Meccano . . . The
> inclusion of the word in the Italian dictionary by Palazzi
> does not in any way alter the position, as he is also
> infringing our rights, and this would have been pointed
> out had we been aware of it.

The word was removed from the next edition of Palazzi's Italian dictionary. Even so, it was clear that Meccano was now such a powerful and famous brand that it had been identified with a whole genre. Frank Hornby's little punched strips of metal held together with bolts had entered the public consciousness the world over.

It had done so not only as a toy, but also as a way of thinking about construction in general. The *New English Dictionary* of 1933 recorded 'Meccano' as a copyrighted trademark and brand name, but also pointed out that it had become 'now commonly applied to a set of metal pieces, nuts, bolts, etc., and tools, specially designed for constructing small models of buildings, machines or other engineering apparatus; any portion of such a set; a toy intended to develop a child's constructive instincts'. It went on to note that the word had also come to be used figuratively. Probably the first such use was in Rebecca West's *Strange Necessity*, in which a character described H. G. Wells's *First Men in the Moon* as 'the complete Meccano set for the Mind'.[4] Meccano had become a description not just of toys, or even a particular kind of mechanical model, but of a whole way of seeing and (re-)creating the world. This was the realisation of Frank Hornby's dream.

He had made a whole new world of play and imaginative creation, Meccanoland, in which young boys became men through playing with Hornby's toys. 'Some boys have lived in Meccanoland for more than twenty years', explained the company's promotional literature,

> and the longer they live there the happier they are. Every day more and more boys are crowding into the country, eager to learn of its wonders. The moment they arrive they feel at home, and they take their places and set to work with a will. They know that they will have the time of their lives; that they will have more fun than they have ever had before . . . healthy boys' fun – fun that makes them glad to be alive; fun that strengthens their characters, sets their brains working, and teaches them something that will turn them into successful men.[5]

This world, populated by boys in short trousers making 'a most topping lot of models', was entirely in keeping with the hopes of Meccano's avuncular inventor. Meccano was a new kind of toy, and the inhabitant of his brave new Meccanoland was a new kind of boy..

1

The Birth of Childhood

Frank Hornby was born in 1863 and died in 1936. His life therefore coincided almost exactly with the Golden Age of children's literature that had begun in the 1860s with the publication of Lewis Carroll's *Through the Looking Glass*, and drew to a close between the wars with the publication of A. A. Milne's last Winnie the Pooh stories, *Now We Are Six*, in 1928. His lifetime saw the publication of stories that would become emblematic of childhood and innocence: *Little Women*, *The Wind in the Willows*, *The Tale of Peter Rabbit*, *The Just So Stories*, *Pollyanna* – so many classics from *The Railway Children* to *Worzel Gummidge*. In the space of this brief span childhood blossomed. Some have even argued that the idea of childhood as we know it began with the nineteenth century. To some extent this is perhaps true since so much of what we now associate with childhood exploded into life then. Yet many of the seeds had been sown much earlier, and as with so many things it was simply that the Victorians bent them to their will.

It is perhaps appropriate to describe the heightened awareness and prominence of childhood during this period in floral terms since it was the metaphor of the garden that came to epitomise childhood. Whether it was the cultivated, manicured, clipped garden of the Victorian schoolhouse with its regimentation and serried ranks, or the arcadian, free, innocent Eden of the kindergarten (literally the children's garden), it was well tended and controlled. Yet it was an enchanted garden, a magical country; a charming hundred-acre wood. It was home to cunning foxes and bears of very little brain, toads in motor-cars poop-pooping past mice in teapots, rabbits in breeches and little girls in pinafores. This was a garden that had matured in only a couple of generations. Yet corners of it are as fragrant and fresh today as they were a century ago.

Of course, this new view of childhood and children was not simply one conjured by writers. It owed its existence to storytellers and educationalists; doctors, social reformers, anthropologists, sociologists, politicians, film-makers, parents – and toy makers. And it developed from a number of social and economic forces as much as it was invented or conjured by creative minds. This same brief period saw the introduction of toy brands and genres of toys that would become famous around the world, many as well known and loved by today's children as they were by those of their great-great-grandparents.

Toys and books largely constituted the first products mass-produced for the children's market. Household names in both literature and toy manufacture sprang up, all the while experimenting with new styles and forms. This in turn broadened the market as writers and manufacturers came to understand the range and depth of children's tastes, and the idea that children regarded the world differently, and consequently had their own distinct requirements.

It is perhaps not coincidental that, growing up when he did, Hornby should make his name creating magical miniature worlds for children to play in, every bit as ingenious as Carroll's, or as charming as Milne's. The world was waking up to the idea of childhood and beginning to see children with new eyes. The result was an outpouring of children's stories, plays, toys and games that would outlive their first lucky recipients. By the time of his death on the eve of the Second World War Frank Hornby's contribution to the imaginative world of children was every bit as significant as those of his literary contemporaries. Hornby has a special place in the story of childhood. First, of course, he invented three icons of the nursery or playroom in Meccano, Dinky toys and his eponymous train sets. Each in its own way helped shape the childhoods of countless children. Secondly, a generation of children had their path to adulthood determined by his toys. Meccano, and to a lesser extent the model-making of the trains and Dinky toys, awakened an interest in science, industry and manufacturing that was almost single-handedly responsible for generations of engineers, inventors, architects and scientists. Lastly, and most often overlooked, Hornby spoke quietly but forcefully to thousands of children in the pages of the *Meccano Magazine*. There was a time before the Second World War during which it was the most popular boys' magazine in Britain. It extolled the power and magnificence of science and technology, all the while capturing the imagination with articles on natural

3

history, geography and such cutting-edge wonders as radar or the possibility of space flight.

This, then, is the story of childhood and children as much as it is the story of one man's life. It is about the stuff of childhood – the toys, rhymes, books and games that burst into the lives of children with such colour in little under a century. They did so with such force and energy that it is almost impossible for us to think of childhood today without picturing one or other of them. Such was the importance of the one-time meat-importer's clerk from Liverpool that images of short-trousered small boys hunkered down excitedly around toy trains or Dinky toys have become synonymous with the concept of childhood. Hornby grew up at a time when such a concept was only just finding its feet. As an adult he led it by the hand into brave new worlds of previously unimagined possibilities. These worlds were expansive, limited only by imagination, and the views stretched out all the way to adulthood – and beyond.

Hornby Trains

Evelyn Waugh regarded children (including his own) with bemused contempt. He felt they were simply poor quality miniature adults. 'I can only see them', he wrote, 'as defective adults; feckless, destructive, frivolous, sensual, humourless.'[1] Though in the twentieth century he was increasingly out of step with prevailing modern thinking on children he was expressing a view of children and childhood that stretched back centuries.

Historians have argued that this kind of view of childhood as no different from other stages of development, one in which children were simply improperly formed adults, was the dominant medieval view, and one which lasted until the nineteenth century. It has been argued that the idea owes its origins to the Middle Ages, when children died early and spent much of their brief lives living with adults struggling against the same great forces of death, poverty and disease. In the view of historian J. H. Plumb:

> There was no separate world of childhood. Children shared the same games with adults, the same toys, the same fairy stories. They lived their lives together, never apart. The coarse village festivals depicted by Breughel, showing men and women besotted with drink, groping for each other with unbridled lust, have children eating and drinking with the adults. Even in the soberer pictures of wedding feasts and dances the children are enjoying themselves alongside their elders, doing the same things.[2]

According to this view, if the experiences of childhood and adults were not identical they were very similar. Their lives were contiguous, and while their experiences seemed to share the same boundaries of life, death and survival there was little notion of childhood until the Victorian age. Children apparently had little to distinguish them from adults. Their clothes were simply smaller versions of those of their adult contemporaries, and any particular or exclusive material culture – literature or toys for example – was almost non-existent.[3]

But this view is misleading. The reality is that from medieval times onwards there *were* notions of childhood as a distinct and separate phase. Shakespeare identified seven ages of man, of which three (babyhood, childhood and adolescence) are distinct from adulthood. The Church and state both distinguished between children and adults, identifying the beginning of the teenage years as the start of adulthood. And if children are absent from most written records they do still feature in a significant number, from coroners' rolls to miracle stories, both of which testify to the unique value and importance of children to adults, including but not limited to their parents.[4] Alongside these ideas grew a nascent children's culture which included both literature and toys. By the turn of the fourteenth century model knights were on sale in London (cast in moulds and therefore capable of being mass-produced). The beginnings of children's literature probably appeared at about the same time. Sigimund Feyerabend, a German publisher, is usually credited with the first children's book, *The Book of Art and Instruction for Young People Filled with Legend and Fables and Folk Tales with Illustrations* (1578). The book was simplified to encourage children to comprehend and appreciate both the subject matter and the idea of reading. It also had moral endings, and was therefore broadly educational in another way. In England, however, children's literature probably had earlier roots in the ribald romances and folk tales which told of Fitzwarin, Eustace the Monk, Hereward the Wake and, of course, Robin Hood. The stories of Fulk Fitzwarin and Eustace the Monk date from around the thirteenth century, and the earliest tales of Robin Hood from around the fifteenth. Many of these were the stuff of the chapbooks and flysheets which were the cheap precursors of magazines and which could consist of political or religious tracts, scurrilous polemics, short fictions and romances or rhymes and fables.

Peter and Iona Opie have also argued that much of this material had a serious role to play in childhood. Modern nursery rhymes often have their roots in these folk rhymes and tales, and they rehearse timeless myths of quest, magic, conflicts between good and evil and other universal themes. This literature schooled children in the important themes of their culture while also providing them with references they could use to understand it. The morals of these tales explain what is good and bad, and even illustrate ways of achieving success by outlining positive human characteristics (or monstrous ones which lead to disaster). Some of these folk tales, such as 'The Friar and the Boy' or the tale of the Swan Knight, even have child protagonists, underlining the point that at a certain level they can be understood as tools with which the young audience could better set about understanding the world and their place in it.[5]

They were also important antecedents in what could be considered one of the great achievements of Victorian culture: the creation of a vibrant and richly textured children's culture, centred largely around the immense variety of brilliant and beautiful children's books had at its root the preservation of these tales, and the tradition of telling them, especially to children. The preservation of these folk traditions together with the creation of a new kind of literature based on them drew children and adults together in a celebration of the ideas of innocence, delight and wonder that became synonymous with childhood. This 'communion of the children's book', as one historian has called it, was one of the central elements in a new conception of the rites of childhood. It was only natural that, just as books tapped into atavistic tendencies towards storytelling and mythmaking as a way of understanding the world, so toys and games would be reworked into new forms, recognising their role in development.[6]

Books did not simply provide occasions for social interaction, of course. They are powerful means of communication and therefore also useful as the tools for social action. The spread of books into new areas of the population was no less radical because these new groups were defined in terms of their age rather than their social status or class. Books offered a new freedom in terms of the imaginary worlds they described, but also, and more profoundly, in terms of the new ideas about childhood they revealed, promoted and responded to. Books were as liberating for children as they had been for adults during the Renaissance or the Enlightenment.

Many books, particularly before the Victorian period, were written in order to be read to children. Books for children to read to themselves presupposed a degree of education and literacy that was still a preserve of only the most privileged, powerful or fortunate. In 1391 Chaucer had written *The Astrolabe* for his son 'Litell Lowys' (aged about ten). The book was a mathematical and astronomical treatise designed to stimulate and develop Lewis's 'abilitie to lerne sciencez touchinge noumbres and proporciouns'.[7] More typical, however, were those writings

8

which targeted children's moral rather than intellectual development. As one historian had put it:

> Early children's literature was constrained by the sense of moral urgency which hung over a child's education.
> Books were written at children rather than for them, and sought to terrify into docile obedience with threats of everlasting hell-fire all those youngsters who obstinately persisted in enjoying their leisure hours.[8]

John Bunyan wrote a book of 'country rhymes' for children which was considerably more menacing than it sounds, but perhaps the best example of this terrifying brimstone bedtime genre would be James Janeway's evocatively titled *A Token for Children: Being an Exact Account of the Conversion, Holy and Exemplary Lives, and Joyful Deaths of Several Young Children*.

The move away from children's books which appealed to adults (or at least to their sense of moral propriety) to those which appealed to children's tastes demanded a more general move towards secularisation in the country at large. It also reflected a shift in ideas about child rearing, and what was good and bad for children. Fantasy, imagination and delight became highly fashionable for both adults and children in the nineteenth century and made the notion of lightly textured children's stories conjuring whimsical worlds both popular and profitable. Prior to that, Janeway's worlds of pain and divine retribution were deemed to be more suitable material for the young and impressionable.

Just as the 'communion of the children's book' had evolved over the centuries to form part of a new conception of the rites of childhood, other strands of culture had evolved simultaneously, and taken their place alongside literature at the heart of a distinct children's culture. Chief among these was play.

There are sufficient toys from antiquity in museum collections throughout the world to indicate that play is an age-old human urge: balls and dolls 5,000 years old; dominoes from the tomb of Tutankhamun; toy animals from the Indian Harappa dating from 2800 BCE; hobby-horses and dolls from the ancient Greeks; gaming pieces carved from wood or bone from the Mediterranean or northern Europe. Many of these playthings were made for adults and only passed on to children when no longer useful, but clearly playing with toys fulfils some basic human needs.

The traditional view is that play was in part shaped to prepare children for the adult world. Playthings address four basic needs: mimicry (of the adult, or 'real' world), vertigo (at times an almost transcendental excitement, or euphoria), competition and chance. Dolls, models or miniature versions of adult tools (such as weapons) clearly mimic the stuff of adult life. Hobby-horses, tops, balls, masks and musical instruments have been used in a variety of cultures over time to transport children and adults alike into light-headed enjoyment through dance or sporting play. Many playthings – particularly games – stress the role of chance as much as skill, while encouraging or even demanding competition. In different cultures and at different times playthings combine these four elements to differing degrees, but they always seem to be there.[9]

These illustrate as well as promote the values of a society, and help to prepare children to take their place in it by rehearsal or play. On the one hand, play is often based on real or adult life: martial combat, child rearing, dancing, sport. On the other, it is not really adult life. It allows children (or adults) to play at aspects of real life while at the same time removing the dangers, threats and consequences of the kind of actions they are enacting. The swords do not kill, the dolls do not cry and the dancing ends with the music. In other words, 'Play schematizes life, it alludes to life, it does not imitate it in any very strict sense.'[10] Play is preparation for adult life, or a temporary release from it.

As a result, medieval children had very few toys that were distinct from the amusements of adults. In the medieval world play was often associated with the time of the year, not times of life such as childhood. The calendar specified activities like dressing up in November and December, football in the winter and playing with whipping tops in Lent. The term 'toy' referred to anything that was frivolous, and included amusements such as anecdotes as well as actual playthings.

Children and adults both played the same games: blind man's buff, closh (a kind of croquet), camping (a ball game with goals), nine men's morris, chess, backgammon, kayles (skittles) and quek (a kind of chequers), as well as running, leap-frog, climbing trees, wrestling and 'sports' such as fishing or hunting. Playthings were also passed down to children by adults when they had finished with them. Among the first of these were carved devotional figures such as Noah's Arks or manger scenes. Originally fixtures in churches for the enlightenment of illiterate members of the congregation, by the sixteenth century these were being sold in miniature form for home decoration. It was only a matter of time before they were eventually passed on to the children to play with. By the late sixteenth century German craftsmen were producing Noah's Arks for children. Now they could play with toy animals at home, while at the same time being pious.

The fashion doll was a toy for women before children were allowed to get their hands on it. Society ladies in the fourteenth century presented each other with them as gifts. This practice was not only charming and amusing but was also useful in providing a record of contemporary fashions, styles or even events. After the death of Catherine de Medici's husband eight dolls were found in an inventory of her belongings, all dressed in mourning clothes. In 1637 the town of Augsburg decided to present the Swedish king Gustavus Adolphus with a cabinet from the University of Uppsala, which included a pair of dolls, a peepshow and a miniature falconry after the style of a doll's house. It would be interesting to know what the architect of the modern European army made of it all.[11] Toy soldiers were more typically popular among princes, who commissioned them from craftsmen.[12]

So perhaps the Victorians did not invent childhood for the concept has a much longer history. For centuries people had recognised children as different from adults – though the conditions of their existence had not always afforded them much opportunity for demonstrating by how much. The French political philosopher Jean Jacques Rousseau recognised that 'Nature wants children to be children before they are men. If we deliberately pervert this order, we shall get premature fruits which are neither ripe nor well flavoured, and which will soon decay.'[13]

From modest beginnings a distinct children's culture had gradually evolved centred around stories and literature and play. It was, however, still relatively small in scale. The real explosion in children's playthings and literature, and in plays, games and diversions conceived of especially for them presupposed a sophisticated market capable of responding to and stimulating children's desire, and meeting their demands through mass production. These conditions, and hence the real growth of children's material culture, occurred from around the middle of the nineteenth century. Moreover, this cultural eruption demanded fundamental changes in the ways in which children were regarded in society. Adults would devote vast resources in terms of time, energy and money to creating and producing such things for children, and then to purchasing them, only if there was a new regard for children, as well as recognition that childhood was something to be cherished and even indulged. Profound social and cultural changes were necessary in order to bring children's culture to fruition. The fact that there were distinct kinds of children's literature or playthings increasingly being produced by the nineteenth century did not mean that children had the time or the wherewithal to enjoy them. Childhood had long been discreet, and had had to fit between the interstices of daily life. Play was snatched where work, hunger, poverty, disease and spiritual propriety allowed. The Enchanted Garden needed tender care and nourishment.

Concern with children's welfare 'was a cause and a consequence of a general upsurge of interest in social conditions dating back to the 1830s'.[14] These gave rise to official enquiries and reports into education, sanitation and welfare, and a range of public and private initiatives constituting more or less palatable remedies from youth groups to labour reforms. Demographic reforms were in part behind this concern: the number of children in Britain had risen significantly as a result of declining infant mortality rates.[15]

In addition to the rising number of children, there had been a growth in the number of people enjoying a childhood, which had not always been the same thing. Changes in employment laws and the provision of full-time education meant that childhood was protected and extended for large numbers of children who would previously have been forced to work. Factory Acts in 1802, 1816 and 1833 re-evaluated the basis upon which children, some as young as five, had been compelled to work alongside their parents in factories and the like. By the 1890s children were not allowed to be employed until they were 12 or 13 years old (unless by dispensation), though this old habit died hard. In addition to working-class children attending 'broken' or 'half-time' schools and working part-time, many continued to work before or after school. (Traditionally, upper- or middle-class children had not had to work until a later age anyway, and had enjoyed longer education prior to the 1870 reforms.)

By the 1870s commercial toy makers were on the increase in Britain as a result of these social and economic changes. In tandem with commercial enterprise was the much older tradition of smaller homemade toys or cheap playthings, invented, made and sold by small concerns or individuals with varying degrees of success. This tradition of local production underpinned the domestic industry and fed into it. Occasionally it threw up products and makers who would go on to achieve significant success in the commercial industry proper. This, coupled with rising incomes, smaller family sizes and increasing indulgence, had helped to promote toy and book buying among large element of the population.

Frank Hornby's place in the history of childhood was assured by the brilliant combination of education and play found in his products. He grew up at a time when these two notions, having so long been considered as mutually opposing forces, were gradually coming to be seen as complementary. In the hands of a number of skilled reformers and visionary educationalists (not to mention sharp-eyed businessmen) this view would eventually come to overturn the notion, stretching back to the Renaissance, that play was the antithesis of learning. More than that it was a harmful diversion which could actually hinder learning in the longer term. Writing in the seventeenth century Cotton Mather (1663–1728) expressed his concerns about his son's development:

> I am not fond of proposing Play to them, as a Reward of
> any diligent Application to learn what is good; lest they
> should think Diversion to be a better and a nobler Thing
> than Diligence.[16]

When learning was focused on classical curricula, or more

particularly religious or biblical texts, play was not only frivolous, it was also vain and distracting. It should be avoided, not encouraged, and children should certainly not be led astray by the creation of light stories, toys or giddy games. Sir Henry Slingsby (1601–58) attributed his son's truculence with the schoolbook to too much enjoyment:

> I find him duller to learn this year than last, which would
> discourage one, but yet I think the cause is to be his too
> much minding play, which takes off his mind from his
> book; therefore they do ill that do foment and cherish
> that humour in a child, & by inventing new sports
> increase his desire to play, which causeth a great aversion
> to their book; & their mind being at first season'd with
> vanity will not easily loose the relish of it.[17]

There was a deep suspicion of play as being the 'devil's workshop'. John Locke in *Some Thoughts Concerning Education* (1693) had been an early champion of the idea that the constructive use of leisure time could be crucial in shaping and developing children's capacities.

> Recreation is as necessary as Labour or Food. But
> because there can be no Recreation without Delight,
> which depends not always on Reason, but oftener on
> Fancy, it must be permitted Children not only to divert
> themselves, but to do it after their own fashion.[18]

That children be permitted to 'divert themselves after their own fashion' was crucial to Locke. He believed that children should have 'divers sorts' of playthings, but not too many, and only one at a time. He feared that too many playthings would 'hinder that

16

great Variety they are often overcharged with, which serves only to teach the Mind to wander after Change and Superfluity, to be unquiet, and perpetually stretching itself after something more still, though it knows not what, and never to be satisfied by what it hath'. Therefore he believed that parents should not inundate their children with too many toys. Rather, children could have as many playthings as they wished, provided they made them themselves.

Clearly there are two strands here which are important to our story. On the one hand, Locke is still suggesting that the play of children should be monitored by adults. They should regulate the number and type of toys played with by their children, and should ensure that they are suitable. On the other, there are the beginnings of the ideas of stimulating play and educational toys that would reach their fullest expression in the early part of the twentieth century thanks to manufacturers like Hornby in Britain and Gilberts in the USA. What is crucial to remember, however, is that for Locke toys are not keys to self-expression, or tools for unlocking the child's imagination, but conduits for certain defined rational and moral values. Locke, after all, disapproved of fairy tales. This is education as a largely one-way process – not the drawing out of anything, but the drumming in of it.

These ideas, passed down in child-rearing manuals continued to be hugely influential in the nineteenth century. The Victorian schoolroom could be an austere or even brutal place, where physical chastisement was justified by the need to discipline children who were not motivated to learn, or even to conform. Hornby later confessed a dislike of his schooling, which is perhaps understandable in this light. The emphasis on conformity was important since education was intended to shape children and help them to grow into young adults. This growth was not through some process of personal discovery or revelation, but by being fed prescribed information and digesting it so that the final outcome could be determined. Learning was geared to creating a certain kind of adult. The process was designed to help children assimilate the information or acquire the skills necessary to prepare them for later life. This was as true for boys being prepared for work as for girls being groomed for domesticity as wives and mothers.

At first, therefore, it was not necessary for education to be engaging since the atmosphere of discipline and authority was there to compel attention. Changes in the way children were regarded gave rise in turn to changes in educational thought, and social reforms enacted by legislation had sought to limit the amount and type of work that children could be compelled to do. As the state (often at the behest of private reformers) sought to protect children, so it also began to take a greater interest in other areas of their lives. Proscriptive legislation designed to protect children from abuse often accompanied prescriptive legislation seeking to provide for them. Housing, welfare, spiritual and physical health and particularly education became particular central concerns of the state.

Very quickly schools had to hammer out for themselves ideas about what was best for the child. As new institutions, the state schools strove to meet the new demands being made of them, and the latter part of the nineteenth century saw a change in the pedagogic approach of Victorian schools. They began to become more concerned with pastoral roles than purely disciplinarian ones. It was at this point that the metaphor of the garden as a symbol for childhood reached its fullest expression. Schools attempted to focus more on guiding and training than bending their charges to their will. Church, state and other interested parties saw formal school education as an opportunity to broaden children's horizons.

This is not to say that state schooling did not remain disciplinarian, or even brutal, well into the twentieth century, for it often, perhaps even typically, did. Now, however, there was usually some sort of Christian or civilising ethic or principle behind any acts of cruelty or stricture. In addition, the mainstream was complemented by more progressive educational teachings, such as Friedrich Froebel's *Kindergarten*. This truly was an idyll, with space to play, music and freedom for children to determine their own learning patterns. Central to the idea of this 'children's garden' was the principle of free play. Enjoyment was both an important precursor to learning, and an element of it. If children were happy and interested they were predisposed to taking the fullest part in a whole range of activities that would be educational. As a consequence the idea of children's culture began to develop. This culture was that which supported and promoted learning, growth and development. It included stories and literature, games, rhymes and sporting play, musical instruments, song and dance, art and toys. This garden was richly planted.

These led to the evolution of the view that play was an essential part of childhood. Not only that, it was an inherent and natural element to growing up. If it was a natural part of growing up, then play must surely perform some function in the process of growth, development and the journey to maturity. Educationalists and theorists had increasingly come to see the importance of play as a key part of education and learning, and throughout the mid to late nineteenth century there had been a considerable growth of literature addressing this point. The result was a number of institutions and organisations that strove to enact some of these principles, many coming from a variety of philosophical, spiritual, religious or political starting points. All, however, shared the central belief: far from being a frivolous diversion as Cotton Mather had seen it, play was a serious business. More than that, play was the *work* of childhood.

The definition of play as work reflected the view that it was not a foolish diversion, but a serious and more importantly valuable business. It also implied a certain amount of effort. Such notions of endeavour were typically seen as positive, since labour was inevitably needed to transform something from the raw to the finished. In Victorian Britain industry was demonstrating its almighty power to transform the world, apparently for ever and ostensibly for the better. There was also a moral dimension. Hard work was good, and was positive not just because of the end product, but in and of itself. Work was stimulating and prevented the body, the mind and perhaps most critically the spirit from stagnating or ossifying. The growth in leisure time and the opportunities for play and relaxation resulting from the industrial reforms and technological advances of the nineteenth century were therefore regarded as a mixed blessing. On the one hand, workers (and this most definitely included children) now had opportunities for something other than work. This could be something that was seen to be wholesome – sport, exercise, access to the finer things, a constructive or improving hobby. It could also, of course, be something quite different – spectating rather than playing games, drinking and gambling and wasting time. There was a conflict, therefore, between the muscular Christian ethic, which promoted wholesome activities and the ancient ideal of a healthy body and mind, and new opportunities for breaking free of regulation and the need to conform to the ideals of one's betters, and instead spending one's time and money in peace and freedom.

Kindergartens, playgrounds and enlightened nurseries (in family homes and public venues) strove to provide the right environment for a good deal of this work to take place. All that was left was to find the tools. At the same time as writers, playwrights and poets had sought to delineate the boundaries and contents of this newly comprehended world of childhood, so businessmen,  manufacturers, inventors, visionaries and charlatans were turning their attention to producing a whole range of items that could rightly fill it. The change in attitudes to children necessitated a reconsideration of the toy business. It was important that business did not neglect this new market, and fail to cater for the distinct needs and wants of children. Victorians were, lamented economic historian G. C. Bartley, 'so accustomed to fix . . .

attention on those articles, whose use is principally confined to persons of adult age . . . that we are apt to lose sight of the fact that children too have their wants, which are to be supplied by those little trifles we call toys, and to ignore the extent to which their manufacture in England is carried on'.[19]

The idea of the importance of play in learning was naturally accompanied by a growth in the range, number and kind of educational playthings. The educational reforms of the later part of the century were a stimulus to the industry in other ways too. *The Times* suggested in 1908 that children attending school would have less time for making their own toys and would have to buy commercially produced ones.[20] Whether or not this was the case is difficult to say, but the changing attitudes to children (and toys) were a great stimulus to the manufacture of toys in Great Britain. As a result the British toy industry grew rapidly throughout the last quarter of the century, aided in part by technological, economic and social developments that were stimulating industry as a whole. These ranged from advances in

production techniques and changes in the cost of raw materials to increased disposable incomes throughout society and a revolution in marketing, retailing and advertising. Finally, the industry was not short of creative impetus.

Toys increasingly found their way into the schoolroom and nursery as educational tools. Debate as to the efficacy of introducing commercially made toys into the classroom raged. By the late nineteenth century there was widespread agreement that play had a role in learning, though this view was not universal. The weakening of discipline was the main grouse of certain religious critics, who felt that at the very least toys should not be available to encourage play and enjoyment on the Sabbath. They, like the rationalists, were increasingly lone voices by the turn of the century and, if not yet in the wilderness, were beginning to feel the chill.

Among those who appreciated the role of play in learning were those who felt that increased verisimilitude in toys stifled children's creativity and imagination, and for that reason commercially produced toys should be kept out of the schoolroom. Opposing them were those who argued for the role of educational toys. 'Children should be lured to knowledge', argued one Mr Macready, writing in the nineteenth century, 'until its acquisition, like that of meaner gain, creates a passion for its increase.'[21]

W. H. Cremer – himself involved in the toy business – hoped that once well stocked with toys, nurseries and schoolrooms would soon become 'the most entertaining of preparatory schools of natural history, science and art'.[22]

There were evidently sufficiently large numbers of people who agreed with this view, and educational toys grew in both number and popularity. By 1914 *Games and Toys* claimed that toy manufacturers had come to accept as axiomatic the fact that 'next to the parents comes the toy dealer as a factor in the education of the youngsters'.[23] Naturally this was not simply a case of toy retailers selflessly looking out for the educational needs of children. They had no doubt realised that toys with a broadly educational aspect would appeal to parents and relatives searching for a present that was not utterly frivolous, and therefore educational merits were useful selling points.

This appeal in part reflected the broad agreement that toys and children's play helped to shape later life. If educational toys helped inculcate certain positive qualities such as logic, dexterity, creativity and scientific, mathematical or geographical understanding then these toys would prepare children for later life. There were touchingly earnest examples of toys being promoted in this way – miniature printing presses to teach spelling, for example – and the Sociological Society even organised an exhibition of toys in 1908. Yet the most obvious

thing that toys could teach – as well as if not better than anything or anyone else – was how boys could be boys, and girls could be girls.

There were, of course, a plethora of toys that were neutral (or neutered) and which appealed to boys and girls in equal measure: farms, Noah's Arks, books, miniature theatres and so on. Dolls were, and still are, seen to be associated with the development (or at least the outlet) of nurturing instincts in girls, and some even went so far as to suggest they might even be useful to instruct girls 'in the art and mystery of gussets, tucks and herringbone hems'.[24] This in itself was part of an older train of thought. In eighteenth-century Nuremberg a toy manufacturer had been mass-producing 'the Nuremberg Kitchen', a toy kitchen designed to teach girls home economics. Boys, on the other hand, were encouraged towards more manly pursuits: sports, construction toys, carpentry and – the boys' toy par excellence – toy soldiers.

One of the most remarkable things about the blossoming of children's culture in the nineteenth century is the way in which it built upon established traditions of literature, learning and play while at the same expanding them to the point at which they seemed to become new forms. The whole process was the result of a confluence of very different factors and forces, but they had the same end result: the creation of a new conception of what it was to be a child, what it meant to grow up, and how the adult world could assist in both processes. Children's culture did not begin in the Victorian age, but its Golden Age did.

The first generations to grow up in it were those born in the 1860s and 1870s. They reached their maturity at the same time as many of the exciting cultural forms that had schooled them. As they grew and developed, so too did children's culture. It matured, for with the further definition of what it was to be a child came the definition of what it was *not* to be one. The concept of adolescence (and the setting aside of childish things that this implied) first became formally established about the same time. Naturally, this implied the end to toy buying for those that were growing up. Notable exceptions to this, however, were those toys that were not limited to children, by either design or appeal. Among these were certain educational toys, or constructional and model-making sets. And any product with a 'kit' design was well placed, not least because it could grow with its clientele as they added 'accessory outfits' to update their kits, or purchased special-purpose sets. Similarly well placed were those toys that appealed to the youth or the adult hobbyist, including toy trains as we shall see later.

The toy industry in particular rose to the challenge of meeting the growing demands of children and their parents for stimulating and diverting material. The industry was changing rapidly, as a result of the dynamic changes in parent–child relations, and as it began to absorb the creative powers of that first generation that had benefited from the richly textured educational environment of Victorian Britain. The industry went on to contribute to one of the largely unsung cultural achievements of the period: the creation of a vibrant and well-crafted children's culture. It was one of the brightest and most exciting areas of the newly discovered garden. New products came and went at an alarming rate, but when new ideas were good ones, and were accompanied by sound business sense and innovation in marketing, manufacture and design, they could make a great impact. They could also make a fortune for their inventors, who could go on to become driving forces within the industry, often presiding over a considerable empire. One such product was Meccano, and its inventor was Frank Hornby.

2

The Birth of a Liverpool Man

On 15 May 1863 Martha Hornby gave birth to her sixth child at her home in Copperas Hill, Liverpool. She was 38 years old; her husband John was 39. Like all his brothers and sisters the child was baptised at St Simon's Anglican church, at the end of the street. The baby was christened Frank Hornby.

The Hornby line (originally de Horneby, or de Hornebie) originated from the neighbourhood of Hornby-in-Lonsdale in north Lancashire. Through the usual mix of selflessness, sycophancy and service to the crown, the Duchy of Lancaster and the Nevills of Hornby they had gradually built up estates, holdings and lands throughout the thirteenth and fourteenth centuries.[1] By the fifteenth and sixteenth centuries the family had extended its branches outward – both geographically and socially. By the nineteenth century the family name could be found throughout Lancashire, from the towns and boroughs, to the sprawling conurbations of Liverpool and Manchester, from hall to hovel. In so far as Frank Hornby held any kinship with his grander namesakes it was a weak and distant one. While the Hornbys of Hornby Castle included admirals and generals, gentleman cricketers and justices of the peace, other branches cast their shadow more modestly.

Aged just 25 Martha had given birth to the couple's first child, a boy whom they christened Charles. Over the next dozen years Martha was almost continually occupied in either nursing her new babies or preparing for the next imminent arrival. In the 13 years between Charles's arrival in 1850 and Frank's in 1863 the redoubtable Martha Hornby delivered five children. By the time of her death in 1908 she had given birth to eight children – the last, Martha junior at the age of 46. She was survived by only five of them. Within a couple of years of their mother's death only Frank, Martha and Emma remained.

Martha Hornby (née Thomlinson) hailed from Whitegate in Cheshire and had married John Oswald Hornby, variously described as a porter or provision dealer, while in her twenties. The couple settled in John's native Liverpool to raise their family. By the time of young Frank's birth the family were living in a small house in Copperas Hill, one of the longer streets in Liverpool. Running from Ranelagh Place to Moor Place, it skirted the high ground overlooking the city centre. The street's recent history told in its character, and the pattern of the area's development mirrored that of the city itself. Originally known as Elliott Hill, the area had been largely undeveloped until the nineteenth century. Before that its most dominant feature was the Copperas Works, a large factory once owned by the former mayor of Liverpool, Mr Hughes. The works were dirty and unpopular, haemorrhaging noxious fluids across the surrounding land. In 1770 the Corporation of Liverpool took action. The owners were indicted for 'carrying on a nuisance'. Thirty-five witnesses were called to a hearing in Lancaster to testify to the harmful effects to people and vegetation arising from the works. It was concluded that the problem could be solved only by the works being closed down. The owners were given two years to remove them. With Liverpool growing steadily and spreading up the hill from the banks of the Mersey and its increasingly busy docks, pressure for land was growing. While some alternative sites for the works were half-heartedly suggested, no one really cared what happened to them provided they were removed.[2]

With the works gone the site lay undeveloped until the beginning of the nineteenth century, when residential housing began to rise up around the edges of the grand Georgian terraces

and avenues. Copperas Hill had been part of the first wave of this expansion, but some parts of the area were beginning to look shabby by the middle of the century. Before the end of it many of them had gone the way of the Copperas Works, swept away by the city's tumbling growth and redevelopment. Any person tempted to make a pilgrimage to the birthplace of Britain's greatest toy maker will be disappointed. Within a few years of Frank Hornby's birth Copperas Hill was demolished.

The reason was simple. In 1863, just after Queen Victoria's silver jubilee, the vast majority of her subjects had been country folk. By the time of her death in 1901 most were living in towns or cities. Not all had moved to the towns; for many the towns had moved to them. England was the first predominantly urban industrialised nation, and this transformation happened quite swiftly. By the 1870s around two-thirds of the population of England and Wales was living in towns and cities. Both the number of people living in the towns and the proportion of city-dwellers to country folk were on the rise. Lancashire was one of the most heavily industrialised regions. Liverpool had a population of 400,000 in 1871 (compared to 300,000 each for Birmingham and Manchester). Overcrowding was a particular problem. While the 1851 Lodging Houses Act had given local authorities powers to build new accommodation for the working classes, Liverpool was one of only three cities to take advantage of this legislation, but by no means to a sufficient degree. The Registrar General had defined overcrowding as more than two people living in each room of a house or dwelling. With rents for one- or two-room slum apartments sometimes swallowing up as much as a fifth of a working-class weekly wage, many were consigned to live in overcrowded and cramped conditions.[3] Urban improvement schemes seldom improved the lot of the working classes, who often needed to live in a particular area – namely near to their place of work in the factory, the docks or the mill. With the clearance of city-centre areas to widen thoroughfares, create municipal buildings and develop railway facilities many found themselves thrown in upon each other in increasing numbers. The decline of an area towards being a slum was very difficult to arrest, as the weight of more and more unfortunates exacerbated the situation. The growth of the railways was a particular problem.[4]

The furious growth of steam power had fuelled the development of the London and North-Western Railway. In 1815 Liverpool had staked its claim as the first railway city of Britain. It hosted the Rainhill trials in 1830 to test the relative merits of steam locomotives. (The city also witnessed the first railway fatality when the unfortunate local MP William Huskisson idly wandered on to the track during the trials and was run down, thereby entering the trivia books.) Opponents to the railways' growth, mainly drawn from the landowning classes who deplored the dirt and noise of the iron behemoths as much as the incursions on to their land by this new, democratic transport, spoke out against the spread of the railways. Lords Sefton and Derby were among the opponents of the Liverpool and Manchester line, fearing, in the words of the contemporary politician Thomas Creevey, 'The loco-motive monster, carrying eighty tons of goods, and navigated by a tail of smoke and sulphur, coming through every man's grounds between Manchester and Liverpool.'[5] Within 15 years of the opening of the Stockton to Darlington Railway around 5,000 miles of track had been laid down, taking in most of the country's main routes and serving many of the great provincial centres.

Though the building of the railways took on a somewhat ad hoc air, they rapidly established themselves as preferable alternatives to the canals for freight and to the stagecoach for passenger transportation. In its first year the Liverpool and Manchester Railways handled around 1,200 people a day – more than twice as many as the coaches had and at a fraction of the cost. By the middle of the century the London and North-Western Railway could justly claim to be the first major passenger railway in the world. As a result it soon outgrew its modest station in the city centre, and in 1861 parliament passed the London and North-Western Railway (Lines near Liverpool) Act. This empowered the company to acquire land between the north side of its existing station in Lime Street and Sydney Street to allow for the expansion of the station. Copperas Hill was one of the streets swept aside by the developments, realising Creevey's fears in a literal sense.

Such developments naturally caused a certain degree of upheaval, not least for the communities that were unfortunate enough to find themselves living in the path of progress. The redevelopment of urban centres to accommodate the railways posed a number of problems, not least of which was the displacement of established communities. By the mid 1860s over 1,800 separate acts of parliament had been passed to sanction the development of land for railway purposes, in addition to 1,300 different amendments to acts. The brunt of this legislation inevitably affected the poorest communities, already living in overcrowded and cramped housing. Many of these areas had begun as respectable housing, but by the mid-century they were being abandoned by the middle classes in favour of the new suburbs. Despite being able to spread into these vacated city-centre areas the working classes still found accommodation desperately hard to come by. Grand civic improvements – railway stations, offices and warehouses, roads, public buildings and even factories – displaced vast numbers of manual and casual workers who needed to live close by their places of work. As a result of improvements such as those to Lime Street Station many found themselves living in ever more cramped and squalid conditions.

That, of course, was preferable to them rubbing shoulders with respectable people. Hand in hand with any new developments was the need to reorganise thoroughfares so as to cause a minimum of disruption to the good citizens of Liverpool. Though Copperas Hill was, for the most part, a reasonably respectable working-class area, some of the nearby streets – in particular around Hotham Street and Gloucester Street – had a less salubrious air. The redevelopment of the area in the late 1860s forced some of the inhabitants blinking into the daylight. Among these were 'the late promenaders of Lime Street' – prostitutes who had previously plied their trade in and around Gloucester Street. 'They were', observed the satirical *The Porcupine*, 'patronised in a business community by a very large number of the well-to-do population of Liverpool.' However, this section of the population was alarmed to encounter the promenaders by the light of day, once the redevelopment of the area had deprived them of their old haunts. Before long the embarrassed Methodist Chapel excused itself from the area, and the nether regions of Lime Street took on all the common marks of urban Victorian sprawl.[6]

It had not always been the case. While the area was not the most desirable, even before it was thrown into the railway station's shadow, Copperas Hill had been a bustling thoroughfare. Though its houses were interspersed with small shops, temperance hotels, refreshment rooms or lodging houses run by stout Scottish and Irish matriarchs, for the most part it was residential. Although home to the odd spinster gentlewoman, fallen into genteel dereliction, it was largely an upstanding working-class area. Its residents were tradesmen of a respectable sort – tailors, jewellers, chandlers, confectioners, stationers and the like. By far the greatest number of residents, however, were like Frank's father John, employed in the provisions trade: grocers, butchers and bakers, victuallers and tobacconists.

Like many in Liverpool they owed their living to the port, directly or indirectly. By the middle of the nineteenth century Liverpool was establishing itself as the most important provincial port in the country. Handily placed for the imports and exports associated with the north-west's textile industry, cereals and meat from Chicago and the eastern seaboard of the USA, and passenger and mercantile traffic to the empire and the world, it was proudly proclaiming itself the 'Funnel of Trade' by the 1860s and employing vast numbers of casual and regular labour in all kinds of work.

John was probably relatively uneducated, a victim of the poor provision of schooling in Liverpool in the early part of the century. A survey carried out by the Manchester Statistical Society in 1833 (when John was eight) suggested that as many as half of the children in Liverpool did not attend school. Yet John was hard working. He worked as a provisions dealer, or porter, as had his father before him. (Though some entries in the street directories or census returns call him a porter, he was more properly a wholesaler, the two descriptions being close substitutes in many cases.)

Porters were generally employed either directly by establishments handling large amounts of meat or produce or by the firms of master porters that operated in the docks. The former comprised local butchers, grocers, markets or wholesalers who employed the porters to bring the meat from the wholesalers and carry it from the carts to the shop premises, though it could also include the large meat-importing firms bringing fatstock into the city by rail or sea. The dock labourers, on the other hand, were responsible for loading and unloading the ships and transporting the goods from the quayside to the dock sheds where they could be weighed, sorted and recorded prior to being transported on to retailers or wholesalers. Though some dock workers were employed directly by the Mersey Docks and Harbour Board, the vast majority were employed by private firms, some of whom were subsidiaries of the larger shipping companies.

The work was very specialised, but it was also hard, dirty and physical, demanding strength and stamina. What it lacked in quality it more than made up for in quantity. Porters working in the docks were usually hired on a casual basis. At the start of the working day porters would gather with other men at stands along the waterfront to be hired by the foremen. The minimum amount of time a docker could be engaged or 'put on' for was a half-day. Experienced and skilled workers were hired first, and while trade was healthy these men were seldom out of work. As Liverpool grew into a centre of the meat trade those working in provisions avoided the bouts of unemployment that beset other trades.

By the 1860s such handlers were plentiful as Liverpool established itself as one of the country's primary meat markets and distribution centres. The development of the railways had transformed the meat trade. Now animals did not need to be driven as livestock to local markets, but could be slaughtered and transported greater distances as meat. Liverpool became an important market, not only for local, but also for Scottish meat sent by rail from Dumfries and Galloway for processing en route to London.

In addition to the meat arriving by rail Liverpool also handled a large amount arriving by sea. Scottish meat came by steamship from the Solway Firth, Irish meat from Dublin. The US Civil War in the 1860s closed the southern American market to northern US meat packing firms, who looked elsewhere for their exports. Three-quarters of all US meat exports during the 1860s arrived in Liverpool, where it was unpacked and sold or redistributed. The work for those in the meat trade was abundant, particularly those handling the meat since the trade involved a considerable amount of distribution and re-exporting. For instance, good quality Irish bacon came into Liverpool bound for the UK market, while the saltier, fattier American meat arrived in Liverpool to be re-exported to Ireland, whose buyers offset its quality against its cheaper price.[7]

While firms of master stevedores were responsible for loading and unloading the ships in dock, it was porters who were tasked with transporting the landed cargoes from the quays to the railway wagons, barges or trucks which took it elsewhere. Meat carcasses were hoisted from the hold in large canvas slings. These were slung from cranes either on the quayside or else on the decks of the ships themselves. Wool arrived in bales; sugar in sacks; fluids such as oil in barrels and other provisions in crates, boxes or chests. Once the stevedores had landed the cargoes the porters set to work measuring, sorting, marking and counting the goods. Sacks, bales or chests could be loaded on to large movable scales fitted with platforms and counter-balanced by hand weights. These scales, owned by the Mersey Docks and Harbour Board, were issued to firms of porters handling cargoes in the docks. The cargoes were loaded on to small flat trucks to be taken to stores

or railheads. As the cargoes were loaded on to the wagons that would take them by road or rail they were then checked by the porters. In the case of cargoes transferred 'overside' from the ships straight into waiting barges the porters boarded the ships to weigh and check them on the decks.

The import-and-export trade boomed in Liverpool and the wholesale provisions trade provided the Hornbys with a fairly comfortable living. For one thing it enabled them to move house fairly frequently in their early years as their young family grew. The christening roll of St Simon's suggests they may have had more than one address in Copperas Hill. John and Martha's first child was born on 24 August 1850. They christened him Charles. Frank never knew his eldest brother since he died of typhoid two years before Frank's birth on Christmas Day, 1861. Three years after Charles's birth the Hornbys were delivered of another son, Henry. He was born on 21 November 1853, and christened five days before Christmas at St Simon's. His baptismal record suggests the family was living at 43 Copperas Hill at the time, though since St Simon's register also differs slightly from the register of birth in details of birthdates for the Hornby family it is possible that this is merely misrecording.[8]

Almost immediately Martha conceived another child and gave birth to a third boy, William, just ten months after the arrival of Henry. Oswald John followed in February 1857, and the Hornbys' first girl, Anne, in August 1858. Six months before the tragic death of Charles Martha gave birth to a second girl, Emma in 1861. Two years later Frank was born.

With five children, the eldest of which was only ten, the

Hornbys presumably needed more space. Once Martha had finished her customary confinement following her most recent delivery and had been 'churched' – that is formally reintroduced into everyday society – it seems the family prepared for a move to another property in Mill Street. This would possibly account for the delay of over five months in having Frank christened. How long they all remained at Mill Street is unclear, but by the time of the birth of the final child named after her mother, they were staying at an address in St Anne's Street, Islington, not ten minutes' walk from Lime Street Station.

Frank was Martha and John's penultimate child. It is likely that he was envisaged as their last, for Martha was in her late thirties, and there was to be a gap of eight years between Frank and the Hornbys' last child, Martha Elizabeth. Despite the tragic loss of Charles in 1861 at the age of just eleven the Hornbys had been fortunate. At the time of Frank's birth Liverpool's population was somewhere in the region of 400,000. Infant and child mortality was shockingly high nationally. Boys were more susceptible, and as many as 72 in every 1,000 died before their fifth birthday.[9] Dr William Farr, superintendent of the Statistical Department, produced a report entitled *March of an English Generation Through Life* in 1872. It revealed that alarmingly few that set out on this march made it very far at all. Farr looked at children in different age groups in the 1860s and extrapolated to see what would become of every million children born if they shared the same fate. Measles, whooping cough, scarlet fever and respiratory infectious diseases would carry off over a quarter of them before they reached five years old. Few of the survivors would be spared an attack of some threatening disease or other.[10]

But Farr's study was based on national averages. It did not reflect the variations in local mortality rates. Liverpool, the report noted, was grossly overcrowded in some areas where mortality rates were high. This was despite the fact that Liverpool was run by an efficient oligarchy, and had appointed a public health officer in 1847. Edwin Chadwick, in his celebrated *Report on the Sanitary Condition of the Labouring Population* (1842), had found two water companies in Liverpool in the mid 1840s which were paying high dividends, and were therefore presumably profitable, but no public fountains or pumps, no standpipes for street cleaning or cattle troughs, and not enough water to put out fires. In Liverpool, Farr noted, nearly half of all children could expect to die before the age of five, and only a quarter would survive to the ripe age of 45.

Probably the Hornbys' income and diet were well enough provided for by John's provision dealing. The work would have guaranteed a reasonable income for an upper-working-class family (though it was occasionally susceptible to fluctuations in trade cycles or even bad weather). It is also likely that John had access to certain quantities of excess food or provisions which would have helped to make up for the strain on resources resulting from a family of seven children. Henry, the first son to make it to maturity, followed his father into the trade, and may even have worked for him. By the 1880s he had left the family home and had set up one of his own with his young wife Sarah.

By this time the family were living at yet another address, 20

College Street North, this time in Everton. Henry, Oswald John and Anne had all left home. Oswald was also working in the same line as his father, as a porter in the Liverpool docks, while Anne had married at the relatively young age of 19. William, the second eldest, was still living with his parents in 1881, as were Frank, Martha and Emma. William had been apprenticed as a joiner, but in the early 1880s was unemployed. Emma, aged 19, was in domestic service as a housemaid, but still living with the family. Martha Elizabeth, aged ten, was at school. Frank, then aged 17 had also begun work.

Loosely speaking, Frank too was working in the same trade as his father, though not as a porter but as a clerk for a local firm of meat importers. His employer, David Hugh Elliott was based in James Street in the city of Liverpool. With grandfather, father and brother working in the import and provisions trades it was perhaps to be expected that Frank would find employment in that line. For one thing it offered one of the most plentiful supplies of work in Liverpool, and had spawned a vast array of clerical, administrative and professional jobs. It is even possible that his father had contacts to help his sons into employment.

That Frank should also have begun his career on the back of imports and exports is appropriate since in a way these were the recurring themes of his life. Not long before his death, when he was campaigning for a seat in parliament, he told a group of old sailors in a seamen's mission that he had always been fascinated by the sea. As a child, he told them, he had frequently gone down to the docks to see the monstrous cargo ships arrive. On these visits he had no doubt also seen the cranes, trains, trucks and engineering which would later feature so heavily in his models and toys.

In many ways the Hornbys were a family for whom the sea was important. Emma, Frank's younger sister, became a Methodist missionary to China. She left Liverpool for Southampton, and from there sailed to Ceylon aboard the SS *Himalaya*. From there she made her way to Ningpo where she served as a nurse or auxiliary as part of the Ningpo Mission under the Reverend Dr Swallow. She was aged 24 when she arrived in China, one of the few unmarried women to be sent out as a missionary by the United Methodist Reformed Church. She stayed in China for around eight years, eventually returning to England owing to ill health. With her she brought a young Chinese girl named Yi-Li So-

Pah who underwent medical training before returning to China.

All the children were christened and brought up in the Christian faith. They regularly attended the Anglican church of St Simon's until it was demolished and they themselves moved from the area. Religion seems to have played a central part in the family's life. Frank remained deeply committed to the church until his death. At what point Emma joined the Methodist movement is unclear, though Frank too seems to have been drawn to it. From an early age he was attracted to the temperance movement. He joined the Band of Hope as a young man and remained a member for some years, though was by nature abstemious rather than ascetic. The family also seem to have been a loving one, and in later years the siblings remained close and saw each other often.

In his adulthood and with his employer's help, Frank went on to be a hugely successful businessman with an extremely strong export trade. The sea helped him make his fortune and he knew it, crossing the Atlantic over 60 times and the Channel on innumerable occasions in the pursuit of his business. In the last phase of his life he campaigned vigorously as an advocate of protectionism. Unrestrained imports were at the root of many of the country's problems and it was only by addressing the 'difficulties of foreign trade' that the country could be made strong again.

In a sense, then, Frank Hornby's life was defined by the fact that he was a Liverpool man, and Liverpool was the city of the sea. Liverpool was home to many of the largest and most important shipping companies in the world. The port handled coastal trade (much of it servicing the larger ocean-going vessels), as well as international trade, and direct sailings were available to almost anywhere in the world. By the 1920s Liverpool was the greatest provincial port in Britain and its principal export port. It handled fast services to the USA, Canada, South America, Europe, Africa, the Antipodes, India and the Far East. Three generations of Hornbys had made their livelihoods from it. It was one of the conduits of trade – the tool with which Frank Hornby made his name. It was also one of the great bases of Victorian sea power and engineering, the twin pillars of the empire. It is the latter of these two that began to cast its spell on Frank at an early stage in those childhood visits to the docks and quays where the giant cranes luffed and jibbed, winched and slung their massive loads on to the rolling stock which trundled through the docks and warehouses. This lifelong fascination with engineering spurred the young Frank on to the journey that would make his name a household word.

3

Frank Hornby Helps Himself

T he greatest invention of the nineteenth century', wrote
A. N. Whitehead, 'was the invention of the method of
invention.'[1] The introduction of method to what had
hitherto consisted of remarkable acts of genius, the fruits of
inspiration or the wages of lives of dogged determination did not
happen overnight. Nor was it the result of an inspired act of
planning, or the implementation of a bold initiative or plan.
Gradually, and in a piecemeal fashion over a period of decades,
the foundations were laid for a technical education system that
could teach the skills necessary for new generations of scientists
and engineers, industrialists and inventors.

Yet one small, and at first sight perhaps innocuous invention
holds a remarkable place in this process: Frank Hornby's
Mechanics Made Easy, later famous as Meccano. One of the key
elements in a successful technical education was the development
and inculcation of certain skills. James Nasmyth, the celebrated
nineteenth-century engineer and inventor believed that the best
way to be taught or trained was through practical, hands-on

experimentation. 'The truth', he stated, 'is that the eyes and the fingers – the bare fingers – are the two principal inlets to sound practical instruction. They are the chief sources of trustworthy knowledge in all the materials and operations which the engineer has to deal with. No book knowledge can avail for that purpose. The nature and properties of the materials must come in through the finger-ends.'[2] Though it was common for those engineers who were self-taught, or who had learned on the job through apprenticeships, to accord a greater value to practical training over book learning, the point was an important one. Over the last 100 years generations of scientists and engineers from all over the world have expressed their debt to the same thing: playing with small pieces of perforated metal, held together with little nuts and bolts. A conference was recently organised by the British Institute of Mechanical and Electrical Engineers to discuss the best ways of promoting science and industry so as to raise new generations of engineers. After much discussion of syllabuses, technical colleges, positive action and recruitment a speaker rose to address the assembly. 'Surely,' he began, 'there is an obvious solution which we are all missing. How many people here played with Meccano as children?' Almost all the assembled engineers raised their hands. 'That', he concluded, 'is the best way to develop engineers.'

For hundreds of children-turned-scientists the story of Meccano, and the man who invented it, is the story of invention of the method of invention. Sir Harry Kroto, 1996 Nobel Laureate for Chemistry recalls in his autobiography the debt he owed to Meccano. 'I had a Meccano set with which I "played" endlessly . . . New toys (mainly Lego) have led to the extinction of Meccano, and this has been a disaster as far as the education of our young engineers and scientists is concerned.'

The education of scientists and engineers benefited greatly from the great upsurge in mechanical playthings and models, particularly construction toys in the late nineteenth century. They complemented perfectly the ways in which generations of scientists and engineers had trained, learned and worked. Many new products had appeared in Germany, the USA and Britain which promised to develop in children an appreciation of sound engineering, architectural or mechanical principles. As toys they offered hands-on learning so that 'trust-worthy knowledge' could 'come in through the finger-ends'.

They contributed to the story of the technological development of the nineteenth century. In many ways this was the story of the struggle to overcome one tradition of scientific discovery and replace it with another: it was the story of the struggle between the amateur and the professional; the dilettante and the specialist. It took the form of a struggle because the amateur – the artisan craftsman, the uneducated inventor, the gentleman natural philosopher – was a potent figure, identified in fact and fiction as the reason Britannia ruled the waves of the new industrial world. These figures were heroes. They owed their greatness to their individual talents and collective genius. In other words, they were heroic precisely because they lacked anything so vulgar and unromantic as training. They had done it on their own, and seemed to suggest that Britain's position at the head of the march of progress relied on an apparently endless supply of genius. As such it was a position that fate had determined, and one that no end of planning or practical common sense by rival nations could threaten. The reality, of course, was that this was exactly what was happening. Denied the advantages of raw materials, skills and expertise continental Europe had set about re-arming itself intellectually throughout the nineteenth century. As Europe made rapid progress it became apparent in Britain that the great successes of the self-taught pioneers needed to be built upon. A more systematic approach to the teaching of science was needed in order that new generations of scientists, engineers and industrialists had both genius and education; theory and practical skills; self-motivation and the strengths of an organised and professional approach to the new technological disciplines.

Even today some tension remains between the self-taught approach of the George Stephensons and the educated one of the generations that followed. The romance and glory of the self-taught tradition has ensured that it continues in an uneasy, more often than not complementary relationship to the educational initiatives that sought to draw out the sparks of genius, or at least provide the tinder.

Meccano is a case in point. It was from the outset an educational toy – originally patented as Mechanics Made Easy – the purpose of which was to help children learn the scientific principles of engineering at the same time as having fun. On the one hand, the story of its invention illustrates the development of technological invention in general. Its inventor was an amateur, with no formal training, who had been encouraged by reading a self-help book lauding the achievements of other self-taught pioneers and inventors. On the other hand, he was working at a time and in a city where the struggle to replace the amateur with the trained specialist was coming to fruition, and the initiatives of the previous 50 years were changing the educational landscape of Britain (and British science and industry) for ever.

When Frank Hornby patented his Mechanics Made Easy he saw it playing a fundamental role in teaching young boys the principles of mechanics. Hornby had taught himself, and was well aware that many of the most fêted and successful engineers had grown up in an environment that was hardly rich in formal technical education resources. Much had been achieved by individuals often working alone, developing theories and devising models and experiments to test them. In his essay, 'Signs of the Times', Thomas Carlyle described the scientific fraternity in 1829, highlighting the negligible role of formal educational training in driving the advancements of science and industry:

> Shall we say, for example, that Science and Art are
> indebted principally to the founders of Schools and
> Universities? Did not Science originate rather, and gain
> advancement, in the obscure closets of the Roger Bacons,
> Keplers, Newtons; in the workshops of the Fausts and the
> Watts; wherever, and in what guise soever Nature, from
> the first time downwards, had sent a gifted spirit upon
> the earth?[3]

The successful establishment of technical education institutions owed much to these amateurs and their endeavours. In fact, long after the establishment of faculties of engineering and technical colleges, the twin forces of industrial and technological innovation were the drive to self-improvement and the exchange and development of scientific ideas. This mixture has no better example than in Frank Hornby's attempt to provide a 'means whereby the interest in mechanical construction from an elementary point of view, is enhanced in addition to providing an interesting means of mechanical education'.[4]

Hornby himself was not an engineer by training. In fact, he professed a dislike of school. Possibly this was due to boredom rather than inability, for he showed sufficient grasp of mathematics to become a clerk on leaving school. No pictures survive of Hornby as a boy, but it is easy to see in the intense and tight-jawed man that he could have been a formidable and wilful little boy if he set himself to it. His determination found a channel other than truculence at school, however. While still  a young man Hornby came under the influence of another former disenchanted schoolboy, the Victorian writer Samuel Smiles. 'In my boyhood days,' Hornby recalled, 'my primitive workshop was my hobby. I think that most boys take up their hobbies in the first place through some accident; and I have always realized that the accident that first aroused my interest in mechanics was the reading of a book that had been given to me.' The book was Samuel Smiles's bestseller *Self Help*.

Samuel Smiles was a Scotsman, born in 1812. By the time of his death in 1904 he had written over thirty books, a similar number of pamphlets and essays and hundreds of articles in newspapers and periodicals. He achieved great success with his biographies of engineers. *Life of George Stephenson* (1857) *Industrial Biography* (1863), *Boulton and Watt* (1865), *Men of Invention and Industry* (1884), *James Nasmyth, Engineer, an Autobiography* (ed.) (1885) and *Josiah Wedgewood, His Personal History* (1894) all sold in substantial quantities. However, it is for his 'self help' series that Smiles is probably best remembered: *Self Help* (1859), *Character* (1871), *Thrift* (1875) and *Duty* (1880).

These works, like his biographies, used the lives of the great and the good to illustrate certain moral principles. It was Carlyle's 'gifted spirits' that were the heroes of Smiles's works, and their stories were reduced to inspiring parables of moral rectitude and virtue in the face of adversity. 'Biographies of great, but especially good men', he wrote, 'are . . . most instructive and useful as helps, guides, and incentives to others. Some of the best are almost equivalent to Gospels – teaching high living, high thinking, and energetic action for their own and the world's good.'[5]

Unsurprisingly therefore, some writers have referred to Smiles's work as 'the Gospel of self help', and his subjects as 'the communion of engineering saints'. Certainly the works have been lauded and derided with the kind of passion usually reserved for dogma. Yet there is little doubting the inspiring influence they have had, not least on Hornby. His mind was set racing by these tales of heroic endeavour and science triumphant. He never forgot the impact they had, and the content and approach of his own *Meccano Magazine* years later owed much to the influence of Smiles's earlier works. These tales were formulaic eulogies to self-taught pioneers toiling in their 'obscure closets', and to their colleagues in what the novelist Thomas Love Peacock referred to as the 'Steam Intellect Societies' – the Mechanics Institutes. Smiles commended these motivated autodidacts, while decrying the stultifying and overrated influence of 'book-learning'.[6]

These societies performed a number of functions. They were born of the century's reforming concerns, and aimed to help working men come to understand the conditions under which they were living and working and appreciate the driving forces behind them. Secondly they served as an outlet for working-class interest in science. Lastly they embodied the widely held view of education as an ennobling and liberating force.[7] It is likely, however, that they were not particularly successful as educational organisations. James Hole, secretary of the greatest of the mechanics' institutes, the Yorkshire Union, felt that the best hopes for the improvement of education among engineers and scientists lay in the development of new university faculties.[8]

One problem with the institutes was the fact that their fortunes reflected those of the economy as a whole. When employment was high so the membership of the institutes grew. When the economy was in decline – for example in the 1830s – and political science promised more practical solutions than natural science, their membership too declined. The institutes themselves, though sometimes suspected of being cells of radicalism or sedition, rarely added a political aspect to discussions of the industrial processes. Some even degenerated into working-men's clubs, offering the kind of attractions of the pier or the music hall – popular music, ventriloquism and mesmerism – in addition to (or instead of) science.

Perhaps more crucially, the institutes were virtually working alone to make up for a dearth of education among their members. If they were not acting in a vacuum, the air was certainly pretty thin. There was no primary education system upon which they could build. Most of their members had been working since an early age, with little schooling. Attempts to turn this experience into a positive asset by relating the subject matter of the institutes' lectures to practical everyday life in the factories, mills or workshops proved difficult. Even the development of examinations and diplomas under the aegis of the Society of Arts could not overcome the indifference to formal technical education on the part of the vast majority of the leaders of industry. In due course, however, they would prove to be the foundation of technical education in Britain.

In the meantime advances in engineering continued to be driven by the twin forces of self-improvement and the moves towards the development of institutions to provide for the organised and co-ordinated education of those in industry. Smiles, himself a secretary of the Leeds & Thirsk Railway, nicely articulated these twin forces. *Self Help* had grown from a request to deliver a lecture at an evening class in a northern town. The standard of teaching in these classes was crude ('Those who knew little taught those who knew less'), but most importantly, 'it was done with a will'.[9]

Perhaps, for Hornby, the appeal of this tradition of self-improvement stemmed from its reliance on determination and willpower. Throughout his life he seldom backed away from a challenge. He was not aggressive or combative, but quiet, dogged and steely. He found in Smiles all the qualities which in himself were to be so important and influential.

Smiles set out to record 'what other men had done, as illustrations of what each might, in a greater or lesser degree, do for himself', pointing out along the way, in a suitably Victorian high-moral tone, 'that their happiness in after-life must necessarily depend mainly upon themselves – upon their own diligent self-culture, self-discipline, and self-control – and above all, on that honest and upright performance of individual duty, which is the glory of manly character.'[10] Under headings such as 'Facilities & Difficulties', 'Energy & Courage' or 'Application & Perseverance' Smiles recounted the trials and tribulations of those

· Hornby Trains ·

whose ultimate success naturally qualified them as great and good in a highly edited anecdotal form. Artists, philosophers, musicians, writers and above all engineers and scientists were presented by Smiles as examples of what could be achieved through moral discipline and rectitude.

This counsel fell on fertile ground. The book was – and still is – a favourite among those who used Smiles's assertion that 'help from without is often enfeebling in its effects, while help from within invariably invigorates' to justify some political position. More generally, the book served to inspire generations of young people who were presented with cheap editions specially produced for school libraries or Sunday-school prizegivings.

Hornby himself was given the book as a child, by whom we do not know. Perhaps, if Hornby really was a poor scholar it was his parents who presented him with it. By the time Frank was ten years old John and Martha were both nearing 50. They had brought up six children and lost a son. The strain on Martha of rearing a large family and on John of a lifetime's physical work in the provisions trade was probably starting to tell. A difficult young boy would have been the last straw, and the Hornbys must have been grateful for any help they could enlist. Smiles's *Self Help* was a favourite manual for corrective as well as directive behaviour. 'The book contained the life-stories of famous inventors,' Frank later recalled, 'and described the difficulties they encountered in working out their ideas before success ultimately crowned their efforts. I was very young at the time and this was one of my first books. Nothing that I have read since has exercised such a strong and lasting influence on me.'[11]

For someone like Hornby who had disliked school, but had set himself the task of becoming an inventor, it no doubt came as great encouragement to read Smiles's accounts of 'illustrious dunces', or under the heading 'Literary Culture Probably Overrated', his commendation of a practical education over a scholarly one ('The possession of a library . . . no more constitutes learning than the possession of wealth constitutes generosity').[12] The fact that Smiles showed many great men succeeding despite – indeed, often because of – a lack of formal training in their respective spheres must have given succour to the earnest Hornby, anxious to become a 'proper' engineer. Time and again in *Self Help* Smiles points out that the great and the good of art and science find that, freed of the stiff apparel of the university or school, they are able to give freer rein to their abilities, climb higher, and vault the barriers which have confounded others. 'It is not', he writes at one point, 'those who have enjoyed the advantages of colleges, museums and public galleries, that have accomplished the most for science and art; nor have the greatest mechanics and inventors been trained in mechanics' institutes. Necessity oftener than facility, has been the mother of invention; and the most prolific school of all has been the school of difficulty.'[13]

The Birth of Meccano

Fortified by such encouragements the young Frank Hornby prepared to set out on what Smiles called 'the old road of observation, attention, perseverance and industry' that led to wisdom, understanding and success. Yet, though he was encouraged that he could become an inventor, he was less sure how to become one. With the confidence of a young man he first turned his attentions to the Holy Grail of all inventors. 'At that time,' Hornby later recalled, 'perpetual motion was being very widely discussed, and I conceived the idea of trying to invent a machine that should solve the problem. I felt that if I could make such a machine I should have accomplished something very wonderful. I certainly should!' Frank fared little better than anyone else. He did, however, go some way to accomplishing something wonderful. 'In the end I failed, as thousands had done before me; but in the effort I had learned something of engineering, and had considerably improved my mechanical skill.'[14]

With Smiles's homilies ringing in his ears Hornby knew that failure was often merely an aperitif to success, and that 'the battle of life, in by far the greater number of cases, must necessarily be fought uphill; and to win it without a struggle were perhaps to win it without honour . . . Difficulties may intimidate the weak, but they act only as a stimulus to men of pluck and resolution.'[15] Once again *Self Help* proved to be both a consolation and an inspiration to him. 'Often I used to pick up my book,' he remembered, 'and read of the difficulties with which James Watt

had to contend. He could not get his engines made properly. When the parts arrived, often after weeks of delay, he found that the cylinder was not true, or that the pipes leaked . . . He persevered, however, and finally succeeded; and I determined that I too would succeed.'[16]

Locked in a regimented and unstimulating job he readily poured his energies into his projects. He began to spend all his spare time tinkering in his 'workshop'. In reality it was simply a shed in his back garden, but Frank thought of it as 'my paradise'. Here he worked through various practical problems, happily exploring mechanics and engineering in finer detail. Though not a bad workman, Frank nevertheless had cause to blame his tools, his relatively meagre wage as a full-time clerk leaving him little to spend on equipment. Consequently, the few tools he possessed were old or crude, and no matter how much care he lavished over each of his projects he found that his efforts were all too often in vain as a result. Yet he remained phlegmatic, refusing to be discouraged.

In 1911 Leo Chiozza Mony had published his study *Riches and Poverty*. In it he suggested that the affluent portion of British society could be defined as those who earned around £700 per annum or more, while the comfortable earned anything between £160 and £700. As was typical, the dividing line between comfortable and struggling was placed at the point at which income tax was payable (around £160 a year). A family could probably be raised on around £100 a year without too much difficulty, but for those earning less it could be hard.[17]

Hornby probably earned around £100 a year, though rising standards of education may have driven the wages for lower-grade clerks even further by creating stiff competition.[18] In 1871 B. G. Orchard had written *The Clerks of Liverpool*, in which he argued that it was just about possible to raise a family on the salary of the lowest paid clerk, who earned about the same as some of the better paid artisans. While the salaries could be meagre the profession did offer a degree of respectability. Some argued that class was dependent on income, while other argued that it was the nature of one's work that was important. The economist Alfred Marshall explained it thus:

> If a man's daily task tends to give culture and refinement to his daily character, do we not, however coarse the individual man may happen to be tend to say that his occupation is that of a gentleman? If a man's daily task tends to keep his character rude and coarse, however truly refined the individual man may happen to be, do we not tend to say that he is a member of the working classes?[19]

Though incomes varied across the profession they were generally not large – perhaps around £200 per year at most. However, it was a profession, not just a job. Clerks wore suits to work, worked with their minds, not their hands, and were addressed as 'Mr' rather than simply by their surnames, as servants or factory workers were.

The inevitable result of the likes of Hornby making good their escape into respectable employment was a growing concern on the part of the middle classes to further distinguish between its ranks. By the middle of the century the concept of the lower-middle class had become current. This group included men like Hornby, who probably had not been born into the middle class but whose energies, channelled through respectable professions, went some way towards hauling them into it – even if their incomes struggled to keep them there. Thus Frank, through working for a small firm in a less than fashionable industry, could see himself as a respectable middle-class gentleman whereas his father (and some of his siblings) could not.

The *Fortnightly Review* of May 1899 defined some of the characteristics that marked out respectability. In an article dealing with schoolteachers the *Review* described the average elementary schoolteacher as 'a small middle class person – knowing hardly anything well, parochial in sympathies, vulgar in accent and style of his talking, with a low standard of manners, but withal extremely respectable, correct morally, with a high sense of duty, as he understands it'. Notwithstanding the supercilious and caustic tone it is clear that profession could go some way to conveying respectability and making up for disadvantages of birth. Together with schoolteachers and shop assistants clerks formed the largest white-collar group in Britain. Their ranks swelled as the century wore on since despite the meagre financial rewards their professions offered respectability and the chance of social advancement. Office jobs offered the likes of Hornby a route into the middle class proper.

Hornby certainly seems to have been 'correct morally'. Throughout his life he remained a committed member of his parish church, and was a solid Anglican. His support for the Band of Joy led him to be teetotal throughout his life. He was a generous and loving father, but was otherwise abstemious in his habits, save for a love of fine cigars in later life. Meccano literature also revealed a distinctly high moral tone that presumably was dictated by Hornby's precepts. In his general conduct, however, he remained modest and quiet.

He was also extremely respectable, with a sense of duty that was revealed not only in his business dealings, but also later in his political career. He was not, however, a 'small middle class person' in the sense the *Fortnightly Review* meant. He had a physical slightness which gave him the air of an earnest schoolmaster, but he excelled as a businessman astride an international company, eventually rising to join the ranks of Liverpool's metropolitan elite. As for his education, he successfully rose above the confines of his own elementary schooling to become something of a popular educator in his own right. His efforts at self-improvement were in the finest traditions of English autodidactism.

He did, however, remain parochial in his sympathies, if not in his experience and outlook. He was Liverpool born and bred, and apart from time spent abroad on business and in Westminster as an MP he lived all his days not twenty miles from his birthplace. Even in later years when a successful businessman he retained his strong Scouse accent. A former employee recalled:

> Frank Hornby spoke lucidly and incisively with a noticeable Liverpool accent . . . To my ears a quirk was that he pronounced the word 'put' to rhyme with what golfers do on a putting green, whereas his 'but' came very close to 'boot'. For instance when I showed him my model he might say 'Putt it there boot don't scratch my desk'.[20]

Yet his interests were wide and varied. He was a music lover and a keen sporting enthusiast, a chess player and an accomplished singer. In business his outlook was marked by an internationalism that set him apart from his contemporaries from the outset. In politics he espoused a stout Baldwinesque brand of Toryism which had as much concern for the social dimension of employment or trade cycles as it did for his capital.

But as a clerk on a middling income in the closing days of the nineteenth century his hold on respectable middle-class status was as tenuous as many of his background and position. This, however, did not deter Miss Clara Walker Godefroy, whom Frank met through their mutual interest in the Liverpool Philharmonic Choral Society. Then again, Clara was a woman who was little deterred by anything. The Philharmonic was a prestigious choir and its performances were a highly regarded part of the Liverpool musical calendar. Frank was an accomplished tenor while Clara was a contralto and both could play the piano. The two regularly sang at charity concerts in St Jude's hall, and after meeting during one of the Philharmonic's events in the 1880s the couple began courting.

Like Frank, Clara was living in Everton with her family at the time. They were both in their twenties, though Frank had already begun to lose much of his hair, reinforcing the clenched jaw and slight frown which gave him a slightly older and more serious aspect. Like his brothers he sported a neatly trimmed moustache that he was to have for the rest of his life. Clara was a schoolteacher, the daughter of Mr and Mrs William Godefroy, her father a customs officer working in the port of Liverpool. She had curly dark hair and was a small, stout woman some inches shorter than Frank but with a forceful personality. She reached up to Frank's shoulders, though she seems to have dwarfed him in other respects. She shared Frank's love of music and the arts and had a voracious appetite for both. She was also the perfect foil for Frank, who, despite the air of a Presbyterian minister enjoyed dancing and games of bridge. Clara, in addition to being lively, was both well educated and cultured. The couple married in January 1887.

Frank does not often mention his private life when recalling his early attempts to become an inventor, and it is unclear when he first seriously began to turn his young man's dream into a determined attempt to succeed. He probably began in his teens, shortly after starting work as a clerk. With little to spend he had resolved to save up sufficient money to buy all the tools he required if he was to see his ambition through – one at a time if necessary. This he did, but it was painstaking. 'I despaired of ever becoming the owner of such things as a lathe and a drilling machine,' he recalled later. In due course he did manage to put together a collection of most of the tools he required, but the necessity of improvisation in the meantime set his mind working: 'the weary waiting turned my thoughts in the direction of interchangeable parts that could be used for a variety of purposes, instead of parts that had to be made especially for each particular job. Looking back over those days I can trace in those vague ideas the germ of the Meccano system.'[21]

As the sun began to set on Victoria's reign Frank Hornby's evenings continued to be spent tinkering away in his workshop. His efforts had become more focused, and after his abortive efforts to solve the riddle of perpetual motion he had turned to more realistic, if not more mundane, challenges. These included an automated ticket machine for tramcars, but despite his prescience, this was not where his fortune lay, and the idea was not followed through. Instead his efforts continued to focus on models – particularly mechanical models for his two sons Douglas and Roland.

Roland Godefroy Hornby was the eldest, born on 12 June 1889. The pressures on the young Hornby family at this time were no doubt keenly felt. Still working as a clerk in the import trade, while continuing to nurse his aspirations of becoming an inventor Frank now had a young family to support. Any time he spent on his hobby had to be fitted around his full-time job. That this job was fairly uninspiring was probably quite fortunate. On the one hand, the role of a clerk demanded a methodical and disciplined approach – something which Frank had had to work at after never really getting to grips with schoolwork. In later life his attention to detail, coupled with his nose for business, was to stand him in good stead. On the other hand, Frank had an active mind but his day job as a bookkeeper provided few creative opportunities. It was this more than anything that served as an incentive for his efforts in his little workshop.

Within a year of Roland's arrival Clara fell pregnant with the couple's second child. Frank's income as a cattle salesman's clerk was augmented by Clara's resourceful household management and the little money she had brought to the marriage and saved while teaching. Like most young families, however, the Hornbys were finding that they had outgrown their home in Stamford Street, West Derby. With a baby at the breast and one more on the way they had to begin looking for a new place to live. They moved across the city to Toxteth Park and a small house at 22 Carlingford Street in time for the arrival of their second child, another boy. Douglas Egerton Hornby was born on New Year's Eve, 1890.

As far as Frank's hopes of establishing himself as an inventor were concerned, two boys were a mixed blessing. Without the nannies and nurseries available to more prosperous families, the Hornbys soon found that two small boys are more than capable of expanding to fill all available space and time. The family was a close one and they prayed and played together. Frank was an affectionate father, with a love of music and singing. He was no stiff-collared Edwardian patriarch, but instead loved playing with his children as much as singing and dancing with his wife. He spent hours with his boys, particularly as they grew older, playing, devising toys and games and pottering about in their company. It was through these shared moments that Frank was to develop the invention that would make his name famous to thousands of other small boys all over the world. At the turn of the century Frank was making models and constructional toys for his sons from sheet metal cut by hand.

The story of Hornby's alighting on the basic form of his first great invention has a certain classic ring to it. Increasingly, his spare time was being devoted to finding new ways of amusing his two children, as much because it offered an outlet for his creativity as because it promised 'new schemes for my boys' enjoyment'.

> One Christmas Eve I was travelling from London to
> Birmingham to spend the holiday with a relative who had
> some children. I had stopped and I looked out of the
> window quite idly. We were opposite a goods yard and
> there was a small crane there. It occurred to me that I
> could make a crane like that for the children using strips
> of steel. I sat in the carriage dreaming about it. New
> possibilities kept coming; I saw what this new game
> could mean. I was drunk with delight when I got out of
> the train.[22]

In another account of the same moment Hornby explained that the idea seemed to offer a perfect solution to the problems he had been having in keeping his boys furnished with playthings:

> At that time we were having problems in our little
> workshop through a lack of a number of small parts for
> building up a splendid model crane that we were making.
> I had tried in all directions to buy these parts, but
> apparently nothing of the kind existed. Clearly it would
> be a long and monotonous process to make them, and as
> I thought over the matter on the train I was more
> impressed than ever before with the waste of time and
> labour involved in making a part especially for a single
> purpose. I felt that what was required was parts that
> could be applied in different ways to many models, and
> that could be adjusted to give a variety of movements by
> alteration of position, etc.[23]

Frank's struggles in his workshop had developed not only his appreciation of mechanical form and function, but also more generally his powers of observation. It is the ability to observe, rather than just see, which frees up a creative mind, and which is the hallmark of good inventors. In *A Scandal in Bohemia* Sherlock Holmes explained the distinction between seeing and observing to Watson:

> 'When I hear you give your reasons,' I remarked, 'the thing always appears to me to be so ridiculously simple that I could easily do it myself, though at each successive instance of your reasoning I am baffled until you explain your process. And yet I believe my eyes are as good as yours.'

> 'Quite so,' he answered . . . 'You see, but you do not observe. The distinction is quite clear. For example, you have frequently seen the steps that lead up from the hall to this room . . . how many are there?'

> 'How many? I don't know.'

> 'Quite so! You have not observed. And yet you have seen.'

While poor old Watson frequently failed to see the wood for the trees, Frank had been concentrating on the problems of model-making, and was becoming familiar with the various possibilities and problems. He recognised that what was needed was a system of perforated metal pieces, with the holes evenly sized and spaced, allowing any one part to fit with another. With fixing bolts of a standard gauge this would allow the pieces to be fixed together in a variety of configurations and angles. In this way the pieces, having being used to make one model, could be unbolted and applied to another.

However, Frank's accounts of his inventing Meccano were written some time after the fact, and considerably simplify the process. As he points out, he had been struggling with certain problems in his workshop for some time. Not only was he experimenting, but presumably he was thinking and researching too. At any rate Meccano did not spring fully formed from his head. It may be that Frank had seen the use of models to demonstrate engineering principles before. In 1879 the Liverpool school board appointed a peripatetic demonstrator in mechanics who toured schools accompanied by a pile of apparatus and equipment in a hand-cart.[24] It is quite possible that Frank had seen this demonstrator and his portable mechanics models. Whether or not he had seen this particular technique at school, it certainly had a long pedigree.

The use of standard pieces to make more than one model was not in itself new. In the 1820s William Farish, a Cambridge don, had developed a system for making models to demonstrate certain mechanical and engineering principles.[25] Since 1813 Farish had been Jacksonian Professor of Natural and Experimental Philosophy at Cambridge. His studies ranged across chemistry, physics and engineering, and were limited in their scope and themes only by his intellect and tastes. In February 1820 he gave two lectures to the Cambridge Philosophical Society in which he demonstrated his engineering construction set and the models they could make. 'These', he explained, 'are so adapted to each other that they may be put together at pleasure in every form. Models may be taken down, and the parts built up again in a different form.' In an anticipation of the later uses to which Frank Hornby's Meccano would be put by engineers, physicists and teachers, Farish's models were principally educational aids. They had developed from his work as a scholar and teacher. 'In the lectures I deliver in the University of Cambridge I exhibit models of almost all the more important machines in use in the manufactories of Britain.'

The models were also designed to be made up from an assortment of parts – not for the enjoyment of assembly, but for ease of storage. 'The number of these models is so large,' explained Farish,

> that had each of them been permanent and separate, on a
> scale requisite to make them work, and to explain them
> to my audience, I should have found it difficult to
> procure a warehouse large enough to contain them. I
> procured, therefore, an apparatus consisting of a system
> of the first principles of machinery, the separate parts of
> which the machines consist. Those parts are various: such
> as loose brass wheels, the teeth of which all fit into one
> another: axles, of various lengths, on any part of which
> the wheel may be fixed; bars, clamps and frames; and
> whatever else might be necessary to build up the
> particular machines wanted for one lecture. These models
> may be taken down, and the parts built up again in a
> different form for the lecture of the following day.

In his address to the society he also explained at length the manual that accompanied these models. It contained pictures of each model so detailed that they recorded each machine, and enabled the models to be re-created at a later date. 'As these machines, constructed for a temporary purpose, have no permanent existence, it became necessary to make an accurate representation of them on paper, by which my assistants might put them together without my continual superintendance.'

For Farish it was these drawings which constituted the main subject of his address to the Cambridge Philosophical Society, and which for him were the important contribution to engineering and science. He called his method of illustrating the models 'isometrical perspective'. It consisted of representing the subjects on three axes of 30, 90 and 150 degrees to the horizontal, on all of which axes the drawings give true dimensions. As isometric drawing it was to become one of the standard techniques of scientific draughtsmanship, and is still used today. In concluding his lecture he ventured that isometrical perspective might 'be of some use in rendering more clear and intelligible, communications to societies' such as the Cambridge Philosophical Society. Clearly his audience thought it would, for isometric drawings appear in later papers in the Transactions of the Society for that year dealing with chemistry and engineering.

It is possible that Hornby knew of Farish. For one thing, Farish's invention of isometric drawing guaranteed him a certain degree of fame among engineers, and Hornby, though not formally an engineer, was in correspondence and discussion with eminent engineers during the development of Mechanics Made Easy. It is possible too that Hornby came across Farish in Gregory's *Mathematics for Practical Men*, reprinted as late as 1858, and a staple in lending libraries.

In addition, the toy industry was beginning to turn its attentions to the more respectable kinds of toys termed 'education toys'. There was a wide variety attempting to teach a range of skills, or inculcate certain attitudes or outlooks. By the second half of the nineteenth century construction toys had become extremely popular. In Germany, Britain and the USA alone there was a  flurry of patents for such toys, many along broadly similar lines. Some were variations on the timeless classic the building block. Others were innovative and sophisticated construction systems which ranged from toys and building kits to new ways of tackling construction projects on either a large or small scale. The sheer numbers of applications were staggering, and many were destined to disappear without trace, no doubt often due to the fact that they took simple ideas and made them complicated and unfathomable. Others perhaps were unlucky, for in their design it is possible – if you squint – to see the germ of an idea that could have led to great things. Sadly it seems Henry M. Quackenbush of Herkimer, Emil Jenss of Lübeck and Marcus T. Wing of Pittsburgh, were not destined for greatness. It passed them by to knock on the doors of others. But while Frank Hornby or A. C. Gilbert were to achieve great fame on the back of their products it is perhaps worthwhile noting that there were many more toiling away at the close of the nineteenth century dreaming up educational and construction toys that shared certain characteristics with their more celebrated contemporaries. The similarities were often fewer than the differences, and many clearly lacked the inspired design just as much as the sure understanding of the changing demands of the toy industry, or the children they were trying to reach. Yet they were often groping towards the same kind of light that shone down on Meccanoland. Sadly for him, Henry M. Quackenbush remained in the shadows.

The classic construction toy was, of course, the building block. Cheap and easy to make they had long been valued as educational toys. They required a steady hand and taught the basics of form, control and balance. They were also fairly calm and contemplative toys – at least until they were combined with toy soldiers to create explosions. Apart from requiring children to be still, they demanded patience, hand–eye co-ordination and a reasonably delicate touch if children were to get the most out of them. These were all qualities which parents valued, and hoped their children would acquire through play. It was partly for this reason that William Dewees, writing in 1826, recommended them as playthings that could teach 'gentle manners'. John Locke, as we have seen, hoped that they could help to develop rational thought processes.

Charles Crandall began making children's building blocks in America in 1867. His first blocks used the then novel tongue-and-groove design to fit together. By 1879 Crandall was producing a range of 28 toys, many of them different sets of building blocks. These included Expression Blocks (which allowed children to make amusing faces by re-arranging picture blocks), and interlocking Wide Awake Alphabet Blocks.[26]

Thus while building blocks were timeless classics they were not immune from being tinkered with, changed or given various modern makeovers. Almost all of these were billed as improvements, but the toy-buying public was not always easily convinced.

In 1873 Henry Fairbanks of St Johnsbury, Vermont, patented an 'Improvement in Toy Blocks'.[27] The blocks were wooden and had holes at regular intervals. Rather than having individual connecting rods, each block had a cylindrical spoke at the end which could be fitted into any other piece, including wheels. It could then be held in place with a pin, allowing children to make rudimentary wooden vehicles.

Henry M. Quackenbush also registered a variety of toy building blocks, four years after Mr Fairbanks.[28] Quackenbush, a resident of Herkimer, New York, devised a system of building blocks 'composed of various sizes and shapes and provided with a series of perforations arranged transversely therein, at opposite angles to each other'. The pieces were all three-dimensional and (apart from the wheels) were perforated on each of the four sides, the holes staggered on each face. They were held together by pins that allowed some basic vehicles and couplings to be made, but the overall effect was of building blocks rather than anything more mechanical or sophisticated. He was aware that a number of different patents had already been filed for improvements to building blocks and therefore his claims were modest. Quackenbush made no great claims about the educational value of his toy, and quite possibly saw it as nothing more than its title indicated: an 'Improvement in Toy Building Blocks'.

In 1888 Otto Lilienthal of Gross-Lichterfelde, Germany,

patented his construction set.[29] The system, which lacked a catchy name at the time of registration with the Imperial German Patent Office, was designed to allow the building of various models from strips of various lengths. It consisted of 'building material which can be readily put together and taken apart and can be used in building models of various descriptions, also in furnishing instructive playthings'.

The idea was clearly to allow imaginative children (or their parents) to build different models from the pieces in the kit, and its inventor saw the educational benefits and the amusement of the system arising from the building of the models as much as playing with them once they were built. The patent included a diagram of a sample model of a house with frame, joists, supports and roof structure, but without the wall panels for the purposes of illustration. The system was intended to allow flexibility:

> The material itself can be accommodated in a very small space, and may nevertheless be employed in many different ways. The so built-up models are light and transportable, and can, after having filled their purpose, easily be taken apart, and the material be used again for the building of new models.

The systems consisted of 'strips . . . as well as profiles, and all of various lengths and perforated systematically at regular intervals. These strips are fastened together by clips in different ways according to purpose.' The strips were of metal and grooved along their edges to allow panels of pasteboard or something similar to be slid down between strips to create flat surfaces. The pieces were connected by inserting small V-shaped pins into the perforated strips and fastening them in place with small wedge-shaped pins on the other side.

One crucial element missing from this system was mechanics. The model was basically a construction set designed to allow the building of static models – there were no wheels of any description specified in the list of parts. The fact that the accompanying illustration was of a house underlined the fact that the system was basically for the construction of broadly architectural models.

In the 1890s two German-Americans devised a system which they called 'Improvements in Building Sets'. Architect Edward von Leistner, of New York, and Dr Herman Goetter, a gentleman living in New Jersey, applied for a patent for their system in Britain in 1895.[30] Von Leistner's system was more sophisticated than its predecessors, and did not resemble building blocks so much as delicate latticework. Moreover, its inventors had given a great deal of thought not only to the design of their system but to the range of uses to which it could be put. This was not just a toy, educational or otherwise. Though von Leistner was an architect his invention was not designed for constructing simple buildings or models. Instead he had conceived of it as an educational aid at least as much as a toy, and even hoped that it could be used for larger-scale structures, which he referred to as 'actual constructions'. With this in mind he had created a range of pieces to create geometrically complicated and mathematically exact models:

> Our invention relates to building sets for actual
> constructions as well as for models for technical
> construction bureaus and schools and the improved set of
> building members further constitutes an instructional and
> educational toy. It is the special object of this invention to
> furnish members of a set which bear to each other certain
> geometrical and mathematical proportions, so that,
> practically speaking, an unlimited number of
> constructions can be made with a very small number of
> members of our improved set.

These 'members' were not made from wood, but from metal. For 'actual constructions' the pieces were to be made of 'metal or suitable metal compositions, preferable of cast or wrought iron'. For toys or those models which were to be used for educational purposes in construction bureaus and schools he suggested brass sheeting, thin iron or steel, or better still, aluminium, 'since it is light and it is desirous to have such toys and models for construction bureaus and high schools as light as possible'.

The system comprised a range of pieces including struts, nuts, screws and angle-keys. The struts were perforated with holes of uniform gauge, but were of different designs. These included flat 'longitudinal members', some of which had regularly spaced perforations, and thin rods flattened at each end and with perforations in these ends to allow them to be fastened as crosspieces or braces.

Most significantly the system had been designed according to sound engineering principles. Rather than designing a kit with a certain number of pieces they had devised a way of thinking about construction which, when applied correctly, could allow users to generate whatever pieces they required. The patent included a diagram with mathematical formulae explaining how the size of the pieces and the location of perforations could be determined.

> Thus this mathematical diagram forms a scientific basis for a system of constructing which is great in its conception and simple in its application, and with the described lengths of the members may be formed an almost unlimited number of geometrical forms which by their technical combination built with the elementary members gives a vast number of constructions.[31]

Von Leistner and Goetter conceived of their system as engineering in miniature. As a consequence they also described a number of full-size structures that could be made by scaling-up the pieces appropriately. It was suggested that the system would be ideal for military engineers looking to build all manner of constructions. These ranged from bridges ('of any shape in all places where time does not permit the erection of expensive permanent structures, and in half-civilized regions where building materials are hard to obtain'), to tents that could be carried by mules. The armies of the world, however, do not seem to have shared von Leistner's enthusiasm for a tent that came complete with mathematical equations.

The complexity and thoroughness of von Leistner and Goetter's system was not always typical of the waves of constructional toys that were being hawked around patent offices towards the end of the century. At the same time as the architect and his gentleman partner were devising ways of making tents even more difficult to erect, a locksmith in Germany was patenting yet another improvement in building sets. Emil Jenss of Lübeck applied for a patent for his 'extraordinarily instructive and entertaining occupation for leisure moments' in May 1895.[32] By contrast to von Leistner and Goetter, Jenss was not really bothered about the mathematical relationship between his parts. In fact, he was not much concerned with their size, shape, type or material either. His invention, he explained consisted of

> simple strips, or angle pieces of metal, or whale-bone or
> any suitable material, with holes formed preferably near
> the end, and connected at right angles or otherwise to
> each other by means of tiny screws and nuts. These strips
> may be straight or curved and of any preferred length or
> width or thickness, and are fastened together in any
> conceivable form.

There was still some fine-tuning required if Emil's idea was to go into production. It was not a bad idea, but others had had it before him, and had given it far more thought than the locksmith from Lübeck. Among them was Henry W. Stratton of Boston Massachusetts. Though again his invention was conceived as an improvement in building blocks and puzzles rather than a mechanical construction set, he did hope that it would serve 'the amusement as well as the training of children'.[33]

The pieces were probably to be made of wood since he described them as blocks, and like Crandall's building blocks they incorporated tongue-and-groove fastenings. While some of the pieces had holes allowing pins, axles and struts to be fitted, the variety of models that could be made mostly depended on these tongue-and-groove fixings. The overall result was a toy that could make swings, wooden carts, miniature furniture and the like, but would probably be far too exasperating if you wanted more mechanical models.

Similarly, Charles Burton's building blocks, patented in the USA a couple of years later, though using pins and holes to fix parts rather than tongue-and-groove joints, were still essentially building blocks – fine if you wanted to build houses. Rather than being sited at regular intervals to each other these holes or sockets were located on the blocks according to a mathematical equation.[34]

By the turn of the century more and more inventors, toy makers and engineers were coming to look on constructional toys as a way of developing thinking not just about construction in a general way, but about mechanics, engineering or architecture. There were clearly a great many inventors working on ways of developing building blocks and construction sets to allow children to make a wide variety of models of varying degrees of sophistication out of the same collection of parts. Many of these systems were hamstrung by being either boring or too complicated – or sometimes both. There were far fewer inventors, however, looking to develop a system that would allow mechanical models to be built that would be faithful to the life-size ones – at least in terms of the engineering principles behind them. Two years after Frank Hornby patented his 'Improvements in Toy or Educational Devices for Children and Young People' William Kilbourn of Colorado developed a system that he hoped would succeed in 'not merely providing amusement as a toy, but serving to develop the mechanical ideas of a child or person'.[35] In contrast to many of the predecessors, Kilbourn's system shared with Hornby's the virtue of being mechanical. It allowed children (or more accurately boys) to make model versions of real-life engineering constructions. His patent included example models of a mill, a belt-driven machine-shop, a wind pump and a bridge. In addition to flat pieces with tongue-and-groove joints, here were wheels, hubs, axles, pulleys, paddles or vanes, washers, bolts and screws. Like Hornby's initial patent there was room for later development, but many of the key ingredients were here. In addition to the models included in his patent Kilbourn suggested that the parts could easily be used to make buildings, railways, 'cars, wagons, &c and various other constructions'.

There continued to be no ebb in the flow of patents for construction sets which improved on building blocks, or devised new ways by which children could construct buildings or models of increased complexity. As time wore on inventors came to be increasingly interested in the ways in which kits could be devised to make models that were accurate, miniature versions of real things rather than just representations of them. At the same time, however, they were tending to follow the same approach which stressed that the parts of the kits should be reusable or interchangeable. In part this was just common sense. Many of these systems specified wooden parts, or metal ones. Either way, until the development of low-cost parts (in other words, plastics), model kits that could only make one kind of model would be far too expensive to catch on, and inventors knew only too well that children would soon tire of them. Probably more importantly, their parents would not waste their money on them in the first place.

Therefore, even the construction sets that were still being developed in the few years after Mechanics Made Easy had gone into production, and which used wooden pieces to make buildings or static structures, stressed the fact that their pieces could make a wide variety of models, and that these models would have realistic features. Walter Walther's patent for a 'Toy Building with Regularly Perforated Bars Designed to be Rigidly Connected Together', registered in Germany in 1903 stressed that it made models which closely resembled the kind of joinery used in real structures.[36] The toy lacked the delicacy or sophistication of the metal kits, or the exciting potential of Kilbourn's blocks. It was still just fancy building blocks: the blocks were basically wooden bars with regularly spaced holes to allow them to be fitted together, principally to build the framework of houses. The toy models resembled timber-framed houses without the plaster lining. Still, he hoped that their faithfulness to carpentry techniques, and the adaptability of the parts would teach children something about building, while providing for versatility and imaginative play:

Structures can be put up closely resembling real structures

81

erected by carpenters, and the different parts of which
can be put to almost unlimited use, so that, e.g., a
structural element which in one building is used for a
support, rafter, molding or beam may in another building
represent a nog, strut, girder, sleeper, framing timber,
corbel or joint.

Pins and other pieces allowed the beams to be lengthened, strengthened, or widened, but the pieces, and therefore the models were limited in range, not least because they were all basically wooden blocks whereas others had already begun to think in terms of building complicated moving mechanical models. Construction toys had begun to grow up.

It is interesting that, despite later legal wrangles and bad-tempered claims and counter-claims of imitation and copyright-infringement throughout the industry, many inventors were thinking along broadly similar lines at roughly the same time. By the early 1900s it is quite possible that toy makers working on construction toys would be doing so in the shadow of increasingly popular and well-known inventions, but many of the patents show distinct and sometimes bizarrely idiosyncratic attempts to invent the perfect construction set. While all the patents referred to improvements in the design of one kind of toy or another, many were clearly intended as improvements to building blocks. Other inventors had begun to set their sights higher. They were looking to bring the traditional construction set up to date, to develop toys that captured the spirit of the age, and this spirit was rendered in iron and steel. These toys needed to be made from girders, not wooden blocks.

Marcus T. Wing of Allegheny County, Pittsburgh, Pennsylvania, certainly saw his toy modernising the tradition. 'My improved toy', he declared, 'bears the same relation to structural iron work that toy building blocks bear to structures of masonry.' The models that he suggested could be made from it included bridges, Ferris wheels, towers, elevators, frameworks for buildings and 'various other mechanical, architectural and engineering structures'.[37]

Wing's patent, of course, came some eight years after Hornby's. I am not suggesting that Hornby was aware of these developments, or that he saw the future of the toy world by standing on the shoulders of others. In fact, many of the aforementioned systems were cited in one or other of the legal battles that Hornby was to fight and win in defence of his invention. It is true, however, to say that, as with the electric light bulb or the internal combustion engine there were a number of thinkers working across the world, all independent of each other and all addressing similar problems. That Hornby's name is remembered is due in part to the brilliance of his product. More significant, however, is the matter of genius, and Hornby's lay not so much in inventing as in business. It is what happened to Meccano after its initial invention which marks the product out. Hornby promoted it all over the world by entrepreneurial flair and sound marketing. It did not become famous of its own accord.

That said, it should be pointed out that Hornby's system was brilliant in its simplicity. The success of Meccano was due in part to its perforated strip, and this was something that Hornby came up with on his own account as a solution to the problem facing him and his two sons. 'I felt instinctively', he recorded, 'that I had hit upon the solution of my model-making difficulties. I little thought, however, that this scheme I worked out in my mind during that railway journey was destined to change the whole course of my life and to develop into a hobby that would bring untold hours of pleasure to boys of every nation and every age throughout the world.'

With the idea taking shape more quickly now, Hornby set to work making the components by hand, beginning with the easiest parts. He chose to use copper because it was soft and easy for him to work with. After initially setting about making a random selection of components he realised that he needed to concentrate his efforts, and make components that would be of most use. He began making the strips, finally deciding after some rumination to make strips 2^1/$_2$, 5^1/$_2$ and 12^1/$_2$ inches long, and each ^{1}/$_2$ inch wide.[38] It was laborious work, repetitive, but he kept himself going by trying to imagine how they could be used, and how useful they all might be. He considered the perforations and decided that they would all be perforated at ^{1}/$_2$-inch centres. He decided to use 8-gauge wire for the axles, but could not find any suitably sized bolts or fixings. In the end he made them by hand. Early models were crude, as some of his early illustrations show, but he had the basics of the system in place. He later observed that he had been extremely fortunate that the chosen dimensions of all the components turned out to be the most suitable, though he was probably modestly playing down the hard work and careful consideration he put into choosing them. At any rate these were never changed throughout the life of Meccano.

By 1900 Frank had a sufficient range of components to consider marketing his system. He took advice and went to a patents consultant (fee £5, which he had to borrow from Elliott). He did not have enough capital of his own, for as a 'cattle salesman's cashier', or clerk, he did not have the necessary disposable income. Having borrowed the money for the patent consultant, Patent no. 587 was lodged with the UK Patents Office on 30 November 1901. At this stage Frank had not properly named his toy. The only name appearing on the patent was 'Improvements in Toy or Educational Devices for Children and Young People'.

Perhaps unsurprisingly, given the distinctly uncatchy name with which his invention was saddled in its early days, the patent emphasised the educational and creative roles of the toy, rather than anything so frivolous as fun. 'This invention', began the Provisional Patent, 'has for its  object a toy or educational device for children. There has long been felt a want among young people for some device which will enable them to construct mechanical objects without the laboriousness of turning, boring, and careful adjustment. The present invention is designed to meet this want, and provide the means whereby the interest in mechanical construction from an elementary point of view, is enhanced in addition to providing an interesting means of mechanical education.'[39]

The patent detailed the essential elements of the invention – the regular pierced holes and the provision of slotted holes in the angle-pieces that allowed for adjustments; the uniform dimensions of parts and a fairly crude key system for fixing wheels to axles. The patent also envisaged that the final version might also include a small tool kit (file, pliers, screwdriver and the like) to allow children to modify the parts. (This idea was eventually turned down, possibly because Frank had trouble enough sourcing manufacturers for the components alone, or because the finished kits were to prove expensive even without allowing for tools.)[40]

Though there were no illustrations in the provisional specification Hornby suggested the kind of models that could be made, most of them connected to railways in some way or other, perhaps acknowledging the toy's conception on the train and presaging another of his great products. Though the list of 'railway lines, railway curves, points, inclines, bridges, tunnels, stations, signals, signal boxes' seems a little dull, there are flashes of the brilliance of Hornby's toy that would help to establish it as an all-time bestseller.

Young boys' fascination with railways was almost certainly part of the attraction of the early model kits, and Frank knew his market right from the start; after all, it had been tested on his two sons. In addition to the railways, however, the provisional specification also mentioned warehouses, suspension bridges and even anticipated the development of the range to allow the building of little model railways complete with warehouses, platforms and tunnels made of cardboard 'that will lend itself to painted designs'. All that was required was 'a certain amount of study and ingenuity'.

Such a model railway was still some way in Hornby's future, but this proto-Meccano specification still demonstrated a great deal of foresight, not least in the design of individual parts. The full specification nine months later included drawings of a suggested model (a rail-mounted crane, with the rails in loving detail), together with a fuller explanation and description of the constituent parts. Though the system still had some growing to do before it was rechristened Meccano, it was pretty well formed in the final patent. 'A child of ordinary ingenuity' could build various models 'without the use of special tools. Also various other objects can be assembled or built up by the exercise of a certain amount of study and ingenuity, and consequently the invention constitutes an education device for the young as well as a toy.'[41]

Naturally there were elements of the system that would be refined in the coming years. The patent specified a means for fitting wheels to axles that Hornby had devised, using a pin or 'key' to hold the wheels in place. (Years later it would be alleged that Hornby only abandoned this after seeing a superior design used by one of his American imitators, though this was never established.) However, while the system was crude and the scope of the patent limited, it promised a great deal: junior constructors would be limited only by their imaginations, and because they would not be using special tools, but 'proper' ones, they would acquire the basic practical skills of the engineer or mechanic, while learning the theories that underpinned them.

Having developed the system, Frank turned to its presentation. This was to become one of the major strengths of Meccano in its later years, but his first attempts mirrored the simplicity of the kits themselves. By Hornby's own admission it was all pretty rushed – probably in an attempt to get the kits into a few shops for the Christmas of 1901. Key to any model-building kit is, of course, the manual explaining how the system works and providing suggested models and building instructions. His first booklet was 18 pages long, and presented the toy as 'Mechanics Made Easy – An Adaptable Mechanical Toy'. This was to remain its name for another six years.

Understandably, given the fact that the system was new, a large proportion of the booklet explained how the toy worked, and how the pieces could be used. 'This invention', it began, 'has for its object the Training of the Young in Mechanical Construction,' The introduction repeated verbatim Hornby's aim outlined in the patent to 'fill the want among young people for a mechanical toy' which would enable them to make mechanical models without having to fabricate any parts themselves, adding that it would allow the development 'of the constructive genius of the child, at the same time dispensing with expensive and intricate tools'.

The system was initially probably targeted not so much at children themselves – who could scarce afford such a costly pastime – but at concerned and interested parents. The introduction appealed to their concerns not only for their children's happiness, but also to their regard for the education, and acquisition of skills that would stand them in good stead in later life:

Everyone must have recognized how full of interest to a

child's mind is the 'building up of an object'; how hour
after hour has been pleasantly spent in childish attempts
to make models of things which have attracted his
attention. If then this bent of its mind can be turned into
the right groove, an educational process has been
commenced which may, later on, prove of great benefit.
The aimlessness of an undeveloped fancy will give way to
an organized method, and from confused, hazy ideas will
spring order and precision.

Clearly Hornby saw Mechanics Made Easy as an amusement, but
more importantly as part of a disciplined approach to both leisure
and learning. At the same time he reiterated a common belief that
the cultivation of scientific order in everyday life was something
to be striven for: mechanics as a metaphor for an orderly life.

Upon examination it will be found this invention will
help to train the child's mind on these lines; chaos will
give way to order; a hazy conception to a definite idea;
guess work to accuracy; while at the same time the
various parts will give endless scope to the constructive
abilities of either a child or a grown up person.

The several parts of this invention have been so made
that they easily fit into each other in a great variety of
ways. This being so, it is self-evident they can be used to
construct a great variety of objects. Herein lies the charm
to the child's mind.

Moreover, when one object has been made, the several
parts can be taken asunder, and used again and again in
totally different directions.

> Hence it will be found that even a young child will be
> able to construct cranes, Machinery, Shafting, Bridges,
> Wagons, Railway Lines, Inclines, Signals &c.; and with
> the addition of pieces of cardboard, Railway Stations,
> Towers, Tunnels, &c.

> Another feature of this invention is that it is practically
> unbreakable – notwithstanding falls, blows and constant
> usage – consequently it will last much longer than the
> usual mechanical toy on the market.

There was a list of the parts included, together with a dozen suggested models. These included cranes, bridges and a miniature Eiffel Tower, but the most common models had a railway theme – rolling stock, tracks and signals. Undoubtedly this reflects Hornby's own interests in railway engineering, and is perhaps also a nod of recognition to the toy's conception aboard a train. More importantly it shows that Hornby appreciated his market. The toy was aimed at little boys, and by the turn of the century the developments in railways throughout Europe had spawned a huge growth in toy trains.

Conscious of his lack of formal education or training in engineering, Hornby had been particularly keen to canvass opinion of his new invention from trained professionals. He discussed it at length with engineers and mechanics, often sending them drawings and samples. One such was H. S. Hele-Shaw. Professor Hele-Shaw (1854–1941) had been Whitworth Scholar at the University of Bristol at just 22, and was the first professor of engineering at Liverpool University (1885–1904). His work included studies on friction (which gave rise to both an aeroplane

propeller and a motor-car clutch that were named after him).[42]
Aside from being a president of the Institute of Mechanical
Engineers, and a president of the Institute of Automobile
Engineers Hele-Shaw was an enthusiastic educator and advocate
of technical education. (He was later to be instrumental in
organising technical education in Britain through the National
Certificate System.) Hele-Shaw replied to Hornby with a brief but
complimentary letter which Hornby seized upon as a testimonial.
The letter, dated 5 November 1901, was reproduced in full in his
first instruction booklet:

WALKER ENGINEERING
LABORATORIES
UNIVERSITY COLLEGE
LIVERPOOL, *Nov. 5th, 1901.*

Dear Sir,

Thank you very much for the photographs of your clever
and useful form of toy. When it is on the market I shall
certainly buy a set for my little boy, and feel sure it will
afford many hours of enjoyment both to father and son.
With a little ingenuity and exercise of the imagination, it
should be as good as a fairy story, and what can one say
more!

Yours truly,

H. S. HELE-SHAW

To Mr. F. Hornby

For the time being, however, the limits to this brave new world remained in place. More specifically they were provided by Frank's difficulties in getting his parts made; his difficulty in getting anyone to sell the kits and – unless you were an unusually affluent child – the difficulty in affording to buy one.

Throughout 1901 Frank had searched out local manufacturers and suppliers who could fabricate his components. However, the system of contracting out the manufacture of the various parts could only ever be practical when the volume of parts involved was small. Frank later recalled the difficulties that arose from these arrangements – particularly when demand for Mechanics Made Easy grew. 'At first I had the various parts made for me by different manufacturers. This arrangement worked fairly well for a while, but presently, as the system became known and the demand for parts increased, all kinds of troubles developed. I could never rely on all the parts being ready at the same time; and frequently outfits for which dealers were becoming impatient were held up because one firm had failed to supply a particular part by the time specified.'[43]

In addition to problems with the delivery of the orders, Hornby repeatedly had trouble with their actual manufacture. The early Mechanics Made Easy kits were made from tinplate, with the brass components – such as the wheels – made by local brass foundries. However, the quality of the parts varied and there were occasional discrepancies in manufacture, finishing or even gauge. Not only were there variations in corresponding components made by different firms, even parts made by the same firm could vary from order to order.

Problems of quality and finish beset the industry as a whole. Writing a critique of British industry in the nineteenth century E. E. Williams described a contemporary of Hornby's as making toys well, 'always excepting a certain lack of finish, which English manufacturers seem to regard as the hallmark of excellence'.[44] Yet this lack of finish was not so much a badge of honour among British manufacturers as an indication that the industry was only just hitting its stride. As manufacturers like Hornby and the Britains family became more involved in the industry they brought ingenuity, industry, entrepreneurial skill and a deal of common sense to bear on such problems.

Faced with problems in the manufacture and delivery of his components, Hornby came to the inevitable conclusion: production of the components would have to be centralised. 'Thus I found myself embarked on an entirely new adventure. From being an inventor I became a manufacturer.'[45]

From that moment the direction of Hornby's life changed. As he noted, he had become a manufacturer rather than an inventor; a businessman not a designer. His involvement in the development of his invention was to take on a very different aspect, and his involvement in day-to-day model-making all but stopped.[46]

4

Elliott Hornby Begins Production

T he industry into which Hornby had now launched himself has not always been kindly regarded by historians. The generation writing before the Second World War were very dismissive of the record of late-Victorian British entrepreneurs. They tarred the leaders of industry with the same brush as their political and military counterparts, who through a lack of imagination and understanding had led a generation into the cataclysm of the Great War. H. G. Wells went so far as to attribute this dullness to an inability to slough off the stultifying influences of the Church of England and Oxford University. The less excitable commentators pointed to characteristic failings of small, family-run firms, where family ties were the primary qualification for managerial responsibility. Bad management allied to poor entrepreneurial skills reinforced a generally lazy or indifferent approach to marketing, which looked to imperial markets rather than continental ones, and did little to adopt any techniques which might render products more attractive to new markets. A quaint British obsession with quality regardless of cost, time or the demands of the market did not help. By contrast it appeared that their continental counterparts, most particularly the Germans, had strengthened their business interests in a similar way to their political and imperial ones – through an aggressive and determined approach, and a hard-headed grasp of modern realities. No industry seemed to exemplify this sorry picture more than the toy industry, dominated by foreign imports and characterised by small family firms.

The reality, of course, was far more complicated. While German products had established a dominance in the commercial toy industry, this accounted for only part of the trade. Playthings were not a nineteenth-century invention, and domestic toy manufacture had a long history. Toys had been produced in one form or another since classical antiquity, and there was a distinction to be made between the age-old business of making playthings for children and the relatively new commercial toy business. Such traditional backwaters were often undisturbed by winds blowing through the business from continental Europe.

As we have seen, by the 1870s commercial toy making had been on the increase in Britain as a result of a number of social and economic changes. Changes in social conditions helped to create a market for toys while at the same time stimulating their manufacture. A steady rise in the standard of living accompanied a consumer boom in the latter half of the nineteenth century, which was itself sustained by changes in production which had driven the cost of a range of consumer goods down. Innovations in retailing, marketing, banking and credit went to help those with increased disposable income find somewhere to dispose of it. These changes were not confined to the fortunate few but cut across the social groups to varying degrees.

Further changes in lifestyle (including smaller families and greater living space) laid the ground for a growth in the sale of luxuries. Whether toys count as luxuries in this context is perhaps a moot point, but by the turn of the century the British toy industry was well placed finally to break out of the shadow of German competition. The Great War inevitably provided a shot in the arm, and further impetus was provided by a new generation of toy manufacturers and entrepreneurs. Many of these companies – some with experience of the industry, others entirely new to the game – showed themselves fully equipped to exploit the conditions favourable to the building of large empires within a flourishing domestic industry. In doing so they gave birth to some of the best known and loved products of the last 100 years. One such man was Frank Hornby and his first but by no means last contribution to the toy-world's Hall of Fame would become one of the world's most popular – Meccano.

Hornby's first steps in the industry, beavering away in his workshop to perfect his toy, were not out of keeping with an industry long characterised by small firms and small-scale production. The census of 1841 recorded 2,000 toy makers and dealers, many of which were very small concerns.[1] Though the 1850s and 1860s had seen a number of important toy firms establish themselves, small companies continued to be the norm.[2] Many were so small that they failed to show up on production censuses. In Booth's *Life and Labour of the People of London*

(1903) he noted the relatively small-scale nature of the industry in the capital: at most two or three factories employing thirty or forty workers. The gross output of the industry in the 1907 census of production was only £216,000, reflecting both this small scale of production, and the cheapness of the products.[3] There was nothing in the UK to rival the large French factory of Duprien in Montreuil, which employed around 1,000 people manufacturing tin toys in the 1890s.

Innovation was not in short supply, however. Changes to the patent laws in 1852 resulted in a flood of applications from toy makers, hinting that if nothing else, the industry was not short of ideas. This creativity did not always extend to other aspects of the business such as sales and marketing. The fashion industry or the souvenir and novelty trades were used to promoting their products heavily to capture the public's imagination and sell rapidly changing lines. Toy makers, however, were geared to selling toys for Christmas. They were not looking to sell toys all year round, and seldom appealed to the imaginations of children. Instead they made muted appeals to their parents, and sold their wares through unglamorous outlets such as hardware shops. Advertising was sombre, where it existed at all, and it tended to be in general dealers' catalogues rather than in publications aimed at children. The business still appealed to the parents' pockets, or their sober hopes for their children's improvement, rather than the children's imaginations.

This lack of imagination was also reflected in the export of toys. By the 1860s exports of British toys were worth around £80,000 a year. Most, however, were destined for well-established

Imperial markets such as India, Australia, Canada and the Commonwealth, suggesting the inventors' ideas were not matched by those of their sales force. Other countries had not been so reticent. The Germans in particular had used trade fairs and international exhibitions to market their wares throughout Europe and beyond their imperial territories. The British had remained wary, not least because the spirit of protectionism of the mid-nineteenth century regarded such exhibitions as folly. The Great Exhibition of 1851 seemed to be little more than an invitation to the entry of foreign products, and protectionists criticised it roundly. British toy makers were conspicuous by their absence from the Crystal Palace. German manufacturers, on the other hand, appreciated the role that such exhibitions and competitions could have in terms of publicity and marketing. They were the driving force behind the trade fairs organised in cities like Manchester from the middle of the century. By the 1870s British manufacturers had set aside their diffidence and several won awards at the Paris exhibition of 1878, but it would take British firms fifty years to appreciate fully the role these fairs and exhibitions could have. Once learned, however, manufacturers like Hornby or Basset Lowke showed a flair, imagination and drive that more than matched their European counterparts.

That the Germans had established a prominence in the British market could not be denied, though some tended to overstate it for a variety of political or economic motives. Writing in the 1870s E. E. Williams had lamented that 'to a large and ever-increasing extent our children's playthings . . . are made in Germany'.[4] By 1900 German imports were worth around £800,000.[5] They accounted for over half the total of toy imports into Britain – a share which rose consistently in the months prior to 1914.[6] Added to the influx of products there had been a steady stream of German immigrants bringing skills and techniques into the country, but also acting as salesmen and agents for German firms. Some commentators agreed with Williams's pessimistic view of the situation, and feared for their livelihoods. Changes in printing techniques (for the making of miniature theatres), the introduction of bisque (as opposed to wax) for dolls and the mastery of the tin-toy manufacturers of Nuremberg all hurt competing British manufacturers. (Evans and Cartwright of Wolverhampton, who at their height had employed over 50 workers, were one of the largest casualties.) At a time of militant German military and economic expansion this dominance raised fears that were quite often thinly veiled xenophobia. However, both the reality of German strength and its hysterical depiction by certain commentators disguised a domestic toy industry that was far from suffering. At the same time British toy exports were worth over £350,000 and growing. The industry had, in the words of its historian, reached adolescence; the coming years would see a marked growth spurt.[7] At the forefront of this growth were the manufacturers like Hornby who were coming to overtake the smaller-scale manufacture of playthings, much of which had not changed for centuries.

Brightly packaged, commercially produced toys sold in shops were only one kind of plaything, and a relatively recent innovation. For centuries homemade toys had been bought and  sold. These were the cheap toys sold for a penny in the bazaars or on the street by hawkers and pedlars. Ernest King – who later gave his collection to the Museum of London – bought 1,700 such toys, all for a penny between 1893 – 1918. (Charlie Chaplin earned a modest income as a boy selling three dozen handmade boats a week for a penny each on the streets of London. He had been taught by two itinerant Scottish toy makers, but had to find alternative work after his mother complained about him boiling up the glue in her laundry pans.) The 1907 census put the figure of such workers at around 1,250,000 selling small dolls, flags and other cheap toys.[8]

Despite their numbers the exact value of their trade is difficult to establish. There were other toy sales that were not counted because they stemmed from the fringes of the industry. These included those products that although used or even sold as toys, had not always been conceived or made as such. These included miniature versions of adult wares (e.g. bicycles, vacuum cleaners or carpet sweepers), salesman's demonstrators or spin-offs. On occasion the value of the trade in such articles could amount to a significant slice of the company's business, and indicated the extent to which manufacturers of consumer goods were coming to appreciate the growing youth market.[9]

There were other playthings that had not been specifically invented as toys. These included scientific instruments and a whole panoply of quasi-scientific tools and curios from gyroscopes and magnets to telescopes and magnifying glasses. There was a kinship between these and more frivolous amusements, strengthened by the fact that some of the principal early stockists of mechanical or metal toys were also retailers of scientific equipment. By 1868 one such Liverpool manufacturer and retailer listed among his stock a wide variety of mechanical toys, including boats, telescopes, model telegraphs and tool chests. One of several British award winners at the 1878 exhibition in Paris was the Scientific Toy and General Novelty Co. of London.

Clearly the industry recognised the amusement and diversion that could be derived from scientific apparatus and instruments. There was also a willingness to use science to develop new and popular playthings. Henry Mayhew, writing in his celebrated study of London working-class life in the 1860s, noted this connection.

> Optics gives its burning glass, its microscopes, its magic
> lantern, its stereoscope, its thaumatrope, its
> phantasmascope . . . electricity its Leyden jars, galvanic
> batteries, electrotypes, etc.; chemistry its balloons,
> fireworks, and crackers; mechanics its clockwork mice –
> its steam and other carriages; pneumatics contributes its
> kites and windmills; acoustics its Jew-harps, musical

glasses, accordions, and all the long train of musical
instruments; astronomy lends its orreries; in fine, there is
scarcely a branch of knowledge which is not made to pay
tribute to the amusement of the young.[10]

Despite Mayhew's sniffy feeling that knowledge was being
debased by being made both popular and interesting to children,
there was more broadly a tendency to recognise the educational
value that toys could have.

Such toys constituted a large part of what *Games, Toys &
Amusements* described as 'the costlier and better kinds of
playthings in which we can confidently hold our own'. This was
one of the traditional strengths of the industry in Britain and
included the wooden toys of the Lines Brothers, boxed games and
educational toys. Much of this growth was at the hands of a new
generation of toy manufacturers. The mid-nineteenth century had
seen a number of manufacturers set up business. These included
future giants such as G. & J. Lines, Britains and Hornby, but also
a number of other companies who enjoyed significant success in
the thirty years before the Great War.[11]

Many of these companies had come into being on the back of
the changes in economic and social conditions that had
stimulated an interest and market in toys. The increases in
disposable incomes for families up and down the social scale
provided a welcome stimulus for a whole range of consumer
industries. However, the industries themselves were not merely
passive in this growth. Manufacturers were starting to get to grips
with advertising (which had been taxed until the legislation of
1853–5), and soon showed an enthusiasm for it that was usually

untrammelled to anything approaching subtlety. Hornby himself had a flair for the medium – in other words, he often greatly exaggerated the virtues of his products to dramatic effect. By the 1890s toy manufacturers had an expanding range of organs at their disposal for promoting their wares. Trade journals, a growing children's press, enthusiasts' periodicals and clubs.

Technological developments such as mass production (e.g. of tin soldiers) stimulated interest and developed markets. Britains developed a method of toy-soldier production based on techniques previously used for wax dolls, and further modified it to allow changes to models by modifying parts of the mould to give different heads, arms or legs. Generals became kings with relative ease. The whole system allowed one worker to produce hundreds of figures an hour, and gave the company a great advantage in its efforts to break into a market that was thought to be heavily defended by well-entrenched German toy soldiers. Well supported by a keen attention to detail which matched their eye for innovation, Britains were able to beat back the enemy. It was a winning combination which Hornby would later employ with equally impressive results against another classic German toy, the train set. [12]

By the middle of the nineteenth century the domestic toy industry was growing steadily. Expansion of toys reflects wider growth in consumerism and developments in production and manufacturing – both techniques and processes. It also testified to changes in society as a whole. Rising living standards and increased disposable income, even among the lower echelons of society, had brought commercially produced toys (as opposed to the traditional homemade variety) within the reach of a far greater number of children. The growth of the middle class also swelled the market.

Industrial reforms had created new-found leisure time for the working class, and the growing numbers of toy manufacturers and retailers were only too keen to help fill it. This offer was no doubt easier to resist for the poorer parents. The middle classes seem to have taken their place in the toy shop with as much alacrity and excitement as they did in other areas of life. For the lower orders it could be a little different. Though the falling cost of living cut across the classes, some parents preferred to dispose of their income not in a toy shop but rather in one of the many and widespread new public houses.

At the turn of the century Seebohm Rowntree calculated that the average family might only have around sixpence left after all necessities had been provided for.[13] This did not account for life's little luxuries such as something to drink or to smoke, let alone toys. Of course, if there was a will many parents found a way to provide their children with something special to play with, or else to mark their birthdays or Christmas. In addition there were a number of charitable or philanthropic initiatives set up during the century with the express purpose of providing toys or games for deprived and unfortunate children.

Across the board there was a recognition that toys were worthwhile, and this both fed off and was encouraged by a new breed of manufacturers. It was these giants who more than anyone came to represent the flower of the industry. They combined flair and an understanding of marketing and promotion with hard work, innovation in business practice and good products. No one embodied this spirit of dynamism better than Hornby. The determination with which Frank pursued his dream of becoming an inventor was probably matched only by his enthusiasm. Into his dream of manufacturing a successful educational toy system he swept up not only his family but his employer as well. Frank's marriage, in keeping with the rest of his family relationships, was close and loving. Frank and Clara shared a number of interests including music and the arts (Frank was also apparently a keen photographer), bridge, dancing and entertaining. Clara also shared with Frank his enthusiasm for Mechanics Made Easy. This was just as well during the early years when money and time were in short supply, for without his wife's support and encouragement it is doubtful whether Frank would have been able to carry on, such was his sense of duty.

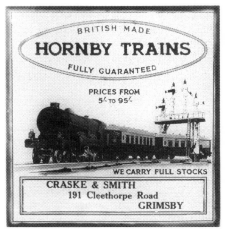

As it was, Frank had abandoned his quest for the Holy Grail of perpetual motion in favour of something more prosaic. He had been spending his time working on toys for his children, and as they approached the age of ten they were increasingly enjoying the time spent with their father tinkering in the workshop and playing. There was a playfulness to Frank's inventing which belied his serious determination, and in many ways revealed the two sides of his nature. In business he was serious and austere. His fob watch and waxed moustache gave him a stern Victorian smartness. Yet in company, particularly that of his family, he was vivacious and lively. He doted on his wife and two boys, and his energies and humour were shared equally between adults and children. He was invariably ready for games and play, and at one Christmas gathering he involved all the assembled house guests in a demonstration of one of his early inventions. He had been working on a toy submarine and persuaded everyone to follow him upstairs to test the toy in a bathtub. This they duly did, and crammed into the bathroom. In the excitement Frank's young niece fell into the bathtub of cold water fully clothed and was soaked to the skin. Sadly the excitement was not justified by the submarine's performance: it sank like a stone.[14]

Because of the nature of Frank's inventions and his enthusiasm for them it was easy for Clara to offer support and encouragement, even in the early days when things were hard. In many ways Frank was a figure who invited trust and support. Though becoming an inventor like his boyhood heroes had long been a dream of his, Frank was not by nature a dreamer. He, like his inventions, was intensely practical. By night he worked in his workshop but by day continued to work for Elliott, and by the turn of the century was his chief clerk. To his goal of succeeding with his toys he brought humour, enthusiasm and determination coupled with the reassuring steadiness of the bookkeeper.

It was perhaps this reliability as much as the strength of his idea which prompted Elliott to back his chief clerk's invention. Hornby, however, did not take any chances. Rather than casually ask for a loan from his employer Frank cannily brandished the testimonial from Professor Hele-Shaw as evidence that his scheme was a certain success. 'I forget what I wrote about Mr Hornby's work and ambition,' Hele-Shaw later recalled, 'but he told me, when he proudly showed me round the Meccano Works during a visit of the Institute of Mechanical Engineers in 1934, that he had been able to borrow £5 as a result of my letter; and with a twinkle in his eye, assured me that it had been promptly paid back again!'[15]

Trust between the two men was not really much of an issue. Hornby was Elliott's bookkeeper; the two had worked closely together for some time and had forged such a strong bond of friendship and mutual respect that Frank later gave his daughter the middle name Elliott. Elliott advanced Frank the £5 required to cover the fees of the Patent Agent and register his new product at the beginning of 1901. The difficulties he had in finding adequate suppliers for his parts and components left Frank with little choice but to begin to fabricate them himself – even the nuts and bolts. He set about it, later recalling that 'This job seemed as though it would never end!' The difficulties Frank had in sourcing components only confirmed in his own mind that he alone knew what was required and that he was the best placed to accomplish it. 'Every day as I laboured on I felt more and more certain that I was proceeding on the right lines and that success was ultimately assured.'

His little home workshop was nowhere near adequate, and so premises needed to be found. Once again Elliott helped his employee, and the two of them went into partnership. Premises were rented next door to Elliott's own at 18 James Street at Elliott's expense. In fact, it was Elliott who bore the brunt of the new venture's expenses and running costs in its early years, and so Hornby's choice of his employer-partner's name for his daughter was as much a reflection of his gratitude as his friendship. The new venture was heavily reliant on Elliott's goodwill and investment. Hornby, of course, handled the accounts (though on Elliott's stationery, and probably in his time) and Elliott put up almost £500 to Frank's £92.

Mechanics Made Easy kits were produced in time for Christmas, though it was something of a rushed affair. The instruction booklet for the early sets featured 12 models, but the majority of the booklet was occupied with a long-winded exposition of the principles and benefits of Mechanics Made Easy. One such selling point was that 'it is practically unbreakable – notwithstanding falls, blows, and constant usage – consequently it will last much longer than the usual mechanical toy at present on the market.'[16] This was just as well since despite certain crudities it was quite expensive. The first kits were priced at 7s 6d, which was a lot to spend on any kind of toy. Indeed, it was more than enough to buy a whole range of quite attractive toys. Hornby's kit, on the other hand was made of tinplate, all save the wheels which he had managed to get cast in the local foundries. The parts were mostly bundled together in a crude box in which they all rattled about.

With the patents applied for and the premises secured Elliott and Hornby set about producing the Mechanics Made Easy kits in earnest. The factory at James Street was in fact simply a one-room workshop-cum-despatch room. The accounts for 1901–3 record that the total wages bill was £49 16s, all of which was probably payable to the single female assistant they hired. It would be some years before Hornby could draw a salary from the company, or Elliott would see a return on his investment. However, for that same period the balance sheet showed a healthy promise. They actually made a loss of just over £20 for the period, but sales amounted to £537 14s 6d (equivalent to around 2,000 kits) and the company had stock totalling a further £129.[17] The potential of Mechanics Made Easy was not obvious in this earlier period. A number of retailers had refused to stock the kits – quite possibly on the basis of their rough and ready appearance. However, Hornby was about to reveal his real talent – business.

These early accounts revealed that from the very beginning Hornby recognised the value of advertising. Right from the start he was spending almost as much on promoting his product as he was on employing people to make it. The first advertisement for Mechanics Made Easy appeared in 1902 in the *Model Engineer and Amateur Electrician*. The advert boasted that as well as providing 'a charming occupation' through the construction of 'an endless variety of models', the toy involved no expense for tools, and was 'indestructible'. As far as the 'endless variety of models' is concerned this was probably a little overselling the kits, but they did afford some popular and fascinating designs. These included a gantry crane with moving trolley that Hornby was so pleased with he included an image of it in both his early advertising and his first instruction booklet. That same year a review of Mechanics Made Easy appeared in the same publication. Under the heading 'A Mechanical Toy for Embryo

Engineers' the magazine reviewed Hornby's 'latest version of the box of bricks'. Despite this remark the review was a good one, even noting that Frank's self-fabricated nuts and bolts were well made and not likely to wear out. The magazine recommended the kit as a superb choice for 'parents and elder brothers . . . at a loss to know what to purchase in the way of toys for the younger members of the family who evince a natural liking for things mechanical'. It went on: 'Models of wheelbarrows, rope tramways, swing and bascule bridges are possible, in fact the scope of the toy is unlimited, and, to prove its capabilities, we built up, in the space of about a quarter-of-an-hour, a representation of the Rottingdean submerged railway.'[18]

Quite what their model looked like using only the parts that came in the Mechanics Made Easy kit we can only wonder at. What was clear, however, was that Hornby's product was capable of capturing the imagination, in the same way that it carried him away. The article also demonstrated the positive role that publicity and marketing could play. By 1904–5 the company was spending slightly more on advertising (£30 17s 6d) than it was on wages (£29 6s).

In addition to advertising, Hornby had taken an interesting approach to finding outlets for his kits. Within the context of an industry that was still largely seasonal the toy trade reflected the more general changes in retailing that were afoot in the country at large. Department stores, the development and growth of chains of shops and the reorganisation of retail outlets and organisations meant that business was rationalised or consolidated in different cities. Overall, however, the trade continued to grow. In addition to the shops, the toy industry continued to employ a large number of street-sellers, who had always been a distinct and important element of the trade. By the eve of the First World War there were nearly 70,000 such vendors working in Britain operating in markets, squares, cathedral courts or shady alleys. These hawkers had originally sold a large variety of toys, but as the retail trade began to stock more playthings street-sellers found it increasingly difficult to compete for trade in more up-market toys such as dolls. Yet they always had an eye on public tastes and were quick to make and sell such trifles as were popular. Cheap penny toys were their speciality, handmade and sold at small profit – but often in large numbers.

Specialised toy shops were still a thing of the future, however. Instead the bulk of the trade was handled by general dealers or fancy-goods shops such as Phillips & Son in Liverpool. Toys could be a useful and profitable sideline for a whole range of retailers, but it was still impossible to earn a living selling toys from a shop all year round. Some of the large new department stores flirted with the idea, but soon retreated with only modest profits or, more usually, losses.

It was such retailers that Hornby approached. With his sample tins under his arms he approached a number of Liverpool retailers. Full of brio he expected to be overwhelmed with the kind of enthusiasm which Clara and David Elliott had shown him. For the first time he encountered criticism and indifference. 'I was firmly convinced', he recalled,

> that I had only to show it to manufacturers and dealers for them to be tumbling over one another to be the first to make and sell it. I was quickly undeceived. The dealers considered it to be crude and unattractive in appearance, and were very emphatic that it was not in the least likely to meet with a favourable reception from the public; and the manufacturers would not even look at it. Although these rebuffs were very disappointing they did not shake my confidence in the ultimate success of my invention. By degrees I succeeded in persuading a few dealers to take it up, in many cases against what they called their 'better judgement'![19]

Initially sales were handled on a franchise basis, with Hornby bypassing wholesalers and selling his product direct to the retailers. Perhaps this was because this was the method by which Frank first broke into the market, and the arrangement suited him. Elliott had introduced Frank to a retailer of scientific apparatus, Philip, Son & Nephew, who as George Philip & Son had a branch in Fleet Street, London, and as Philip Son & Nephew in South Castle Street, Liverpool, and Stoke-on-Trent. They were persuaded to accept a few kits, but initial sales were slow, no doubt in part because of the cost. Other retailers who agreed to handle Mechanics Made Easy in its first few years included the Birmingham Engineering Company, and Osborn & Jordan of Sydney, Australia.

It was also in 1903 that Hornby established what was to become one the great strengths of the Meccano company – the model-building competition. The first was advertised to model makers and hobbyists in the *Model Engineer* in October 1903. The model competitions served three purposes. First, as with most public competitions it whipped up publicity and interest far beyond the kind normally generated by standard advertising. Secondly, these competitions opened up new markets for Hornby both geographically and in terms of the type and range of his customers. Through the competitions he was able to break into new countries, and new markets. One such was that of the (adult) hobbyist. Lastly, Frank, having to spend all his time looking after the business of Mechanics Made Easy, had little or no time to develop new parts or ideas for new models. Perhaps this was a blessing in disguise, since many of Frank's early Mechanics Made Easy models were distinctly crude. 'The exaggerated claims which Hornby attached to many of his own creations,' noted the Meccano historian Bert Love, 'were largely the result of over-enthusiasm coupled with a sketchy knowledge of true engineering principles.'[20] Public competitions provided Hornby with ideas for new models and modifications that would become one of the standard tools for research and development of the product for the rest of its life.

The first competition was for boys under 15 years of age and offered substantial cash prizes of between 10s and £5. Entrants could use any combination of the parts available in the Mechanics Made Easy series (including cardboard 'to make the model attractive' and primitive gears which Hornby had made for the kits by a local clockmaker). All the models were to be sent to Liverpool at the company's expense, where they would be judged pending an exhibition. The competition was a success. Entries were received from the length and breadth of the country, and the exhibition was held at the Mount Pleasant YMCA in Liverpool on 11 and 12 February. In the absence of Hornby's old supporter Professor Hele-Shaw the competition was adjudicated by J. E. Lloyd Barnes, a member of the Institute of Mechanical Engineers. The winning entry was a gantry crane made by an E. H. Edwards from Wolverhampton, but other entries included cable-powered tipping wagons and motor-driven cranes, as well as a model of the Eiffel Tower with a working lift, and a large model of two of the cantilevers of the Forth Rail Bridge entered by the Technical Department of the Bedford Grammar School.

The competition illustrated Hornby's grasp of marketing and advertising, as well as his continued desire for academic respectability for his educational toy. He was delighted to receive an entry from a school. The fact that his kits were being used in schools was every bit as rewarding as the demonstration afforded by the competition and exhibition of the great range of models that his kits could make. (He was so delighted by the model of the Forth Bridge, which was, needless to say, far better than anything he had made, that it featured in his promotional literature for some years to come.) The competition was limited to under-15s in recognition of the potential complexity of the models and the kit. However, it also demonstrated the fact that the market for Mechanics Made Easy (as with some other, mainly educational toys) was not limited to children. There had been in the last decade or so a further extension of the (commercial) toy habit. Since the last quarter of the nineteenth century it had extended down the social scale; now it was breaking out of the confines of childhood. *Model Engineer and Amateur Electrician*, in which Hornby had placed his first advertisements and which promoted his competition, was not a children's magazine but a hobbyist's paper. In October 1895 the inaugural issue of *Hobbies* magazine was published to cater for the growing interest in formal leisure activities. These in themselves were nothing new. (The first use of the word to denote these pastimes came in Scott's *The Antiquary* in 1816.) Many – like pigeon fancying, whippet racing, gardening, or decorative fretwork – had their roots in older traditions of animal husbandry, horticulture or carpentry. By 1895 *Hobbies* could observe, 'It is but very rare nowadays that one encounters a person who does not possess a hobby of some kind.'[21] The first issue ranged across such pastimes as fretwork and carpentry, amateur photography, magic lanterns, stamp collecting, sports and bent ironwork.

Some contemporary observers were unsure as to whether hobbies were in themselves a good thing, or even harmless since they absorbed energies which might be more profitably employed, principally for work. A German observer writing about British workers in the first half of the twentieth century noted that, 'for a man who takes a passionate interest in dog-racing, or football or making models, the job becomes of secondary interest. Sometimes the hobby can become so absorbing that it takes his mind off his work and lowers his efficiency.'[22] Others disagreed, pointing out that these energies when not employed for work were often spent in drinking and indolence. In such instances hobbies were preferable. Writing in 1922 in her study *The Young Industrial Worker*, Margaret Phillips made a distinction between 'personal interests' which were largely in the way of diversions (but included basic interests such as sex), and 'objective interests', which included more studied pursuits. She went on to say that for men these might include 'engineering and mechanical invention connected with their work', while in the case of girls 'housecraft or clothes'.[23]

This was an important distinction, for it drew attention to the fact that hobbies could serve different purposes for different people. For some it was undoubtedly a release from the boredom or the activities of their daily occupations. For others hobbies could serve to develop the skills that their jobs required, or further develop interest in their kind of occupation. Many chose to spend their leisure time on hobbies related to their work, with the crucial distinction that it was by their choice and on their own terms. This could have a very positive effect. Some workers acquired a great deal of knowledge about the machinery and processes they used, often becoming quite jealous of new machinery. Some foreign observers were impressed by the healthy interest of British workmen in machinery and technological problems associated with their work. At exhibitions and trade fairs they could be seen excitedly discussing the various merits and failings of British or American machinery with a knowledge and understanding at the very least as good as their managers'.[24]

Whether they were good or bad for employers, hobbies were certainly growing through the last half of the nineteenth century. Organised sport – particularly football – had taken off in the 1880s, helped in no small part by the development of new media that promoted and stimulated interest. New publications appeared at an astonishing rate covering football, cricket, rugby, cycling, athletics and field sports, while traditional newspapers devoted more and more space to the coverage of these activities. Increasingly interest in such sports as football revolved around

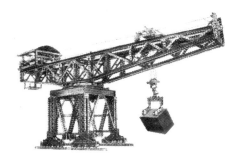

spectating rather than playing, and the newspapers catered for the enthusiast whose energies were devoted to being well informed and acquiring knowledge rather than skills. While some questioned whether 'spectatorism' was healthy, others pointed out that this sustained interest and acquisition of knowledge still required discipline, though it was intellectual rather than physical. Similarly, collecting had long been valued as an intellectual pursuit, and one associated with the development of knowledge, taste and connoisseurship among the travelling gentry on the Grand Tour long before it became a hobby for large numbers of the population.

Clearly hobbies could be extremely useful in developing certain disciplines and attributes, and the new range of magazines and papers focused on this aspect. The acquisition of skills or knowledge thus afforded is one of the defining characteristics of a hobby. First, they must be freely chosen. Secondly, they are organised and require discipline, in terms both of the individuals' application and their organisation into a local, regional or national framework of societies, leagues, competitions and clubs. As a result they demand sustained interest and a certain degree of knowledge. Lastly, they provide for the creation or discharge of some physical, intellectual or emotional tension.

Their proponents argued that these characteristics could only have positive effects on the development of people's characters. One of the aims of *Hobbies* magazine was to promote hobbies, and through a series of articles and features to help people find the hobby that was best suited to them. Hornby too recognised the positive effects hobbies could have in developing a disciplined and methodical approach, particularly in children: 'Every healthy boy has hobbies, and I often think that the earnestness and thoroughness with which he follows them is an index to the kind of man he will make when he grows up.' Hornby was also an astute businessman, and recognised the importance that hobbies had as a foundation for the industry, and the need to foster and promote them among children. 'A boy without a hobby always seems to me to lead an aimless and rather miserable existence; and whenever I come across such a boy I long to sit down beside him and talk to him, find out what his interests are, and start him off on a suitable hobby. It always gives me the greatest pleasure to see a boy following his hobbies with keenness, trying to find out more about them, and to improve his knowledge and skill in every possible way. I know that this keenness will become part of the boy's nature, and that when he grows up he will tackle the serious things of life in the same splendid spirit.'[25]

This positive attitude towards any kind of hobby was not just sound business sense. It was Frank's boyhood interest in mechanics and engineering which had brought him his fortune. As a result Hornby – 'The Boy Who Made $1,000,000 With a Toy' – was well aware that great things could grow from the apparently trivial, particularly when the pursuit of such pleasures bred determination and other moral virtues. Smiles had taught him that much. In a passage headed 'Might in Little Things' Smiles had recounted Benjamin Franklin's response to a sceptical contemporary who had asked him what use his work on electricity was. 'What is the use of a child?' Franklin retorted. 'It may become a man!' As a description of the toy maker's philosophy, Hornby could not have done better.[26]

Among the toys that most successfully bridged the generation gap and appealed to children and adults alike were model trains. Hornby's early Mechanics Made Easy literature showed a distinct bias towards trains and train sets, probably not least because his toy had evolved through playing with his two sons. The appeal of trains reflected the growth of the railways in the latter half of the century, and toy manufacturers had been quick to respond to the upsurge in interest. Toy trains had been produced since the mid-nineteenth century at least, and ranged from crude pull-along engines, to more sophisticated steam-powered models known as

119

'little piddlers' (for their not-so-endearing habit of leaving stains on the floor). By the latter half of the century tin toys had become extremely popular, and the great German manufacturers such as Mattheus Hess, Gebrüder Bing, Guenthermann, Karl Bub and George Carette (all of Nuremberg) were well-established manufacturers of tin toys, with trains a popular line.[27]

While the model-making competitions helped to promote the kits, they also served another purpose, eventually forming the basis for enthusiast clubs and societies that would stretch beyond the confines of childhood and educational benefit. What lasted into adulthood was the love of the models themselves, and the challenge of bettering those made by others. This was the final strength of Hornby's competitions. Models from the competitions were exhibited, but also incorporated into the manuals for later kits. In this way Hornby was able to appeal to the competitive instinct in modellers to outdo each other, which also provided a spur to the further development of the system.

Hornby now further expanded the kits and increased the range of parts. By 1905–6 both the system and the company were developing, though the latter progressed cautiously. Neither partner was yet able to take a salary from the venture and Hornby remained in the employ of Elliott as his manager. Still, sales were growing and now amounted to over £700, though high running costs meant this translated to only a meagre net profit of under £100. But at least the company was now trading at a profit. Elliott felt able to reduce his liability in the company and tentatively approached Frank. They agreed that he should withdraw a little under £100 of his capital stake, though Frank kept his capital in. Frank could have done with some return on his efforts, for although the company was now dealing with nigh on twenty retailers, had a growing sales return and for the first time a net profit, Frank's own circumstances changed. On 27 July 1905, 45-year-old Clara gave birth to their third child, Patricia Elizabeth.

Despite his added family responsibilities the Mechanics Made Easy trade was well enough established for him to give up his 'day job' with Elliott. It was Frank's turn to scale down his commitment to his partner, and in 1907 he resigned from his post as Elliott's manager to devote his time to looking for larger premises in which to start his own factory proper. Mechanics Made Easy now had retail outlets across the country and Hornby had broken into the market in France. As early as 1904 he had produced a French-language instruction booklet. His horizons had broadened.

5

The Birth of an Empire

In his later years, when Hornby was campaigning for the Everton seat in the 1931 general election he addressed a meeting in the Sailor's Welfare in Liverpool. In his address he made much of the fact that he was an experienced seafarer himself, having made over 60 Atlantic crossings. At a time when such a crossing could take anything between two and four weeks this was no mean achievement. Yet although the sea had always held a fascination for him, these crossings were not made for pleasure, but in the relentless pursuit of his business. Like others who had set out with such purpose across the ocean, Hornby was fashioning an empire.

His transatlantic crossings were necessary if Hornby was to ensure that his interests in the USA were established properly, and managed correctly. Hornby had always been a very involved and directorial manager, and while he delegated tasks and responsibilities he never surrendered either the power within the company or the central principle that he was its guiding genius. He cast a long shadow travelling across Europe and the USA to ensure that the company's growth was trained and channelled according to his own precepts. He was a father figure and his concerns were not simply for the growth and development of his progeny, but also for its security, since from the very beginning Hornby had recognised the central importance of protecting one's intellectual property. Even when a struggling clerk desperately trying to support his dreams as an inventor and a young family, Hornby had the presence of mind (or the good advice) to consult a patent agent. He had had to rely on the support and generosity of his employer to meet the £5 fee at the time, but within a very few years it became obvious what a sound and crucial investment this had been.

There had always been an international, or even internationalist, aspect to Hornby's view of business. Perhaps in some general way this was inevitable. Hornby was a Liverpool Man – it was the slogan he would later use when he ran for parliament – and Liverpool was the City of the Sea, the 'funnel of trade'. Hornby's father and brother Henry had both earned their living as dealer in commodities which almost all came off the ships berthed in Liverpool. His brother Oswald had also worked in the docks as a stevedore, and his sister Emma had sailed half-way round the world as a missionary. The Mersey prided itself on being the heart of the British import and export business, and it pumped relentlessly – people to the New World, meat from the Americas, products and dreams all over the world. When Hornby went down to the docks as a young boy he saw in the ships, cranes and locomotives, and in the docks and harbours, all the engineering marvels that were the currency of empire. In time they would be the inspiration for his fortune. He also saw that Liverpool was just one end of the process. Ships swarmed into Liverpool like so many leaves growing over the rim of the horizon, but the fruit lay out of sight.

Hornby had also had his imagination fired by Samuel Smiles's portraits of the industrial revolution's 'Communion of Saints'. Many of these celebrated industrialists and inventors had erected monuments visible in all four corners of the world, their engines had traversed the whole globe, inscribing their fame upon it. Britain's greatest export in the nineteenth century had been the notion of the power and possibility of science and industry. Hornby had drunk it all in, and realised that it was inextricably linked to the idea of an empire upon which the sun never set. Victoria's empire was built upon science and industry, and so was Hornby's.

And yet Hornby was international in his outlook in a very practical and concrete way too. Unlike so many of his contemporaries, Frank had recognised the need to build a strong domestic business, but to do so as a foundation on which to build outwards. His aim was to spread beyond the confines of the domestic or even imperial markets and to compete with the European giants, especially those in Germany. To do this he needed to be strong: to have a strong product; a strong manufacturing base; a strong market share; and a strong grip on the reins.

Despite initial reservations on the part of retailers and manufacturers Hornby's faith in his product was being rewarded. Mechanics Made Easy had returned its first real profit in 1906 and sales had been strong enough for Frank to leave Elliott to concentrate on his toys full-time. From the outset Frank at least had believed his product was a good one. Through force of determination, enthusiasm and a little native flannel Frank had managed to persuade a sufficient number likewise.

To create a strong manufacturing base Frank knew he needed to move to larger premises, and to find a space large enough to enable him to manufacture all of his components himself, rather than simply having one small room in which to assemble and pack kits comprising components sourced from often unreliable contractors. In 1907 Hornby signed a three-year lease on a one-room factory near the heart of Liverpool among the old Georgian warehouses and small factories in Duke Street. Street directories record the firm at 12 Duke Street, while the company's accounts and correspondence list the registered address as 10–12. In reality the building was something of a muddle.[1] Hornby described the set-up as 'a very crude affair – so crude, in fact, that looking back I often wonder how we produced anything at all'.[2] Initially Elliott & Hornby, Machine Tool Manufacturers shared 12 Duke Street with a firm of coopers, but within a couple of years they had all of the cramped premises to themselves.

Hornby transferred old stock to the new premises and proceeded to fit out the factory with some basic plant – hand presses, 'a lathe or two, and a small gas engine, which in spite of its many protests we succeeded in persuading to provide the necessary power'. In addition were some metal-cutting saws and guillotines, grinders and milling machines. The machines were bought as cheaply as possible and the whole move involved a bank loan of over £1,500. Owing to the age of the machines the manufacturing process provided Hornby with what he called 'plenty of excitement'. At least he was not now on his own. As part of the expansion Hornby had taken on some skilled assistants to operate the new machines, and some manual staff to work in packing and despatch and to handle the less-skilled work.[3]

Cleaning the brass components in vats of acid was especially hazardous, and it fell to Frank's unlucky chief assistant to stay behind with his enthusiastic boss to clean and lacquer the brass wheels and other parts. 'We had no proper system of ventilation,' Frank cheerfully recalled years later, 'with the result that the fumes from the acid often nearly choked us. When matters got too bad we had to suspend operations abruptly and dash out into the open air to recover, and at the same time give the air in the room a chance to recover!' Despite this and other hazards the company was now on a sound footing. Having gone some years without seeing much return on his investment (other than the satisfaction of seeing the business grow), Elliott was now able to further reduce his capital stake in the company, while Hornby increased his. Hornby's increased capital investment was made possible by the fact that there was now a £340 profit accruing to the partners. In addition Frank was at last able to draw a salary from the company. In the year to March 1908 Frank drew £3 per week for 38 weeks, before being able to give himself a rise to £5 per week for a further 10 weeks. This put him just over the income tax threshold. It was enough to furnish his house and even retain a servant. He was now probably matching the salary he had earned with Elliott, though he was not quite in the bracket of 'smaller businessmen', who F. G. D'Aeth, writing in the *Sociological Review* of 1910 estimated earned around £300 per year on average. At any rate, in the space of few years Hornby had established a strong market share for Mechanics Made Easy, renamed Meccano in 1907. Annual sales now totalled £2,957.

Typically, Hornby realised that further capital investment in the business was required if it was to grow. Though he had increased his own stake the kind of sums he needed were beyond his means alone. Legislation in 1900 and 1907 had led to a growth in the number of small companies registering as limited liability companies in order to re-capitalise and secure funds for further investment. A number of the more ambitious and progressive toy firms went down this route even earlier. Britains had secured capital funds of £18,000 by becoming a limited company in 1895. Hornby's were more modest at £8,000, though by no means the smallest.[4] He went to see his bankers Hill & Sons to discuss the possibility of limited liability. Having persuaded David Elliott to part with £5 on the back of a throwaway testimonial from a local academic was one thing, but these were somewhat higher stakes. Hornby, however, was an accountant and knew what bankers wanted to hear. The company was a new one but already had sales of £3,000 in the previous year; new premises, an enthusiastic workforce, growing markets all over the world, stock assets, patents pending. Needless to say, Hill & Sons agreed to become one of the backers together with Hornby and four local businessmen. George Jones, a photographic manager from Tranmere, Arthur Hooton, a bank manager from Liscard,

Owen William Owen, Hornby's solicitor, and a bank cashier from Birkenhead rejoicing in the name of Edward Holt Diggles Warry.

Elliott, still a partner with Hornby but now pretty much asleep was allowed to retire for good as part of the settlement. He received £1,600 worth of preference and ordinary shares in the new Meccano Company as the assets of Elliott and Hornby (including Frank's patents) were bought by the new limited company. Hornby received debenture shares worth £2,400 and 4,000 ordinary shares worth £1 each, a reflection of the fact that the patents were his.

Hornby Trains

The re-branding of the product was a smart move, not simply because Mechanics Made Easy (and Simplified Mechanics, which he had briefly tried as an alternative shortly before Meccano) was unwieldy. Meccano was catchy and sounded like a cross between 'mechanics' and 'dynamo'. It suggested movement, science and whirring motors. It also had a whiff of the theatrical about it, and sounded like the stage name of some vaudeville magician or illusionist. All in all a great name for a magical model-making toy. It was also a canny switch for another reason. Meccano had a faintly foreign sound. As Bert Love suggested it sounded 'Esperanto-like' which may have endeared it to the rapidly growing number of foreign Meccano enthusiasts who were now taking up the hobby, and beginning to enter the competitions in growing numbers.[5]

From early 1905 Hornby had been making inroads into foreign markets with his system. While this increased his market Hornby was not about to allow it to weaken his control over his business. Part of maintaining control lay in protecting and controlling his assets, and managing them shrewdly. Right from the beginning Frank had recognised the importance of patents, and consulting a patent agent had been one of the first investments he had made in the name of Mechanics Made Easy. Patents have two basic functions. First, they serve to protect an inventor's work from being stolen, copied or passed off as original by another. By registering a patent through a patent office in a particular country an inventor protects his invention from imitation in that country. Secondly, patents function as assets in an invention, converting into a monetary value the intellectual property rights an inventor has over his invention. By patenting an invention an inventor registers the fact that it is his idea, and as its creator he has rights to the fruits of his ingenuity. These rights can be sold at any stage, but in the meantime they constitute assets.

Minor improvements in the Meccano range were protected by patents as Hornby tried to ensure that his assets were safeguarded. The name Meccano was registered in 1907 in Britain. Within a few years Hornby followed this up with a flurry of patents across the world, all seeking to register the term and the toy as his. Within a year of the British patent for Meccano it had been registered in France and Belgium. Canada followed in 1909, Argentina in 1911, and Australia, New Zealand, Austria, Italy, Holland and Germany in 1912. Before the outbreak of war in 1914 Switzerland, Spain, Norway, Denmark and India had been added to the list. In a little over twenty years the name Meccano was registered on every continent.[6]

The pattern of these patents illustrated the development of Hornby's sales. Initially a large part were in the 'imperial' markets of Great Britain and the Commonwealth together with English-speaking markets in North America. Yet what marked Hornby out was the progressive attitude he had to marketing and promoting his products. As with other members of the new breed of toy makers he had never dealt with wholesalers, preferring instead to deal direct with the retailers themselves. For the likes of Walter Lines this meant that one could bypass the untrustworthy wholesalers, whose interests lay in sourcing the cheapest toys, or those on which they could secure the best profit margins. For this reason many manufacturers suspected that wholesalers preferred to keep their options open (and one eye on the continent). Hornby's preference was probably simply good business sense, coupled with a legacy of having found it difficult to find supportive wholesalers in the early days of Mechanics Made Easy. Dealing directly with the retailers in effect created Meccano franchises. Hornby literally cut out the middle man, and reserved to himself some control of retail prices. If the retailer became a recognised stockist Meccano would offer them a whole range of support and perquisites. These included advertising literature, tailor-made shop-window and point-of-sale displays, advertising in Meccano publications, supplies of the *Meccano Magazine*, a free colour booklet on Meccano lines and a trade folder. This tied retailer and supplier together in a mutually beneficial pact. In exchange for loyalty and assiduously promoting the company's lines the retailer received customer support and became the conduit for a whole range of services and promotions not commonly available elsewhere.

Overseas markets were developed aggressively, with advertising literature produced in 16 languages. The system of franchises was also the base upon which Hornby built his foreign markets. As the products began to attract attention abroad and sales increased Hornby appointed agents in each country or region to co-ordinate marketing and distribution. Agents were given responsibility for their country or a group of countries. Within their areas they had sole responsibility for developing the business. They were also the sole licensees, and as such were the channel for distribution of Meccano products to retailers that they managed to interest. Again this tied supplier and agent together in a reciprocal relationship. It was in the agent's

interests to develop the business as much as possible, since in addition to a quarterly allowance paid in advance he also received a commission on sales in his region.[7] A typical example was the arrangement with J. Lord, a Manchester man who won the franchise for Egypt and the Levant in 1928. In addition to a $7\frac{1}{2}$ per cent commission on sales he received a 'special allowance' £37 10s in advance. In 1933 his commission was reduced to 5 per cent, while his advance was increased to £62 10s. This was presumably in recognition of healthy sales in the area.

The agency system, as with the franchise system in Britain, was extremely effective. Agents stood to make considerable sums of money, particularly in areas with a strong educational, engineering or colonial expatriate community such as the Argentine, South Africa or India. It said much about Frank's style of business and management. There was a strong personal or face-to-face dimension to the conduct of sales which reinforced its dynamic expansion rather than limiting it. This was Hornby's preference. Possibly this reflected the strong personal relationships with backers like Elliott or retailers like Phillip & Sons which had underpinned the Hornby's business in its early days. Hornby could be fiercely loyal, and if he took a liking to someone he could also be impulsive and generous. For this reason as much as the rich financial rewards many agents remained with the Meccano company for thirty years or more.

The agents were crucial to the success of the business for a further reason. In addition to handling business development and distribution they had a third role. It was the responsibility of the agents to protect the company's image and copyright in each country. It was also in their best interests to try to prevent inferior imitations being 'passed off' as Meccano, thereby impinging on their sales of genuine kits. Meccano therefore had in place a system committed to combating all competitors (or imitators as Frank preferred to call them). He had obviously been wary of imitators from the outset and so had protected his product through patents. 'Probably no article or commodity of outstanding merit', he noted, 'was ever produced that was not imitated by envious competitors. Meccano is no exception to this – in fact I do not know of any article ever made that has had to submit to so much imitation, most of it unfair and much of it unscrupulous.'[8] In fact other companies such as Britains found their products being paid the sincerest form of flattery through imitation. Britains' success in making toy soldiers had been largely responsible for the formation of over a dozen imitating companies making toy soldiers prior to 1914. That said, Hornby was not simply bristling at seeing other competitors in the field. An avid cricket fan, no doubt his gentleman's sense of fair play was aroused by increased imitation of Meccano, yet his concerns with competition were based on more concrete legal principles. From the time Meccano took its place in the field alongside other educational and constructional toys its advantages in terms of design and refinement became clear. From that point Hornby witnessed with alarm the number of imitations springing up around the world. Over the next sixty years the company devoted increasing time and resources to battling subtle and not-so-subtle imitations of Hornby's brainchild: Mechano (Austria), Mekkano (Iceland), Meccano (Persia), Super Mecano (Argentina), Mikana (India), Mecana (Chile), Meccanodoos (Holland), Mecanic (Germany), Meccastar (Egypt), Pequeno Ingeniero Meccano (Uruguay), Betta Fit Meccano Sets (Australia). In addition to those products which tried to invoke or suggest the increasingly famous and recognisable Meccano brand name, there were also those products which simply copied Meccano's format: Engineer (Canada), Buildo (USA), Tecnic (Belgium), Tekno (Norway), Tecnico (Switzerland), Makeets (South Africa), Benco (Germany).

133

Some companies, occasionally in all innocence, did not even bother to make any pretence. Meteor, a Dutch construction set, simply marketed itself as 'de Hollandische Meccano'.

In such instances it fell to the agents to bring imitators to book. The usual approach was to discover a potential infringement of

copyright, often by word of mouth. The agent, or two assistants incognito would then enter the shop posing as confused and ignorant shoppers looking for Meccano for a young relative. If they were offered some cheap imitation they would purchase two copies, one of which was sent to Liverpool for examination. If after examination Meccano felt they should act, legal proceedings were initiated. Such was the number and range of imitators that the company did not always spring into action. Arthur E. Harris, Meccano's long-serving agent in Johannesburg described such a case to his bosses in Liverpool:

> A day or so ago we found the stores were offering an
> outfit, boxed with an illustrated paper covering entitled
> BOYS MECHANIC SET. The article is so badly
> manufactured, unattractive in appearance, crude and so
> desperately feeble an imitation of Meccano that it is an
> insult to the Public to offer it to them, and while you may
> possibly feel it can be entirely ignored, we feel that we
> should bring it to your notice.
>
> It is being manufactured in a very small concern in one-
> story premises in a room perhaps 50 feet square, who

have a few hand presses and among other things are
making hair pins, pins etc., and even if such a concern
had violated any patent rights they would not be worth
powder and shot.[9]

Occasionally the agents would be offered 'locally made
Meccano'. In such instances it was more difficult to prove that
retailers were attempting to pass off inferior imitations as
genuine, since they specified the products were locally made. In
addition Meccano was becoming so successful that it was now
the benchmark against which all other construction kits were
measured and defined. The very name Meccano had become
synonymous with construction toys of a particular kind, and was
being used as a generic term to describe a particular kind of toy.
'We would say', commented one Meccano agent, 'that
uneducated [shop] assistants regard Meccano as they might, say,
dolls, for instance – and would talk of locally made dolls in the
same breath as locally made Meccano sets.'[10] Goldies Store of
Australia described the Australian Ezy Built ('Australian &
Guaranteed!') as Meccano 'not as wilful misrepresentation, but
merely as giving the public some idea as to what an Ezy Built set
looked like'. D. Rámon Marco of Barcelona developed a clay
statue kit which he described as 'Mekano de la Figura' ('The
Figure-making Meccano'), explaining that 'owing to the wide
diffusion of the name "Meccano" I believed that it was a generic
word which suggests to everyone the idea of a constructional toy'.
Meccano's legal team in Liverpool were wary of attempting to
bring legal action simply on the basis of the use of the term
'Meccano' as descriptive for toys of a certain kind. They pointed

out that this was one of the drawbacks of the word 'Meccano'. Against its brilliance as a brand name should be set the risk inherent in registering as a trademark a 'fancy word resembling a word in common use, and reasonably descriptive of the article'. Meccano countered that, in addition to being the name of the product, Meccano was also the company's name, and therefore needed special consideration. Therefore the company brought a range of actions against companies such as Perfumeria Floralia Sociedad Anonima who manufactured a soap called Mecano in 1927, or the Mecandex Company of France, who made printing equipment. At the behest of

Meccano's legal team Mecandex withdrew the name. 'Meccano, like "Kodak",' the company argued, 'is one of the few trademarks that are universally known all over the world.'

The fact that 'Meccano' was becoming a generic description of a whole branch of mechanical toys was a sign of strength as well as something to be guarded against, and should be viewed accordingly. Indeed, confronted with one particularly poor imitation one agent ventured to suggest 'the thought does flash in front of one's mind if there is any harm being done by keeping the word Meccano alive and bringing it before new customers whose amazement would be beyond description when they see the proper Meccano outfit'. In this particular case the imitation was so spectacularly poor that Meccano were actually amused by 'the ambitious description "locally made Meccano"', going on to state:

As a product this outfit speaks for itself on sight in no uncertain terms, and the straits to which the toy-buying public has been reduced could be no more eloquently illustrated, we should think, than by this very paltry equivalent for a guinea spent.[11]

More than this, though, 'Meccano' had become shorthand for a way of regarding engineering. From being an attempt to replicate mechanical engineering, engineers were now using Meccano as a template for engineering proper. George Fischer Steel and Iron Works, Schaffhausen, Switzerland, marketed a prefabricated constructional building technique in the 1930s. Though it was full-size they described the result of employing their scaffolding system as 'gigantic Meccano'. The newspaper *La Suisse* carried a front page illustration of a podium built using this system to carry 2,000 people at a young Christians' convention at the Palais des Expositions 'construit à l'aide de tubes métalliques demontables "Meccano" monstre'. Despite the fact that the company were only using 'Meccano' as a simile, Meccano attempted to sue, but did not have a strong case in Swiss law.[12]

Such exchanges demonstrated two things. Firstly it was apparent just how easy and desirable it was to imitate Meccano. Workshops could be set up quickly and easily, and materials brought in to churn out cheap copies from a back room of a shop or a makeshift warehouse. When legal proceedings were served on imitators it was sometimes difficult to apprehend those responsible since the operation could often be no more than one man working from a garage to supply family shops or itinerant

vendors in rural villages, shanty-towns, favelas or one-horse
dorps. Percival Page of Page & Co., Bondi, Australia, was caught
selling inferior copies and argued he was 'selling it for a soldier
who had gone to New Guinea and had grown out of it'. Secondly,
the attempts to enforce patent rights show how far Meccano
travelled as a toy, both geographically and technically, in a short
space of time.

The company had expanded. In 1907 Hornby had brought out
the first booklet under the new Meccano name: a 'Kindergarten
Drawing Book', which was a small kit produced until 1910. In
1908 a lurid cover for the 'Manual of Instructions to Meccano
No. 3' had featured both the names Mechanics Made Easy and
Meccano, plastered all over the cover around an Edwardian boy
and girl leering out from behind the title. The girl had presumably
wandered on to the cover by mistake, since the models contained
in the booklet remained unabashedly boyish in their appeal (all
except two were old models anyway), and the cover even bore the
motto 'The Best Boy's Toy'. Entries from competitions formed the
basis of a handful of new model booklets, but Hornby's energies
were taken up managing the growth of the business within the
confines of a factory at Duke Street that was demonstrably too
small. In 1909 the company moved to an old carriage works in
West Derby Road, which allowed the company to produce more
components in-house. The company underwent something of a
makeover with a new logo (which was to last more or less
unaltered until the present), and the introduction of more
elegantly designed packaging. In 1913 the Meccano Boy first
appeared in his Jaeger jumper. Short-trousered and wearing a

chequered-trimmed jumper (later to reveal itself to be yellow with the advent of colour brochures), he would become a staple feature of Meccano merchandising for years to come, invariably pictured next to an implausibly large Meccano model looking very pleased with himself.

Meccano was now producing ever more sophisticated kits as ideas from modellers fed into the creative design process of the company via competitions and the hobbying fraternity. Meccano was advertised as a 'fascinating hobby for all ages' and one which 'outshines all other hobbies'. Still with a nose for what would appeal to boys, aeroplanes were appearing on Meccano advertisements as early as 1910. The thrill of flying had not really captured the British imagination at the time of the Wright Brothers' flight in 1903 (the *Daily Mail* had reported it briefly under the heading 'Balloonless Airship'). It was only when Blériot flew across the Channel in 1909 (and Selfridges exhibited his plane in their window) that aeroplanes captured the imagination, and as ever Hornby was on to it.

Following on the attempts of the Kindergarten set to tap into the vogue for educational toys Hornby next addressed the older market. Three kits, priced at 70s, 35s and 10s, were brought out as part of the Hornby System of Mechanical Demonstration. The purpose of the kits was

> To provide an economical and yet very effective series of
> apparatus for demonstrating the main elementary
> fundamentals of mechanics and mechanical science. The
> scheme is intended to cover the requirements of ordinary
> elementary schools, though it is by no means limited to

such an application. The present models used in the
teaching of mechanical science such as those in use in
Evening and Secondary Schools are very costly . . . We
have introduced three separate Outfits to meet the
requirements of the three higher standards of elementary
day schools. 'A' section relates mainly to constructional
work . . . 'B' section embodies a series of simple movable
parts in engines; while the 'C' section is designed to
afford scope for the teaching of elementary laws of
mechanics.

The booklet came complete with a two-page explanation of the
metric system, and models ranging from simple jointing exercises
to pantographs, epicycloidal gears and centrifugal governors.[13]

Hornby was nothing if not opportunistic. He replaced the
Kindergarten set with a Royal Meccano set in 1911 in time for
the coronation of George V. As his range of kits evolved, so the
company and its business grew. Agents were developing the
market abroad to keep pace with the growth of Meccano at
home. Staffing had increased in line with the move to larger
premises, and the structure of the company was becoming more
defined, with manufacturing, sales and clerical staff. Frank was
now managing director of Meccano, and drawing a comfortable
salary from the company. Meccano was now in a position to be
disdainful of small one-room concerns with only a few hand
presses, only ten years or so after Hornby had set up his own
small factory in Duke Street. The company's letters to agents or
tone in legal proceedings was now that of a large international
firm based in Liverpool and supervising a worldwide business

empire. There was more than a hint of self-assurance, haughty amusement and even contempt for some of the quaint foreign attempts to join in the games of genuine Meccano Boys.

Yet for all that the company could occasionally afford to pat small amateurish imitators on the head and send them on their way, generally speaking Frank remained as dogged in his preservation of his property as he had been in first creating the company. He could from time to time console himself with the thought that 'It is very rarely indeed that an imitator meets with real success, for of necessity he is always following in the rear of the article that he is imitating, and is always handicapped by his own lack of initiative.'[14] However, Hornby was mindful that money was at stake, particularly in the lucrative markets of North America and Europe, and he did not hesitate to act if he felt there was a point to be made. The United States was a market for Hornby. He had made a point of personally supervising the establishment of the business there. In 1908 he had first attempted to interest American dealers. In August 1909 he had appointed the Embossing Company of New York as Meccano's sole agents, and that first year they sold $6,886 worth of kits.

In the development of the US business Hornby showed the same grasp of marketing techniques as he had in the UK. Over a period of about seven years he claimed that 'not less than £100,000 has been spent on newspaper advertising, pamphlets, folders, leaflets, showcards, demonstrations, models, travelling expenses, [printing & advertising] blocks and expert advice'.[15] For every kit sold in the United States 10 per cent of the selling price was to be set aside for advertising. The Embossing Company even managed to exceed that allotted figure between 1909 and 1912. As a result the Embossing Company achieved impressive sales results. Mr Trumpore, a buyer of toys and dolls with Halne & Co. of Newark, New Jersey, and H. B. Claflin & Co. had been in the business for 23 years, but was struck by the impact Meccano made in the USA. Speaking in 1916 he said:

> I have been a student of the toy business, of course, all the time I have been in it, and realised the growing demand for a toy that would both instruct and amuse, and it seemed to me that this was the best thing at that time that had ever been brought to my attention. It was, in fact, the pioneer of all such toys.[16]

From initial sales of just under $7,000 in 1909 Guy Hillis, the Secretary of the Embossing Co., was able to report increasing figures throughout the time of the company's Meccano franchise: $23,743 in 1910; $49,422 in 1911 and $114,192 in 1912. Hornby maintained that all spare cash was reinvested in the business to further stimulate its growth. 'The only remuneration I was receiving at that time [1908–12] was £416 a year, and this was divided between Mr. D. H. Elliott's business and Meccano Ltd. I received no further remuneration in connection with this business until 1912, when a 10% dividend was declared on the capital, all surplus profits being put back into the business.'[17]

The growth of the company did not go unremarked. American toy manufacturers had begun to take note. Francis A. Wagner was a manager of the European financial office of the American National Cash Register Company, and was based in Germany and England. On his way home to the USA he had seen a

Meccano set and bought it for his young son. Intrigued and impressed he set about refining the set, copying the parts, manuals, models and instructions almost exactly, while introducing one or two modifications himself. As the American Mechanical Toy Co. Wagner set about manufacturing and marketing his version of Meccano. When Hornby found out he immediately set off for New York and initiated legal proceedings.[18] He was evidently impressed by Wagner's American Model Builder. He grudgingly admitted that 'except for the inferior finish of the parts and the generally less attractive arrangement, one of these imitation outfits might easily have been mistaken for a genuine Meccano Outfit'. In fact, Hornby is probably being a little unkind to the American Model Builder. Wagner had introduced a number of changes which turned up on Meccano a year or so later. Most notably these included the introduction of a collar-band with a set-screw to control the fixing of the wheels on models, certain wrapping designs and the use of hinged box lids instead of sliding ones.[19]

Hornby's case against the American Model Builder, however, seemed to be a strong one. The literature in Wagner's sets was identical, featuring the same models in the same positions, the same design, and trumpeting 'American Model Builder – by some

called Meccano'. The 'some' presumably referred to Wagner, since even the copy in adverts for the two systems was the same, the American Model Builder sharing with Meccano the tag-line 'The Greatest Game Ever Invented For Boys'. (One advertisement even boasted that the American Model Builder 'Makes Mechanics Easy'.) However, the case dragged on for nine years and cost Meccano a fortune in legal costs. Wagner cited numerous mechanical, construction and educational toys as evidence that Hornby was not first in the field with Meccano and therefore could not patent any ideas or principles embodied by it. Along with references to Quackenbush, Kilbourn, Wing, von Leistner *et al.*, Wagner cited 16 other patented toys that he suggested anticipated Meccano, some by as long as 23 years. These included people who had actually patented some elements which Hornby claimed to be his own, and took in a range of toys from a model suspension bridge patented in 1881 to Otto Nentwig and his interlocking building bricks. In the end the court decided that,

> Even if every element of the claims were found in the
> prior articles, invention would still exist if by their
> combination a new and useful result is attained, or an old
> result in a new and materially better way; and that we
> think has been accomplished by the invention covered by
> the claims in issue.

The court rejected the suggestion that there was a particularly close correlation between either techniques or end uses in any of the cited predecessors. Moreover, it noted that while some shared principles may be found in Meccano, the fact that Meccano had done so much to promote, develop, and refine these principles was crucial. Wagner appealed and over the next few years

Hornby shuttled back and forth across the Atlantic until at last the case was settled in his favour by a majority decision.

It was something of a pyrrhic victory. Between 1914 and 1919 the company spent over £14,500 in legal expenses. The action against Wagner cost Meccano thousands of pounds, and in the end damages were settled by the two sides negotiating an amicable settlement. It was a courageous case for Hornby to have fought, and he did so out of a sense of principle. Less determined or stubborn men might have thought twice about continuing when the costs began to mount. They might even have been daunted by the prospect of fighting a legal case in a foreign country on the notoriously difficult ground of intellectual property. Hornby had been anxious when he arrived at the New York offices of his legal advisers. Though a company director presiding over a rapidly expanding business empire he was not a widely travelled or cosmopolitan man. The case, however, was a point of principle, and his pride in his invention ran deep. The lawyers assured him he had a good case, and since it would be heard by a district court in Ohio advised him to hire a firm of Cincinnati lawyers, Healy, Ferris & McAvoy. By the end of the case Hornby was greatly impressed by the American legal system, as he had been fascinated by it during the course of the trial. In recognition of the fair treatment he had received, his growing admiration for the Americans he had encountered, his respect for the legal system and his pride in the verdict he had all the papers, briefs, transcripts and documents from the case bound into volumes and sent home. They took up four large volumes 'looking like so many family Bibles!'.

The case had the effect of deterring a number of other imitators and some dropped out of the toy business. Others stood and fought. John Wanamaker and his Structo Manufacturing Company, who made Steel Builders and Accessories took Meccano on. After a lengthy and expensive trial which failed to resolve the issues to Hornby's satisfaction (but left the company with a bill of $4,604.78 payable to the Federal Trade Commission) Meccano cut a deal. They made Structo Manufacturing agents for Meccano in the USA. The deal had all the hallmarks of Hornby's cunning eye for business. Structo received $50,000 – the profits from a $125,000 order which Meccano placed with them for parts and accessories in 1920. In exchange Structo passed on all rights to Steel Builders and ceased its manufacture immediately. They also passed on to Meccano all order books and client lists, together with any existing or subsequent interest in mechanical construction toys.

Many felt aggrieved that Hornby was claiming for himself and Meccano much of the rights in and business of mechanical construction sets. This had been the main plank of Wagner's case. However, as the judge in the Wagner case had pointed out Meccano was the standard in mechanical toys, and had done so much to define the genre that it was only right. What the case underlined was the fact that other inventors were capable of ideas that were as good as if not better than Hornby's. Wagner's refinements to Hornby's clumsy arrangement of pins for fixing wheels on to axles was as elegant as it was simple. Hornby's real gift, however, had been in promoting and developing his business, and though there remained aspects of the actual product which could be improved upon, it did not really matter. Meccano was king. In the 1930s the company took action against the French company Société Française du Jouet Metal, whose Constructor kits had ruffled feathers in Liverpool. The company's managing director M. Poumeyrol, took a stand against the pompous English company attempting to tell him what to do. In a bad-tempered meeting at the company's stand in a trade fair in France an uncomfortable representative of Meccano had to endure a defiant and proud rebuttal from M. Poumeyrol. Poumeyrol refused to back down in the face of claims that his product copied Meccano until he discovered to his irritation and anger that his printers had been foolish enough to copy Meccano literature verbatim. He was not pleased at having to concede that he would change the literature, but refused to change the colours of the parts to please Meccano.

Meccano had had a presence in France from the outset, with entries for the early competitions being submitted from the other side of the Channel. In 1912, however, Frank had sought to set

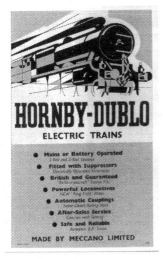

up his European operation on a more sound footing in collaboration with his sons Roland and Douglas. Frank's sons had both been educated abroad for a period after leaving the Liverpool Institute. Douglas had studied in Germany and Roland in France. In due course both took charge of Meccano offices in Paris and Berlin so it is possible that Frank had been grooming his sons to join him in the business. Roland, the elder son, had a lot in common with his father. Like Frank he had a serious aspect, and the same sleek features and steady gaze. He was invariably impeccably dressed, and his formal well-tailored dark suits underlined the air of the dependable serious man of business. Douglas, on the other hand, took more after his mother. He was far heavier set than either Frank or Roland. His presence was physical and emanated less from an intense sense of authority than from an amiable sense of humour. Unlike Frank or Roland, who appeared in photographs or around the factory upright, guarded and slightly reserved, Douglas had the open-shouldered and relaxed air of an affable bon-viveur. His features were rounder, and like Clara a smile was usually playing around the corner of his mouth, or twinkling in his eye.

His informal air belied the fact that within a few years of joining the company alongside their father the two young men had, along with the rest of their generation, been sucked into the maelstrom of the Great War. While at the Liverpool Institute, as was customary in older public schools, the two boys had served for a time as cadets. After a period in the Territorials the two had enlisted in the regular army shortly after the outbreak of war in August 1914. Both joined the illustrious 6th Battalion of the King's Liverpool Regiment (King's Lancashire Rifles), and were posted to France in 1915 in time to take part in the first Battle of Ypres. Roland was involved in the what one unnamed NCO described as the 'horrible slaughter for Hill 60', a piece of high ground near Zillebeke overlooking the Comines rail cutting. In all 22 men were killed and 62 wounded. The hill was captured, but within a few days had fallen to the Germans once again, and remained in their hands until 1917. Roland subsequently transferred to the Royal Flying Corps, where the danger reflected in the highest mortality rates in the war eventually told. He returned to England suffering from shell-shock. He finished the war as a flying instructor. Douglas was commissioned early in 1916 and posted to the 11th Battalion of the Lancashire Fusiliers as a transport officer until 1919.[20]

The outbreak of war had cut short the expansion of the Meccano range, which in 1912 had included the addition of an electric motor. The business, however, was not curtailed. After putting £500 into setting up Meccano (France) in Rue Bleu, Paris, Meccano had also opened a German Office in Berlin. It was the latter which was set up to manage the manufacture of the motors under contract by the famous Märklin Brothers, whose celebrated tin toys featured motors. In 1914 Frank had also begun to look for new premises. Rather than taking on yet another old vacant factory the company now had sufficient strength to consider buying a plot of land and building a factory to suit. The financial year up to March 1914 had brought in sales of £120,000 (almost £4,500 of which was accounted for by Meccano Motors). After finding a site in Old Swan the deal was done early in 1914, and construction of the new factory planned so as to allow for a seamless transition from Derby Road. With two overseas factories Frank was now making a number of foreign trips every year – at least two to both Paris and Berlin. He was in Berlin visiting his factory in 1914, unaware of the events that were about to unfold in Sarajevo. He left the city on the last train to carry English passengers to Holland, though his British Berlin staff were not so fortunate. His manager was interned for a year.

The opportunities provided by the war to domestic manufacturers did not go unnoticed amid the momentous developments of 1914. On 7 September 1914 *The Times* noted that the war provided an excellent opportunity to undermine the German share of the market. Manufacturers leapt with indecent haste on the chance to present the buying of their toys as a blow

for the war effort. An advert run in the *Meccano Magazine* in 1916 boasted, 'Meccano Beats Germans Hollow!' Part of the flag-waving included the creation of Lord Roberts workshops. These workshops, named in honour of the Victorian hero of the Indian Mutiny and Kandahar who had died in 1914 while visiting the troops in France, were intended to provide work for disabled ex-servicemen. Plans for such a workshop were put together for the new Meccano factory at Binns Road. The rise in anti-German feeling was an opportunity for British firms to encroach upon German market-shares, though those firms who obtained their raw materials from the continent, or who acted as wholesalers for German products, were a little more ambivalent about fanatical flag-waving.

Most of these had been sold by 1914, however, and the Americans and Japanese moved to fill the gap in UK toy imports left by the Germans. Domestic manufacture continued apace. While it seems incongruous, if not to say in bad taste, that toy manufacture continued during the war, the industry was one singled out by the government as an area which could help to stimulate the war effort. Any toys that had previously been imported from Germany could or should, in the interests of the war effort, be made in Britain.[21] Into this category fell the first tin trains which Hornby produced in time to exhibit at the 1915 Industries Trade Fair (another government initiative for a bit of jingoistic trumpet-blowing).

The fall in imports and rise in raw material costs meant that toy prices rose immediately war was declared. Though some companies sprang up in the hope of making a quick profit, generally speaking the problems outweighed the opportunities. Rising labour costs or shortages and the loss of skilled workers might have done for some firms. In addition, the rising cost of raw materials (metal, paper and wood for making and packing toys) and difficulties in obtaining transport to distribute or export toys severely curtailed manufacturers' profit margins. Operating under the auspices of a clause in the Army Act, the government had the power to requisition material for the war effort, often paying well below the market value. (In March 1915 two army officers requisitioned a million and a half sandbags in Liverpool in one afternoon, paying about a third the asking price.) The government therefore had the whip hand over manufacturers, and requisitioned large amounts of leather, wool and steel.

It was unsurprising, therefore, that the changes introduced in the Defence of the Realm Act of 1916 were far more popular with industry. The Act introduced a system of 'costing' which shifted the emphasis from requisitioning raw materials to contracting manufacturers to supply finished products. The system established costs and values for commodities and products requisitioned by the government. These costings included calculations for the prices of raw materials, costs of production, and an amount for 'reasonable profit' due to the manufacturers. 20,000 firms were either hastily set up or else converted to cater for the demand for munitions alone. Inevitably there were often wide variations in efficiency. Sometimes this was due to the size of the businesses, their inexperience in the manufacture of munitions, or simply the fact that in some cases they had been created as much by the huge government incentives as by a desire or ability to operate as competent businesses. Around £2 million was made available to fund the creation of adequate munitions manufacturing capabilities and it was perhaps inevitable that at least some of this money went towards making the fortunes of a number of businessmen. The creation of profiteers and the large gains made by many businessmen were perhaps the price paid for the development of a war machine capable of equipping an army of 4 million men in a couple of years.

The difficulty in continuing toy manufacture meant that many companies were only too happy to switch to munitions work. Meccano switched a good deal of its capability to munitions in 1915, but did continue some toy manufacture. Its first tin train, as we have noted, came out around this time, and a grand £200 model-making competition was announced. The first prize was an impressive £50, and over 10,000 entries were received. This time the results were published in a *Complete Book of Prize Models* as well as in the big *Manual of Instructions*. The cover to the leaflet announcing the winners again showed Frank's eye for publicity. In addition to featuring a model helter-skelter which had caught his eye, it also featured Charlie Chaplin, for no very clear reason other than celebrity association. In 1917 Frank even tried launching a Scientific Competition to complement the general model-making competitions which ran successfully throughout the war.

Naturally there were critics of this new breed of rich industrialists, particularly among the more fiery and vocal elements among the Labour Party, not wholly tempered by the fact that the wealth of some profiteers was as short-lived as it was undeserved. The government maintained a diplomatic silence, running the war in accordance with the principles of laissez faire, rather than through co-ordinated government action. The natural outcome was the creation of a successful entrepreneurial group. If taste suggested that profiteering was unseemly, a mix of patriotism and pragmatism suggested that it was unavoidable in the circumstances. In exchange for the maintenance of this balance a good many of the newly affluent supported Lloyd George in later years.

Frank Hornby was not one of them. In the last trading year before the outbreak of war Meccano Ltd recorded net profits of £54,034 9s 9d, with sales of just under £120,000. Yet rises in costs of materials had undercut any huge profits the company might have hoped to make. None of the war years was as profitable for Meccano as the year 1913–14 had been, and the war served only to give the workforce greater organisation and negotiating power. Generally speaking, workers in the toy industry had always been badly paid, though there was variation throughout the industry. Women could earn anything between 14s and £2 a week for a skilled job. An unskilled man could earn around 30s, his skilled colleague nearly £5 a week. The workers were badly organised and there were little or no collectively negotiated pay agreements in the industry. Employers resisted the setting up of a trade board to manage such things, fearing it would drive wages up, but when they began to rise at the end of the war anyway, the employers changed their minds hoping a board would at least bring uniformity. In 1918 female workers at Meccano went on strike demanding pay in line with other Liverpool toy firms. In 1920 a Toy Trade Board was founded, and the industry entered a new phase.[22]

6

A Junior League of Nations

The First World War had had profound effects upon the British toy industry. While it may not have resulted in great profits, it had spawned a host of new companies all trying to take advantage of a market suddenly bereft of the once-dominant German imports. Moreover, what the government contract had not provided by way of excess profits they had in terms of the skills and training of the workforce and even the investment in capital equipment of the factories. While the formation of a trade board had promised the industry and its workforce a greater degree of organisation, so too did new trade organisations such as the All British Toy Association or the Incorporated Association of Toy Manufacturers (formed in 1918).

The dearth of German imports had also provided a shot in the arm to manufacturing generally. Patriotism and self-interest combined in the war years, and a number of manufacturers – Hornby included – lobbied for extensions to the protection of domestic manufacturing through tariffs once the war was over.

British manufacturers had not been slow to take advantage of developments and move quickly into the spaces in the marketplace left vacant by their erstwhile German peers. At the close of the war in 1918 one-third of British toy production consisted of dolls and light metal toys – precisely the kinds of toys in which the Germans had specialised for years. Manufacturers feared that wholesalers would turn once again to German manufacturers to supply them since the German toys might not only be cheaper but would almost certainly be of better quality than the new British versions. While Woodrow Wilson touted his beloved League of Nations as a way of punishing Germany while providing a basis for future European harmony, manufacturers in the toy business just held out for the punishment of Germany, and their continued exclusion from the British marketplace.

Hornby, meanwhile, had been extremely fortunate. Though his two boys had run to the colours in 1914 they both returned home safely. Hornby's only real wartime casualty was his German business concerns. It would be a long and arduous struggle to have his interests returned to him. The factory had been confiscated and his business manager interned in 1914. Though his manager was repatriated after a year, the Meccano operation had been confiscated and subsequently acquired by the German toy giants Märklin. They were not restored to Hornby until 1928.

Frank, however, suffered a far greater loss shortly after the close of the war. His only daughter Patricia died in 1919 aged just 14. Frank and Clara had doted on Patricia. The loss was even harder to bear since neither Frank nor Clara was with her when she died. They had been on holiday when she took ill at her boarding school in Liverpool. Her eldest brother Roland was at her side when she died of poliomyelitis. Frank never fully recovered from the loss. The jocular and good natured humour which was the counterpoint to his serious and determined professionalism struggled to take him through the loss of his only daughter.

Ironically, the business was doing better than ever, though this was no consolation. The British toy industry underwent a boom after the cessation of hostilities. Wartime investment in infrastructure and workforce and the better organisation of both labour and business interests within the industry that had grown out of the war placed well-run companies like Meccano in a strong position to take advantage of the head-start they had over the Germans. Hornby hoped that the industry could maintain their advantage, though he feared that the German producers (and the Americans and Japanese) would soon catch up:

> Just now is a critical time for industry in this and all
> countries. Trade in the home market, as we all know, is
> fraught with all kinds of troubles with labour, raw
> materials and the reduced purchasing power of money,
> while trade with foreign countries is hampered by
> constant and disconcerting changes in rates of exchange,
> tariffs, freight charges, delays and, in some instances, the
> prohibition of imports under certain difficult conditions.
> The only right course, as I see it, is to produce goods of
> the best possible type and to give a square deal to the
> trade, the public and our employees so that when the
> nation sails into calmer waters Meccano Limited will take
> the high place in British industry which I am convinced is
> its natural destiny.[1]

Meccano was practising exactly what Hornby preached. The company now had a workforce of 1,200. The factory had been expanded with a new 30,000 sq. ft. wing, taking the factory size to 154,000 sq. ft. This new wing was for the production of toy trains. 'Before the war,' Hornby boasted,

> this class of toy was almost entirely imported from the Continent, and it was apparently accepted as a fact that it was impossible to manufacture goods of this type satisfactorily in this country. The war has created new conditions, which have brought with them new opportunities, and I believe that it is now possible to produce clockwork trains and other metal toys equal to anything previously imported, and at prices which will make them commercially profitable. The types which we have so far produced, and which are already selling well have been designed and perfected in our own factory. The Hornby clockwork train is quite a departure from the recognised type, and I am convinced that it has a wonderful future.[2]

Hornby expressed his hopes for the future in a new in-house publication entitled *Meccano News*. It was intended as a trade paper and a publication for Meccano employees (one article explaining the shelving of plans for a refurbished canteen), but no other issues seem to have been produced. Details of staff departures, savings schemes and outings were reported together with the expansion of Meccano trade and the company's fortunes in Belgium, America, Italy, South Africa, France, Australasia and elsewhere. Issue 1 appeared in November 1920, but there were no more, it presumably falling victim to the downturn which hit the industry in the early 1920s. The postwar boom in toys lasted little more than two years. Many of the opportunist manufacturers who had recently sprouted were swept aside. Meccano had deeper roots; all the same it felt the recession's blows. Manufacturers of dolls and metal toys (the Germans' old favourites) bore the brunt of the downturn. Hornby had to make drastic cuts to the company. Only a year after boasting of its size and new buildings the workforce was cut by two-thirds, from 1,454 in 1921 to just 453 in 1922.[3]

One of the features covered in the inaugural edition of *Meccano News* was advertising and promotions. In a piece which pointed out that Meccano literature was being produced in nine languages including Chinese the paper drew attention to the mascot of the company, 'Meccano Boy' – 'a sturdy, happy-faced young man. With joy and fun oozing from every feature and limb.' It was Meccano Boy, and the vast and dynamic department responsible for him, that was to play such an important part in the company's revival and progress once the business picked up after 1923. Meccano had a progressive and dynamic approach to the marketing of their toys, and the Meccano Boy was the embodiment of that. Meccano's sales were based not simply on the strengths of the product, or on global franchising, marketing and promotions, but on a relationship not just with its customers but with young people generally.

Excellent customer support had, of course been a feature of the company. Boys could write in and ask for information, tips and help. They could also send broken parts and receive replacements at a fraction of their list price. It was this point of contact with the company – or more properly the company's recognition of its importance – that set Meccano apart. Boys could almost imagine Hornby sat in his mechanical wonderland answering letters like some Liverpudlian Santa Claus. The company realised this and were quick to develop it both in their approach to business and their depiction of it in their promotional material, which appealed directly to boys, as in *Dick's Visit to Meccanoland* (1925):

'Who started Meccano? Who's the inventor?'

'Why, Frank Hornby, Dad,' Dick quickly replied. 'Every boy knows about him. He says he has a million boy friends!'

'I shouldn't wonder if he has,' I said.

The growing popularity of Meccano was reflected in the response from the public as much as in sales. Entries to the competitions and correspondence to the factory asking for advice on modelling, engineering and even careers pointed out to Hornby that his product had struck a chord with boys. There were great opportunities for the further development of the business. With these opportunities, however, came responsibilities. For thousands of boys Hornby had come to be a friend, even a father figure. He was part teacher, part toy maker, and as such was a trusted confidant, a respected role model.

Children felt they knew him through his toys, and well they might. The growing correspondence the company was receiving underlined the fact that Meccano was more than simply a toy; it was becoming a phenomenon not confined to the world of toys. Hornby turned his attention to meeting the demands of this phenomenon, not simply through the development of the product, but through the development of a Meccano philosophy. To the toys must be added service, and a service that was geared to children. Hornby had made his toy, and his toy had made him money. It had also made him friends, and Frank recognised that he had a responsibility to them. He also recognised that this unique relationship was perhaps the greatest asset the business had. In maintaining it he developed his brand yet further.

With Meccano's competitions receiving entries by the thousand Hornby's claim that Meccano was now the 'greatest of all hobbies' had a certain ring of truth to it. In addition to the committed modellers and the formal educational market of the Hornby System of Mechanical Demonstration, Hornby had been at pains to promote his products to a general audience. He hoped that they would marvel at the models contained in the Meccano manuals of instruction and through building them would gain a grounding in engineering principles, and in making subsequent modifications would begin to think critically and eventually creatively, like inventors.

Moreover, lest he confined Meccano to too technical a market he was keen to suggest that it catered for at least one universal boyish urge: 'Every boy is interested in knowing "how things work", and why they work in their own particular manner.'[4] The educational appeal of Meccano was therefore a general one that extended to 'every boy, even those who have no special aptitude for engineering, and who certainly have no interest in taking up engineering as a career'. It was a three-dimensional scientific reference book, an essential guide to working things. It could teach specific techniques, or general skills such as observation, critical thought, logical planning, problem solving. Aside from being brilliantly suited to many needs – teaching the blind, say – Meccano's voice spoke to something in every boy.

The tremendous response to the Meccano competitions must have confirmed in Hornby the feeling that his toy had a universal quality, and perhaps it did. Even at a time of desperate carnage and suffering there were those whose faith in technology and science to right the problems of the world remained unshakeable. There were even those such as the futurists in Italy who had their faith in science strengthened by the war, and the seeds were sown of a feeling that the postwar world, whenever that might start, would be built on a solid foundation of rational, modern science. The attraction of science in art, literature, music and even the study itself, was underpinned by a tremendous excitement about engineering, flight, navigation and all the paraphernalia of war that Meccano was only too happy to meet. New model catalogues featured tanks, artillery, planes, armed motorcycles and Maxim guns. But while Meccano continued production of toys throughout the war, shortages – particularly of raw materials – and the difficulty of conducting business with Europe focused his attentions on America.

The Meccano offices in Berlin and Paris had been primarily that – distribution and administration centres. All production of Meccano kits remained at Liverpool, and the Paris and Berlin branches served as the hubs for the European market. The success of the product in America under the licence granted to the Embossing Company from 1909, however, had illustrated the market that existed in the USA for Meccano. It made sense if at all possible to establish a manufacturing base in the USA that could serve the markets in North and South America. In 1916 The Meccano Company Inc. was set up, with offices in Masonic Hall, New York.

Correspondence that he had received from young modellers over and above the competition entries stimulated the drive for some publication to share information – particularly about kinds of models and problems.

> When a boy takes up a hobby, whatever it may be, he
> feels a desire to meet other boys who have interests
> similar to his own, and to compare notes and talk things
> over with them. This is particularly the case with
> Meccano. No Meccano boy is content to play a 'lone
> hand' for long; he soon wants to meet other boys, to see
> their models and to show them his own, and to discuss
> plans and schemes for other bigger models.[5]

This, coupled with the fact that production was perforce scaled down during the war prompted Hornby to add yet another

163

publication to his catalogue. Published by the new American arm of the company, the *Meccano Engineer* appeared for August–September 1916. It was largely an advertising sheet for Meccano parts and accessories, together with trailing the competition. The *Meccano Magazine* which followed a month later in Britain in October had the avowed aim 'to help Meccano Boys have more fun than other boys'. It was not much of a magazine, running to only four pages, and was printed on poor quality paper due to wartime shortages, yet subsequent issues were largely advertising sheets together with turgid homilies by Hornby to his invention and Meccano Boys everywhere.

The first issues of the *Meccano Engineer* and the *Meccano Magazine* were both free, but the success of the latter prompted a second issue. From that point on it became a bi-monthly publication. Hornby regarded it as a tool for maintaining customer service as well as promoting his products, and referred to it as the 'greatest of all service organisations'.[6] The early issues dealt solely with Meccano, but having taken his first few steps into the world of model trains in 1915 the *Meccano Magazine* was the perfect opportunity for tying the two branches of the business together. The success of the magazine was for Frank partly due to the fact that it served as 'the organ in which Meccano Boys and Hornby train enthusiasts throughout the world find the connecting link between their hobbies and true engineering, and partly to the opportunities it affords its readers of discussing not only their models, but also their own aims and ambitions, with the Editor and his staff, whose interest in their lives has given the Magazine great social importance'. It was designed to fill the gap between the professional engineering press, and the picturesque coverage accorded the more spectacular engineering projects in the popular press. The magazine could illustrate the kinds of machines boys were building models of, together with explanations of specific and general engineering specifications, principles and functions. From a magazine designed to help boys get the most enjoyment from their hobby it evolved into the world's first and only children's engineering magazine.[7]

The reading of periodicals was firmly established as children's activity, and the interwar years were something of a golden age for children's popular magazines. Competition in the market was high, and Meccano was distinguished from its competitors by being factual. There were no ripping yarns about school life, or boys' own tales of derring-do on the North-West Frontier. Though many had forecast that the magazine would be a disaster without the ubiquitous adventure stories and fictional element, Hornby resisted. Short stories were tried, but eventually were limited to occasional tales with scientific or engineering themes. As with other non-engineering features, such as the rambling observations of the music-hall entertainer Wee Georgie Wood that had followed the Meccano-themed *Babes in the Wood* (or *Meccano in Fairyland*) pantomime at the Palace Theatre in Manchester in 1917, readers were not slow in expressing their disapproval. *Meccano Magazine* was an engineering magazine and should stay as such. After all, there was no shortage of 'funnies' or story-papers, and children could (and often did) read more than one magazine or paper if they wished.

Between the wars children's magazines became as near to a universal part of childhood as possible. Worthy improving papers had been around before the war. For girls these included the soporific *Girls' Own Paper* (for 'girls' of indeterminate age, with features on how to start district visiting of the poor, set up sewing circles or mothers' meetings) and the *Girls Realm*.[8] For the boys the japes of Billy Bunter and his public school tormentors in the *Gem* and the *Magnet* were almost racy in comparison. Almost, but not quite: an indication of just what a rotter the bully in the *Magnet* was was the fact that 'he spelled worse than badly'. After the war, however, children's publishing changed for ever. The increases in employment and wages that had been brought about by the war affected both adults and children. Naturally there was some 'trickle-down' as working-class parents found themselves with more disposable income, but even young people had increased earning power. The lack of unskilled labour for munitions work during the war had led to exemptions from school for children under a system of Labour Certificates. Between 1915 and 1917 the number of these certificates of exemption rose by 22 per cent, increasing the earning (and spending) power of a significant number of working-class youngsters.[9]

DC Thomson was the main figure in the boys' magazine world from the immediate postwar period. In 1919 it brought out the

Dixon Hawke Library (about a detective named Dixon Hawke).
But the 'big five' were yet to come. In 1921 the *Adventure*
appeared, followed by the *Rover* and the *Wizard* within a year.
The *Skipper* (1930) and the *Hotspur* (1933) were the last in the
stable. Aside from *Dixon Hawke* and *Skipper*, which finished in
1941, all the magazines ran until the late 1950s and into the
1960s. All were story-papers and vied for the children's penny
with other DC Thomson publications (*Vanguard*, *Red Arrow*,
Beano, *Dandy*) and Amalgamated Press's rival offerings
(*Champion*, *Triumph*, *Playtime* and *Tiger Tim's Weekly*). DC
Thomson's magazines were hugely successful, and of the middle-
class children's papers only the *Boys' Own Paper* managed to
weather the assault from this new band. To this list of titles could
be added others – the *Ranger*, the *Startler*, the *Thriller*, *Bull's Eye*.
The choice was enormous, and in a survey of London children in
1933 over half read more than three comics or story-papers a
week, and a third half a dozen or more. Only fretwork and
carpentry were more popular pastimes for boys. In 1938 almost
3,000 children were surveyed. The results revealed that boys read
more weeklies than girls, and the high-water mark was 12 years
of age. At this point a boy would read between three and four
titles a month.[10] This was all put to work by Hornby. Meccano
took out adverts in these boys' newspapers, with the effect that
the company had adverts running in papers with a combined
circulation of 75,000,000.[11]

As Hornby's aspiration expanded so too did the magazines.
Between 1916 and 1920 they had been free, supplied to young
enthusiasts on the basis of postage and packing only. It was

difficult, however, to remain free (and therefore small) while fulfilling the three-fold purposes of advertising, communication among the fraternity and a general pastoral role for inquisitive young people trying to find out more about science and engineering in the modern world. In 1921 Hornby took the bold initiative of recruiting to the company a popular writer. Following a share issue which increased the company's capital from £5,000 to £100,000, Hornby hired Ellison Hawks as advertising manager to develop the company yet further. Hawks was the author of a number of popular children's books on diverse topics (mostly non-fiction) including science, astronomy and natural history. He was given the responsibility of managing and developing the company's promotional activities, including both the *Meccano Magazine* and its other after-sales programmes. The magazine grew. At its peak it ran to over 100 pages with a three-coloured cover. The range of articles on 'boys' interests' was pretty broad – models, sports, toys, engineering, wonders, stamps, photography and even a page of jokes called 'Fireside Fun', though they always remembered that it was an engineering magazine for Meccano Boys (and their fathers). Initial issues had been free and were bi-monthly until July–August 1922, by which time the price was 1d for eight pages. In September 1922 it became monthly, and in 1924 the price rose to 2d per copy, though now there was a colour cover.

Among others, Hawks recruited a young enthusiast by the name of Hubert Lansley. Lansley had been producing his own Meccano paper, *The Meccano Engineer*, as a schoolboy. He had managed a circulation of well over a thousand at its peak in the early 1920s, churning the paper out from his bedroom, and in addition to his editorial skill had shown a flair for marketing and self-promotion which attracted the attention of Meccano as well as a number of children's journals and local papers. He sent a copy of his *Meccano Engineer* to Meccano; Hawks replied. Typical of the Hornby philosophy, Hawks's letter began by pointing out that 'Meccano' was a protected name and Lansley was in breach of copyright, but went on to invite him to the factory. In due course Lansley joined the marketing department of Meccano as a 17-year-old. The editorial team comprised experienced and talented journalists such as *Yorkshire Post* veteran W. H. McCormick, *Meccano*

Magazine's assistant editor and T. Stanhope Sprigg who went on to a career in Fleet Street. The company also included a number of other teenagers working in a variety of roles from model-makers to office-boys, many as young as 14.

The youth of the likes of Lansley and the skill and judgement of Hawks helped give *Meccano Magazine* appeal to its young readers. Hornby was keen that the magazine should have a friendly tone which would encourage young readers to write in. In this it reflected his own slightly diffident avuncular air while at the same time being a quite shameless publicist of his toy and its qualities. In this he was something of an old-style marketing man, by turns economical with the truth or liberal with flourishes of dramatic exaggeration. Adverts for Meccano kits were frequently misleading, not always apparently inadvertently. In his 1916 Manual of Instructions he included 35 models which required special parts such as braced girders, sprockets and chains which could not actually be found in the sets which he suggested the models were based on.[12]

That said, there was a distinctly moral or upright tone to the magazine, implicit in its underlying belief in the ability of boys to transform themselves and the world through disciplined application to science and industry. Much of this was the sort of Smilesian philosophy of the grace of engineering and its power to transform the world through the sacraments of biography, discipline, hard work, practical effort and the like. Hornby even repaid his own debt to Smiles in the pages of *Meccano Magazine* when it ran a series on the 'Lives of Famous Inventors' in the 1927 run. Hornby was also capable of the kind of indignant posturing that Smiles sneaked into his books – particularly in his denigration of competitors. In the decade or so after the outbreak of the First World War when a significant part of Hornby's time was taken up with legal proceedings (or travelling to them) it is understandable that he devoted special attention to rubbishing imitations of his toys – even when they were occasionally quite commendable. He also reserved a special mention for 'inferior' foreign toys, which betrayed his staunch commitment to the protection of domestic industry through the control of imports. This belief in protectionism remained with Hornby until his death.

But by far the most distinct aspect of the magazine's moral philosophy was the central importance of the 'correspondence friendships', as Hornby called them, that grew up between editors and readers. By the 1930s the editor was receiving around 200 letters a day, and Hornby wrote with evident satisfaction that the postbag was 'unique in its intimate character'.

> Correspondents are of all ages, living in all parts of the world. Many of them write monthly, or even weekly, and their letters make it clear that their correspondence plays an important part in their life . . . They are written simply in the spirit in which one writes to a friend – that is to tell of one's everyday doings, and of little personal incidents that may be of interest.[13]

Hornby laid out a very definite role and approach for *Meccano Magazine* which reflected his personality, and his vision for the role of the company in the lives of children. All letters were replied to in the language of the school playground ('Dear Smith . . .'). Patricia Darby was a female employee charged with replying to the letters. She had joined the company as a shorthand typist and was based in the advertising department. 'I was given the task of trying to decipher the names and addresses,' she later recalled, 'written in either weak pencil or in ink which spread all over the porous paper. There were hundreds of these to deal with and send out, and it almost gave me an early dislike of kids.'[14]Each child received a personal reply to his letter 'in the spirit in which he writes – and, equally important, in his own language – no matter whether it be to ask for advice in some difficult situation that has arisen, or merely to announce the arrival of a family of baby rabbits!'

The idea was that the magazine would take into account the

age(s) of its readers and give 'helpful advice at important periods in their lives'. The advice offered to readers therefore even included careers advice. A section entitled 'What Shall I Be?' included articles on professions and a review of the 'prospects' in each. The idea and the intent found favour with, among others, Lord Baden-Powell. His approval delighted Hornby, who reprinted his comments in the 'Life Story of Meccano' in the *Meccano Magazine* in 1932. 'With your widespread influence on youth,' the Chief Boy Scout observed, 'you have an unrivalled opportunity of giving sound advice to boys as to shaping their futures. I am therefore glad to see that you are doing this, and cordially wish you a full measure of success.'[15]

The idea of the magazine providing some pastoral care and advice for its readers even went beyond the printed word. A number of 'correspondence friendships' became actual friendships when boys attended the factory on visits and were shown round. Factory visits were a feature of life at Binns Road. Hornby 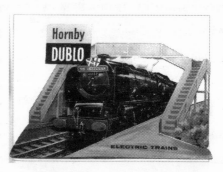 had realised the value of inviting celebrities to visit the factory and each visit was well reported in trade and local press or promotional literature, whether the visitors were the somewhat bemused South African cricket team or child actor Jackie Coogan. Coogan visited the New York factory in 1926. At least according to Meccano's mutually sycophantic blow-by-blow record of the visit produced for promotional purposes (*Jackie*

Coogan Visits a Meccano Factory) Coogan was something of a Meccano enthusiast. (For his part Hornby confessed himself struck by Coogan's strong character, intelligence, personality and 'genius'.) Like all good movie stars Coogan had returned from a European trip with a sophisticated affectation. Where Fred Astaire sported brown suede brogues, Coogan returned with a Meccano habit. 'Everyone in Hollywood', his father explained to Hornby, 'knows of Jackie's keenness on building Meccano models.'[16]

More typically, however, visitors to the Meccano factories were neither sportsmen nor Hollywood actors but ordinary children, invariably trailing their father, pipe in his hand and a reverent look on his face. Hundreds if not thousands of these visits to Binns Road took place over the years, and the factory became fixed in reality as much as in imagination as the embodiment of Meccanoland – at least on earth. In 1925 a promotional publication from Binns Road even tried to capture the magic of a child's visit to the factory. In *Dick's Visit to Meccanoland* a typical dad (at least typical for a Meccano Boy in the 1920s) spends an unexpectedly enjoyable evening playing with his son and his Meccano: 'I forgot all about going to the club, and Dick and I had the jolliest evening – the first of many such evenings we were destined to spend with Meccano.' Impressed by the toy, and swept along by his son's enthusiasm, the father trades his gentleman's club for a trip to Binns Road. On arrival an attendant conducts them to the Meccano Model Room to wait for Mr Hornby ('What a sight!'). Binns Road is heaven, or more accurately heaven is Meccanoland:

Some boys have lived in Meccanoland for more than twenty years, and the longer they live there the happier they are. Every day more and more boys are crowding into the country, eager to learn of its wonders. The moment they arrive they feel at home, and they take their places and set to work with a will. They know that in Meccanoland they will have the time of their lives; that they will have more fun than they have ever had before. Meccano fun is healthy boys' fun – fun that makes them glad to be alive; fun that strengthens their characters, sets their brains working, and teaches them something that will make them into successful men.

The sun never sets on Meccanoland, where there is always life and joy. The gates are never closed, and the only passport you require to enter this wonderful land is a Meccano Outfit. Get your passports today, boys, and don't stay another minute in the dreary world outside.[17]

The place of the factory emotionally and philosophically at the heart of Hornby's vision of Meccanoland reaffirmed Hornby's personal link with his little friends and enthusiasts. The factory cultivated a reputation for being a magical place, a strange mix of genial toy making and strict Edwardian business practice. Overgrown children rubbed shoulders with reserved and austere managers. Mr Hewitt the company secretary was an intelligent and cultured man who had lost an eye – reputedly the result of a broken spring while playing with a clockwork train as a boy. 'It did not', Lansley observed, 'put him off messing about with mechanical toys the rest of his life.' George Jones, the assistant managing director (and reputedly the man behind the name

Meccano) had been with the company almost from the beginning. The staff nicknamed him 'Felix the Cat' since like the cartoon character he just kept on walking. He prowled around the factory floor on noiseless rubber-soled shoes with his hands clasped behind his back, occasionally pausing behind workers to watch in silence while they worked. After a few minutes he would walk off without a word. 'As frequently you had no idea he was there it was a bit unnerving to say the least,' observed Lansley. The advertising department was presided over by Hawks, whose desk was positioned to give him a good view of the whole department. Cyril Cox began with Meccano as a 14-year-old office-boy working in an office just above Hornby's. 'As boys,' he recalls, 'if we made too much noise Mr Hornby would come out and complain to the advertising manager, and we would get a telling off.'[18] Hornby was remote from the majority of his staff, especially the young ones, and much of the day-to-day management was conducted via the departmental heads. Lansley recalled Hornby as

> rather an awesome figure, upright as a ramrod with a
> balding head and a fair moustache waxed to fierce
> points. He was obviously very conscious of his
> importance and achievement as a self-made millionaire
> and a great benefactor of the youth of the world.
> Nevertheless he was affable and popular with his staff.
> To me of course, he was a god, and it was with great
> trepidation that I entered his office with some message or
> other.[19]

Hawks and his team further strengthened the paternalistic

feeling of the company approach by their commitment to the idea of Hornby as a genial god, and Meccano as the tool of his great works. He was the beneficent Toymaster, and Meccano was not simply a toy. It was the embodiment of a moral vision, and the main tool by which that vision could be realised. In a promotional publication entitled *The Story of Meccano by the Meccano Boy*, which appeared in different forms either side of the Great War, Hornby trumpeted the attraction of Meccano to boys: building ('It's jolly building Meccano models') and playing ('and it's rare fun making models that work'). More than that, 'Meccano is a Real Help to Parents', not least because it was a present that was durable. But of course it ran far deeper than the 'lowest grounds' of cost. Meccano's true gifts were beyond price: 'Meccano is more than a pastime. It is a great moral force for the training of a boy. No boy who uses Meccano can be a bad boy.'

The toy teaches boys to think, to be patient, thorough, ordered and methodical, to care for their precious toys and to be inventive. It could also launch a boy on a prosperous career. It was more than a toy. Perhaps it was even a way of life, at least for a few. But it was also less than a guarantee of goodness, a saviour of civilisation. Whether everyone at the company fully subscribed to some of the more outlandish claims on Meccano's behalf it was certainly a powerful and effective branding for a toy. There was enough in the myth of Meccanoland to make those that could afford it want to be part of it.

> I am the Meccano Boy. I am always bright, keen and
> happy. All the boys, big boys and little boys, young boys
> and 'old boys' like me. Everybody knows and loves my

happy smile. That is why I want you to know about
Meccano, which is the jolliest, manliest game ever.[20]

This moral aspect might seem trite and pompous today but it was
by no means extraordinary, and certainly was not specific to
Meccano. Youth movements such as the Boy Scouts or the Boy's
Brigade had this exact same mix of religious and civic piety. They
would make boys better too, by stamp collecting, carpentry,
music or ruddy-cheeked games. In short, they too agreed that a
well-managed hobby could be the making (or saving) of a lad.
This quasi-religious piety permeated all manner of youth
movements, clubs and societies. After 1918 up to 30 per cent of
cinema audiences were under 17. Cinema managers vied for the
young audience, providing incentives by the way of a free orange,
a bag of sweets or a pencil. As with attendance at football
matches for young men, the cinema experience was lengthened
and made to last a whole week by the collecting of memorabilia
(cigarette cards, photographs and the like) or joining 'star clubs'.
These clubs had a strong moral tone to them, despite being based
around the cinema, and shows would begin with the national
anthem, the club song and some wholesome pledge.[21]

It was against this background of a drive to help and focus
young boys that the Meccano guilds – 'the most remarkable
brotherhood of boys in the world' – were formed in 1919.
Meccano clubs had appeared within a very short time of the
hobby establishing itself. These clubs centred on schools, youth
clubs or churches and were run by teachers, priests, parents and
boys themselves. The Meccano guilds sought to encourage local
clubs the number of which grew to over 500. Each club had an

adult leader, but the remaining officials and members were boys. Subsequently many of these clubs became affiliated to the guilds as the fraternity reached outwards. By the 1930s there were over 100,000 members of the Meccano guilds worldwide. These 'guilds' were so called because Hornby wanted them to be based on the 'splendid ideals and traditions of the old guilds – good fellowship and comradeship, and unselfish working for mutual benefit'. They came to be described as a Junior League of Nations since they had global moral aspirations. The membership application set out the three objects of the guild as being:

1. To make every boy's life brighter and happier.
2. To foster clean mindedness, truthfulness, ambition and initiative in boys.
3. To encourage boys in the pursuit of their hobbies, and especially in the development of their knowledge of mechanical and engineering principles.

Application was a formal process requiring witnesses, and members received certificates and badges. Each badge was triangular, its three corners representing the three ideals of the guild. In *How to Run a Meccano Club* the company in the guise of Hornby explained all manner of things from how to generate publicity and manage club funds to the different topics which were worthy of discussion at Meccano club meetings. 'Entries need not always be connected with Meccano. For instance one member may win a scholarship of merit; a second may invent something of considerable importance; or a third may perform some brave deed.' Here was the stuff of Meccano Boys – scholarships, inventions and stirring heroism. The article warned against cheapening the record by including anything unworthy. (Hence, presumably, the injunction that any inventions must be 'of considerable importance'.) The paper offered advice that was both practical and liturgical.[22]

By the 1930s there were over 400 Meccano guilds in Europe, North and South America, Africa, the Middle East and the Antipodes. A Meccano magazine was produced in Spanish especially to cater for the South American market. In 'the Dominions' the Meccano guild was in its element, organising competitions and exhibitions judged by Governors General and members of the diplomatic corps. Success with Meccano was a first step in the civilising process. The Earl of Athlone, Governor General of South Africa, while judging a Meccano competition expressed the view that, 'No exhibitor who has shown himself capable of the painstaking work, intelligent curiosity, and determination to make good, indicated by these models, would be likely to fail in interest, or perseverance, or conscientious method in any walk of life.'[23]

The principles of the Meccano guilds extended quite naturally to Hornby's other products, most notably trains. In 1928 the company founded a sister organisation for train enthusiasts: The Hornby Railway Company. By 1939 it had over 10,000 members spread through almost 400 branches worldwide. Members collaborated on a variety of model-railway projects including site visits and modelling activities. The activities of both organisations were avidly and breathlessly reported in *Meccano Magazine*. Soon the organisations took their commitment to the ideals of youth movements to their natural conclusion. They branched out into other social activities – sports, camping, rambling and the like.[24]

The carefully cultivated image of Meccanoland and of Meccano as a wholesome hobby for boys called Dick or Alan making 'a most topping lot of models' created a mythical world, while at the same time curiously locating it firmly in the middle-class middle-England of the interwar period. Of course, the literature for Meccano differed in each country, and it evolved over the years, but key elements endured. The American Meccano Boy did not have the Jaeger pullover with its chequered trim, but he did have a neat bow-tie. Meccano was a toy for a certain kind of boy.

The price of Meccano had made it almost from the outset a middle-class toy. Indeed it was often beyond the reach of many (even middle-class) children, and arrived as a present from an indulgent adult, if at all. Throughout the 1920s it sold best in those large urban centres where a healthy preponderance of industrial and engineering industry accompanied a sizeable, wealthy, middle-class population. The company performed an analysis of its sales in the 1920s (as it presumably did in every other decade). While the figures for London are not known, the cities of Glasgow, Liverpool, Manchester and Birmingham were at the heart of Meccano's sales in this period. If one were looking for a physical centre to Meccanoland, the industrial centres of the north-west and the midlands were the places to start.[25] By volume of sales these cities were the core of Meccano's market. In 1925 Glasgow with a population of 1,034,000 was accounting for £7,928 in sales of Meccano goods, Manchester, Liverpool and Birmingham had sales of over £5,500 each. The effect of the

Depression was a slight decline of sales in each of these cities in 1927, but sales were again increasing the following year. In 1928 it was Manchester that headed the gross sales figures with £8,340.

The management of Meccano were also interested in finding out where their products were most popular or alluring. Therefore they also worked out the sales figures per head of population. With a population less than a third that of

Birmingham or Liverpool, Newcastle's sales figures grew from only £1,659 in 1923 to £3,361 in 1928, the highest sales per head of population at over £12 per thousand people. Manchester, Bradford and Sunderland were not far behind. Newcastle's neighbour Gateshead, just across the Tyne, was a consistently disappointing market for Meccano, in terms both of volume and sales per head of population. Smaller and traditionally poorer than its neighbour its sales figures served only to underline the point that being part of an industrial conurbation with a proud tradition of engineering was not in and of itself enough to create a market for toys like Meccano. Disposable income and a willingness to spend it freely on luxuries and consumer goods was crucial.[26]

Income, disposable or otherwise, was in many ways a salient feature of Meccano Boys. Meccanoland was not in and of itself exclusive (the only passport needed was a Meccano outfit), though the expense of Meccano acted for some as an invisible barrier across its open doors. It did, of course, have members from all backgrounds, but the pursuit of Meccano as a hobby demanded resources as well as resourcefulness. It was not alone as a hobby in this respect, but it was a distinctive quality for a toy. There were working-class Meccano Boys and middle-class boys with few privileges, but the toy was marketed to children who were lucky enough to be able to afford it, or whose parents valued its benefits enough to dig deep.

Devotees of Hornby's trains needed to be similarly fortunate. The trains were not the most expensive toys around, but they were sizeable. They presupposed a house big enough to accommodate them (or parents indulgent enough to work around a large layout on the dining room table or parlour floor). Early 0-gauge sets could typically feature a basic 4-ft (1.3m) radius track layout, and stations could be almost 3 feet (1m) long. The first electric locomotive introduced in 1925 was $9^3/_4$ in. (25cm) long. With the introduction of electric trains there was also a new requirement in mains electricity. All this pointed to a large modern house – or a change in the range and requirements of toys. It is not difficult to guess which solution came from the fertile brains in Meccanoland.

7

Hornby Trains

Beside those spires so spick and span,
Against an unencumbered sky,
The Old Great Western Railway ran,
When someone different was I.

John Betjeman, 'Distant View of a Provincial Town'

With the exception of the teddy bear and the building block there is probably no toy which conjures so eloquently a vision of childhood as the toy train. And in the steam train 'puffing its sulphur' in the country station there are few images which capture so well the time and place that was Britain between the wars. Here are the milk churns waiting their return to the local farmer, and the goods yards bustling with wagons and trucks; the spinster with her bicycle, the businessman with his *Times*; the rangy baggage porter; the art deco mainline station and the red-tiled branch-line ticket office; the shrill screech and the lazy whistle. Trains run through British culture every bit as much as they run through the British countryside. They were born there; perhaps they will die there, too. There is something British about trains – or something about the British that trains elucidate. It could be Britain's air of lost power and former glory, faded beauty and pride. It could be the sense of order, or the fact that the people know how to queue. At any rate, trains are part of us. Betjeman knew this better than most. He wrote poems on trains and from trains, about stations and branch-lines and railway companies. Yet no one captured the spirit of the railway better than Hornby. He was and is synonymous with model trains. Despite having already made his fortune with one bestselling toy it was his train sets that made his name famous the world over.

Writing in *Games and Toys* magazine in 1914 the well-respected commentator Sidney Myers of L. Rees & Co. identified the most popular toy of the year. He chose the train set, which to most people meant a clockwork train, although also more expensive mechanical models were available. Early toy trains included carpet trains (with neither motor nor mechanism) made by German manufacturers, many of whom were based in Nuremberg. One of the earliest was Mattheus Hess, who began producing tin toys in the 1820s. By the 1880s celebrated manufacturers like George Carette, S. Guenthermann (both of Nuremberg) and Theodore Märklin (Württemberg) had begun manufacturing toy trains of one form or another.

Among the most celebrated were the Gebrüder Bing manufacturers of Nuremberg. From the late 1870s the Bing brothers had a tremendous reputation for manufacturing train sets of very high quality, which included very detailed and well-crafted stations. Among the first British companies of any renown into the field was Basset Lowke. Wenman Lowke was the son of retailer J. T. Lowke of Northampton. Like Hornby he was interested in model-making, but realised that there was little in the way of materials available to model-makers. He began making parts and fittings in his spare time to sell to modellers. Lowke was quick to learn, and far from parochial in either his outlook or his aspirations. Beginning in the early years of the twentieth century he quickly established a fine reputation for his model trains and boats. He adopted the continental practice of producing a catalogue, and by 1910 his had over 450 pages. In 1904 he published a German-language catalogue which helped strengthen his links with the continent. Lowke bought in models from the celebrated German manufacturer Bing, but eventually went one better, employing George Carette, onetime supplier of Gebrüder Bing. By the outbreak of the First World War the company had agents in Paris and The Hague, and like Meccano had recognised the value of competitions in stimulating business and publicity, organising a model engineers' exhibition from 1905. Like Hornby, Lowke was not averse to trumpeting his own innovations, even if there remains some doubt over the veracity of his claim to have manufactured the first scale model of an English railway locomotive.

The first Hornby trains appeared on the market in 1920. Hornby suggested that their origins lay in the development of the Meccano system, and this is hardly suprising since there was always a heavy presence of railways and rolling stock in the

Meccano models and literature. Despite this, accurate or realistic models of railway engines had been slightly beyond the grasp of the clumsy Meccano pieces in its first few years. By the First World War, however, the introduction of an architrave piece (much like a braced corner bracket) suggested to model-makers at Meccano the shape of a locomotive cab. A model was made using this part together with another special part for the boiler. The team were evidently pleased with the results, and but for the munitions work then dominating Meccano's time probably would have been keen to push through the development of the trains in order to capitalise on the lack of imported German toy trains, the absence of which Hornby had described as 'the greatest grievance of the youngsters of that period'. The ideas remained on the drawing board immediately after the war as Hornby concentrated on re-establishing the Meccano business.

When the trains did go into production they showed their kinship to Meccano. Locomotives, tenders and trucks were made of standard parts that could be dismantled and re-assembled, and replacement parts could be bought from the company. The locomotive came in black, red, green or blue but was not styled in the livery of any of the railway companies. Instead the wagons had small metal letters attached by clips which denoted railway companies such as London and North-Western (LNWR) or Caledonian (CR).

The new Hornby train could travel under its own power thanks to a clockwork engine. Hornby had chosen to make the trains in the standard 0-gauge (where tracks were 1¼ in. (32mm) apart). The set came with two types of curves which made circles of 4ft or 2ft (1.3m or 0.65m) when assembled. The trains made an immediate impact. Typically Hornby attributed this to the popularity and credibility of the Meccano brand, though the absence of superior or at any rate established and respected continental competition was probably as significant a factor in Hornby trains' early sales figures.

Though Meccano operations had grown far beyond the small workshops of the products' early days, this new toy was every bit as personal an invention as Meccano. Though it was born of a number of minds and perfected by teams of model builders, designers and marketing men, it was founded on the principles upon which Hornby had built the Meccano system. The first of these was that the product would grow and develop.

> From the outset we determined that the Hornby
> miniature railway system should be just as perfect in its
> way as Meccano, and the ideal that we kept in mind was
> of a gradually growing and developing system that
> ultimately would be capable of reproducing in miniature
> practically all the everyday operation of actual railways.[1]

This had the obvious advantage of encouraging continued investment of both money and time by the hobbyist and customer. The sets could evolve and develop a character that reflected the personality of the hobbyist as much as their spending power. A Hornby train set would never be complete; a model layout never finished.

The second principle was a central commitment to accuracy. This was originally defined in the same way as with Meccano – that is, accuracy was not equated with verisimilitude, but

187

faithfulness to mechanical and engineering principles. There was
to be an honesty of design that was based on function rather than
form. However, this was soon modified to emphasise a
commitment to accuracy of representation. 'Before long we found
that the building of locomotives and rolling stock on the
Meccano constructional plan was proving a handicap to the
development of more realistic and true-to-type models.' These
'true-to-type' models required specially made components that
were then assembled into a ready-made model. This emphasis on

 realistic representation was crucial.
Britains had stressed their careful
attention to detail with regard to toy
soldiers, and had emphasised it as a
distinction between their products and
foreign ones (which often had incorrect
uniforms or details). Hornby clockwork trains were marketed as
'British and Guaranteed'. Similarly Hornby incorporated a strong
British flavour to his model trains by decking them out in the
smart livery of the British companies. The early trains carrying
only railway-company letters were superseded between 1925 and
1926 by models in the livery of the LMS and LNER companies.
Next Great Western colours were introduced, followed by
Southern Railway colours in 1928. The range was eventually
extended to include most of the major companies: Great
Northern, London & North-Western, Caledonian, Midland, or
London, Brighton and South Coast Railway Systems.

The 1925 catalogue listed some models which closely resembled
German-made trains, and interestingly enough the page did not

bear the proud boast 'British and Guaranteed'. Perhaps these toys were bought in from Germany and repackaged under the Meccano brand although, given Hornby's keen advocacy of British-made products and his repeated defence of the domestic market against foreign imports, it seems unlikely that he would have been selling toys made under licence or agreement abroad. On the other hand, deals between Meccano and foreign suppliers for parts, or even wholly assembled toys, might explain Hornby's reticence in backing legislation which called for the clear marking of foreign-manufactured toys. (Changes to rules regarding the marking of merchandise introduced in 1932 specified that all toys over the price of 2d must be marked as foreign or else bear indication of their country of origin. Despite repeatedly calling for the protection of the domestic market against such imports Meccano (together with Britains) had never been active supporters of the legislation.)

New promotions, as ever, centred around crucial periods for the toy industry – most notably Christmas. This meant extra work for staff like Patricia Darby, working in the advertising department preparing copy for adverts. It also meant overtime, paid at the princely sum of 1s 6d a night for staying behind two-and-a-half hours until 8 p.m. One such promotion was for a new model of the *Princess Elizabeth*, which in November 1936 had set a new speed record. Such records and statistics were the food of young boys' railway enthusiasms. The LMS train, driven by T. J. Clark had travelled 400 miles non-stop at an average speed of 70 mph, while hauling a 260-ton load. The famous Beattock Bank and Shap Incline had been torn up at a speed of 66 mph. To every schoolboy whose nostrils flared in anticipation of the acrid-sweet smell of steam this was stirring stuff. And if it stirred schoolboys, it stirred Hornby's marketing brain. Hornby boasted that many new products in the line were the result of children's requests for models of actual trains or accessories that had caught their imagination.

> The suggestions put forward in the letters arriving day-by-day in large numbers from all parts of the world are carefully tabulated, and when it is seen that there is widespread demand for a particular item, the production of this is carefully considered. If the idea proves practicable, designs are got out, and before long the new accessory or piece of rolling stock is being turned out by the thousand, to the great joy of the boys who suggested it.[2]

In 1929 Hornby began producing trains specific to particular railway companies. Instead of simply painting identical locomotives in the livery of different train companies, they were now producing engines specifically for each company: LMS Compound, LNER Shire, GWR County and Southern L1-class engines. This illustrated both the company's eye for detail and commitment to the market, since many children and collectors had a liking for trains of particular companies and appreciated the realism. By being in touch with their customers' appetites the company was able to ensure that it remained ahead of the market with each promotion. Whether it was as a result of such canvassing that the *Princess Elizabeth* was produced is unclear, but the Hornby company wasted no time. Despite the fact that the company hurried to get the model into the shops at the time that the LMS was promoting the real thing, the *Princess Elizabeth* was probably the finest 0-gauge model Hornby produced. It was expensive by Hornby's standards at five guineas, though still cheaper than many continental rivals. The *Princess Elizabeth* was in the shops just months after the original locomotive's triumph. Patricia Darby worked on the advertisement, which for that added whiff of authenticity even featured the driver's laconic tribute: 'Driver Clark Says It's Fine!' While Driver Clark struggled to contain his excitement the campaign and the overtime went into overdrive. 'Rumour has it', recalled Ms Darby, 'that my mother hears me saying in my sleep, "Driver Clark Says It's Fine!"'[3]

The Christmas rush was a strain on the workforce. Prior to the Second World War the company provided few extras beyond a football team and a works canteen (which could be booked in the evenings for private functions), and the overtime pay helped considerably. Catherine Mills, who joined the company in Hornby's day as a 14-year-old remembered Christmas fondly since 'it meant extra in our pay packets', The work could be monotonous on the shop floor, though. The production line included a conveyor along which passed the toys. The workers – all unmarried women at this time – had to work hard to avoid letting the toys pass. It was Catherine's job to stand at the end of the line and collect those that had been missed. 'You had to be very fast indeed in those days.' She was paid 8s 1½d a week in 1931 plus overtime, which rose every birthday up to a maximum of £1 5s 1½d. Every hour a buzzer sounded and the women downed tools for a five-minute break. 'We all looked forward to that five minutes every hour.' When Catherine married she was forced to leave the company, which like many other employers of the day, frowned upon married women working.[4]

The overtime (which extended to 4 p.m. on a Saturday) ensured that Christmas promotions could be brought on to develop sales. Unsurprisingly Hornby was less reticent than Driver Clark when it came to his trains' accurate detailing. Much of the designing was carried out in the Works Drawing Office at Binns Road, under Mr Helsby, the works' manager. Here Meccano ensured that their Hornby trains were precise replicas. They were brilliant in their own right, and captured the beauty of the originals, while adding the magic and wonder that can only come with miniatures. They tried to capture almost every detail, and where that was not possible, capture the spirit of the thing. They were miniature celebrations of the train, romantic or modern, steam or electric. One of the strikingly realistic early models produced in 1925 was not of a steam loco, but that of the Metropolitan Railway's electric train. It was, appropriately enough, the first electric Hornby train – 'The Latest Hornby Thrill!' It was modern, sleek and inspiring: 'They felt so sure on their electric trip / That Youth and Progress were in partnership,' Betjeman wrote of the line.[5] The Hornby model had electric lights in both the locomotive and coaches which could be switched on and off, and connected to the mains supply (another indication of its modernity) via an adaptor which plugged into a light socket.

Once Hornby had moved his trains from the construction-kit form to what he called 'true to type' trains the emphasis on detailing had two strands. On the one hand, attention to detail meant realism, but it also meant capturing the essence of the original and creating a true miniature. Upon seeing his model of the Metropolitan Electric loco for the first time, despite it having only four wheels, Frank was impressed with it. Hornby visited Meccano's London office and told the manager, R. L. Cooper, that he would like to see the prototype. He was taken to see the real train, and when it emerged exclaimed, somewhat surprised, 'Why, it's just like ours!' The idea that the *model* was the definitive article, the standard by which the original should be judged, reflected the hard work and attention to detail that Meccano's modellers and draughtsmen put into each new model. It also illustrated Hornby's own sense of order or priorities.[6] Unlike the Meccano models, the genius of which was that they could be expanded, developed and invented by precocious or ingenious boys, Hornby trains were born of a professional approach. The model of the Metropolitan train was based on original drawings supplied by the company itself.

Lines of goods wagons offered the same scope for realism. Just as the locomotives and carriages were picked out in the distinctive livery of railway companies with their Pullman cars, so too the goods trucks bore the true-to-life details – 'Seccotine Sticks Everything', BP Motor Spirit, Sir Robert McAlpine & Sons, Crawford's Biscuits. It was the job of the Meccano advertising department to write to these large brands. True to form, Hornby did not ask for permission to use their names to make his toys more realistic. He asked the companies if they wished to pay Meccano to advertise their products using his replicas. (The same approach was used for Dinky Toys.)

The attention to detail was not limited to the trains, however. It included the stations – a piece of the magnificent fabric of the railway's golden age every bit as much as the sleek and powerful behemoths that slid through them. The modern 'through station' and signal box marketed for the Dublo sets in the late 1930s were modelled on Mersey Railways' striking art deco stations at Hoylake and Moreton. Earlier stations for the 0-gauge sets included name boards and *trompe l'œil* bill posters. 'The bare and desolate appearance that characterises the station platforms of so many model railways', explained Hornby, 'has always seemed to us to be a serious defect, and we determined to do what we could to improve matters in this respect.' Miniature platform accessories were introduced: milk churns, barrows, luggage and so on. By the mid-1920s the range was highly developed, and the list of rail, points and crossing parts alone ran to some 50 entries.

Hornby Trains

Rolling stock and accessories were no less impressive. Signals, lamp standards, telegraph poles, water towers, buffer stops, turntables and practically all the furniture, fixtures and fittings of the British railway scenery were available in miniature form.

The trains were timely arrivals in the market at a time when their German counterparts could not be obtained by a hungry audience. The market was strong for trains, not just because there was a dearth of toy trains, but also because trains were extremely popular in their own right. It was a golden age for trains. Film-makers, writers, composers and poets fêted the power, beauty and influence of steam travel. More than anything the railway was one of the most potent images of modernity, and had been ever since the 'locomotive monsters' so detested by Creevey had torn up the countryside in the mid-nineteenth century. The interwar years constituted the Age of the Train (despite what a track-suited Jimmy Saville might claim years later). This was a time when the GPO could commission an august composer (Sir Benjamin Britten) to orchestrate a film about a mail train, and a renowned poet (W. H. Auden) to provide the eulogy to its mundane but heroic toil:

> *Pulling up Beattock, a steady climb:*
> *The gradient's against her but she's on time.*
> *Past cotton-grass and moorland boulder,*
> *Shovelling white steam over her shoulder.*[7]

The 1920s saw a great upsurge of interest in trains. The centenary of the Stockton and Darlington Railway in 1925 was a spectacular celebration. Railway companies and locomotive works sent examples of their locomotives old and new to the pageant at Darlington. In 1927 the two rival companies operating between London and Scotland – the LMSR and the LNER – began long-distance races to compete for the accolade of the fastest service. The LNER sent a *Junior Scotsman* non-stop from King's Cross to Newcastle ($269\frac{1}{2}$ miles) ten minutes before their west-coast rivals sent their *Royal Scot* from Euston to Carnforth (236 miles). Soon *Royal Scot* was running non-stop as far as Carlisle (300 miles). In 1928 the LNER began the 392½ mile non-stop *Flying Scotsman* run from London to Edinburgh, which became a regular feature of the summer timetable. These races captured the public imagination until the two companies agreed between themselves to fix an established timetable for each route in the interests of safety. However, the glamorous trains of the 'Big Four' companies (LNER, GWR, LMS and Southern) continued to fire the imagination. The most famous of them all was the *Flying Scotsman*, but in addition to the London Midland & Scottish *Great Scot*, the Great Western operated the *Cornish Riviera Express*, and the Southern the *Golden Arrow*. Companies prided themselves on the speed, punctuality or luxury of their trains. Named after their routes, their stops or their connections with steam packets and liners these trains came to conjure an image of the countryside they ran through: the *Wild Irishman* (Euston to Holyhead), the *Grampian*, the *Tinto* (named after the Lanarkshire hills), the *Harrogate Pullman*, the *Southern Belle* (London to Brighton). Trains became the country, for they not only traversed it but embodied it. Even as late as the 1960s Betjeman, the self-appointed bard of Englishness, could write

> *'Unmitigated England'*
> *Came swinging down the line,*
> *That day the February Sun*
> *Did crisp and crystal shine.*[8]

To meet the hunger for all things railway Hornby continued to develop and expand his railway products. In 1926 the Hornby control system was introduced. The system involved a series of wires running from the track to a miniature lever frame which could be housed in a signal box, much like the real thing. Clockwork trains could be controlled (stopped, reversed and restarted) by means of a special control rail connected to the system. The system was ingenious, if a little complicated, and really demanded a permanent layout since it would have been much too infuriating to erect and dismantle time and again. This was a particular concern where space was at a premium (or parents were indulgent enough to allow a layout to remain erected in a parlour or bedroom). The control system lasted for the best part of a decade.

For reasons of space if not cost, Hornby train products had remained beyond the reach of many children. However, the huge government house-building programme between the wars meant that many families suddenly had both space and amenities. Around 4 million homes were built between the wars, many with sufficient space to accommodate children in relative luxury, and most connected to the national grid. In 1910 only one in five homes had electricity; in 1939 the proportion was three-quarters. By the time of the arrival of Hornby's electric train set in the 1920s many homes had both the space and the electricity to run them. Further miniaturisation in 1938, with the introduction of the smaller Dublo scale trains, broadened their appeal. Moreover, these new houses in the suburbs were interconnected by railways and bus. Public transport was central to life in the suburbs to the extent that it was as much a part of the world of 'Dunroamin' as the clipped lawn and the modern tiled bathroom. It was an artery as much as a *cordon sanitaire*. The railway was the means by which father travelled to his office, so it was natural that its model version was the preferred way of transporting little Tommy to his imagined worlds. Even the sales literature for new estates of semi-detached houses often showed children playing with Meccano sets and model trains.[9]

By 1930 the Hornby range was extensive. The development of electric trains added a new dimension to the hobby. On the one hand, they enabled a greater variety of track layouts: since the electric-powered trains could negotiate gradients far more effectively, modellers could incorporate inclines and even underground track sections. More fundamentally, it meant that the locomotives did not need to be wound up and therefore could run and run. As Hornby put it, 'The un-railway like spectacle of a train stopping half-way between stations owing to the clockwork having run down is avoided.' After little more than a decade it was possible to build a complete model railway with a main line, branch lines, stations, sidings and pretty much all the scenery and accessories to conjure up a realistic and convincing miniature world. Generic lead figures to people this world needed to be bought from toyshops until the introduction of Hornby's own range: stationmaster, guard, porters, ticket collector, engine driver, hotel porters and so on. But 'the trains must have a reason for running' Hornby observed, and a set of miniature passengers was duly added to the range. The attention to detail seemed to become a challenge to replicate in miniature anything and everything that was familiar from the railways of Britain. Small-scale reproduction posters of popular or familiar advertisements were available, and could be attached to hoardings, fences or bridges. Nothing was overlooked. A watchman's hut and a platelayer's hut were even available, together with cuttings, sidings, cabins and sheds – many wired for electric light for an added touch of realism.

In 1930 Hornby train sets produced more sales than Meccano kits. Meccano accounted for £142,282 worth of sales, while Hornby recorded £149,338. Only in exports did Hornby fail to outperform Meccano. Hornby sold £42,843 in 1930 compared to Meccano's £134,472. Generally, Hornby found it difficult to build an export market comparable to its steady and impressive growth of sales in the domestic market. In the year Hornby died his trains recorded £187,630 of domestic sales, plus a further £25,985 abroad. The sales were, of course, on the back of Meccano's sophisticated and determined marketing campaigns. The train sets were, in the way that Meccano kits had become, a status symbol. Their price gave them a cachet. One young boy was reduced to tears by the response he received from a young urchin to whom he gave his Meccano set.[10] More than that, though, the toys were marketed well.

Realism was not the only feature in the Hornby's marketing plans. Hornby Train Week began in 1925 and was, according to an early trade guide 'a never failing method of creating interest' and generating publicity. During Train Week the advertising output from the company was intensified and large layouts and models were created for exhibition at dealers and toyshops. These dealers and outlets were then promoted, both through Meccano's own literature and that of the shops. Special display boards were available (at a price!) upon which dealers and retailers could mount layouts for display. In addition, special window display plans were devised by Meccano's model-makers in much the same way as for the large Meccano displays and supplied to retailers in a special folder. The Hornby Train ranges also enjoyed the same type of Meccano-produced literature. *Our Selling Service* (1928) detailed all the promotion facilities that Meccano could offer retailers, including 'stereo' images and advertising blocks, showcard and window bills ('These are Meccano Days') and lantern slides (supplied free on loan upon request). Each glass lantern slide featured the Hornby (or Meccano) image in colour, together with a customised element featuring the retailer's name and address. The lantern slides were then shown in cinemas and theatres.

In addition, Meccano were producing the *Hornby Book of Trains* as well as the *Meccano Book of Engineering* throughout the mid to late 1920s. The first edition of the *Book of Trains* in 1925–6 ran to over 40 pages. In keeping with the style of *Meccano Magazine* the books combined extensive catalogue advertisements with twenty pages of railway history and articles on early locomotives, the first railway companies, colliery engines and, in a way that Samuel Smiles would have appreciated, biographical sketches of early rail pioneers such as Trevithick, Stephenson, Matthew Murray and William Hedley. The 1926-7 edition looked at technical aspects of the railway, and the following edition looked at the life history of a typical railway locomotive, from design, through foundry, machine shops and boiler works, to assembly, trial, painting and commissioning.

In addition, as a sister organisation to the Meccano guild, the Hornby Railway Company had been formed in 1928. As with the Meccano guild the organisation catered mostly for boys who wished to share their enthusiasm with like-minded boys. Via the Railway Company they could obtain detailed information about layouts and seek assistance with technical problems. Again mirroring the guild, local branches of the Hornby Railway Company were formed under the auspices of an adult chairman (like their members, they were invariably male). Aside from a variety of model-making activities, the Railway Company enabled youngsters to gain unrivalled access to actual train yards, engine sheds, stations and railway company premises. Clambering about in their duffle coats and caps, members could indulge their curiosity or research possible layouts and details for their own use. There was also a correspondence club as part of the Railway Company, again allowing for the sharing of information, photographs and news. As with the Meccano guild, the Railway Company strengthened the idea that model-making was engineering in miniature by bringing together enthusiasm for them both.

The Hornby range continued to increase and new techniques such as tin printing were brought to bear on the trains, together with greater attention to the detailing of scenery and accessories. Hornby trains were on their way to becoming the household name that Meccano had become. Indeed, with the introduction of the smaller 1/76th scale 00-gauge (Dublo) trains in 1938 Hornby would achieve with trains exactly what had been done with Meccano: the creation of a set so fine that it would become the industry standard, and with that would become synonymous with all toys of its kind. The Dublo range was probably the finest of its kind, and Hornby Trains became a generic term for 00-gauge model train sets. Sadly, though he may have had more than

HORNBY

an inkling that this was about to come to pass, Hornby would not live to see the introduction of the Dublo range. Yet before he died he did see the successful marketing of his last great contribution to the lives of children, and the life of playthings.

As part of the drive towards greater realism in his train sets Hornby had introduced his own range of 'Modelled Miniatures' in 1931. These accessories comprised half a dozen cast figures for peopling stations and bringing the layouts to life. The first set included a train driver, stationmaster, ticket collector, a guard, and two different porters. They were hand-painted and beautifully detailed as one might expect. Having added railway workers the countryside was brought to life with farm animals, and finally the train line was given passengers. With a flourish typical of the attention to detail some of the early passengers were hitchhikers. The interwar years had seen the rediscovery of the countryside in the political rhetoric of the likes of Stanley Baldwin, but through a whole variety of forms, from the intellectual celebration of 'tramping' to the pastoral eulogies of everyone from Vaughan Williams to A. E. Housman. London Transport and the Shell motor-oil company had been quick to exploit this by running campaigns which called for greater access to and enjoyment of the countryside, and the Federation of Rambler Clubs and the YMCA and Youth Hostels movements were at the forefront. On one dining-room table could be found so many classic images of the 1930s.

Further figures were produced by neatly repainting the same figure in a variety of ways, but the real leap came with the introduction of vehicles. For four shillings a lucky child could get six vehicles intended to perk up any railway layout (though, bizarrely, the first group also included a tank). Ironically, given Hornby's at times self-righteous railing against foreign imitators, the range was a direct response to a range of American miniature vehicles known as Tootsie Toys. The Dowst Brothers of Chicago had been making their Tootsie Toys since the early 1920s. Unlike tinplate toys these diecast toys were capable of some fairly intricate detailing. Hollow-casting (used to make lead soldiers) involved pouring molten metal into a mould to give a hollow casting. Die-casting involved the molten metal being forced under pressure into a die. The die could be made of two or more parts and constituted a 'negative' of the final model. Typically it was made from wood, with additional details (such as door handles or chrome detailing) added with wire. The level of detail was limited only by the ability of the zinc alloy metal to run freely around the die and pick out the nooks and crannies of the mould. To create a suitably detailed die was delicate work and required not inconsiderable model-making skills. For this reason – and the fact that a new die was required for each casting – the process could be expensive. The effects, however, could be impressive. Once the metal had cooled the die was opened to reveal the model. Because detail in their surface was three-dimensional, the models were far more realistic than the tinplate toys whose details were painted or printed on the surface.

The level of detail made possible by the die-casting process meant that models could faithfully replicate the intricate styling of 1930s vehicles. Indeed, they could do it so accurately that American automobile manufacturers were soon using diecast models to promote their real vehicles. Citroën had similarly used French-made 1/43rd-scale die-cast models to promote their cars in 1928, and die-casting was quite well established in France between the wars. M. de Vazeills had diversified his metals business into die-cast toy manufacture in the early 1920s. His Solido models – so named because of their solidity – had been innovative and detailed, featuring opening doors and sprung wheels. The 1933–4 *Hornby Book of Trains* included the full range of Modelled Miniatures, which even included a small pull-along train complete with Shell Petrol tanker and crane, and a set of the distinctive Hall's Distemper advertising figures. By 1934 the range had been renamed Meccano Dinky Toys, and later simply Dinky Toys.

The toys rapidly established themselves as collectable, despite the fact that, unusually for Meccano products, they were not the correct scale to ideally complement the railways – either in 0-gauge or Dublo format. Despite that they made sales home and abroad of over £50,000 in their first year, and just under £75,000 in their second. With all three classics now firmly established the Meccano company had a trio of recognised brands that together sold £398,962 in 1936.

8

From Meccanoland to Westminster

At the close of one of A. A. Milne's Winnie the Pooh stories, *Eeyore Joins the Game*, Piglet is typically worried about his friend Tigger. He asks if Tigger is all right, really.

> Of course he is,' said Christopher Robin.
> 'Everybody is *really*,' said Pooh. 'That's what I think,'
> said Pooh. 'But I don't suppose I'm right,' he said.
> 'Of course you are,' said Christopher Robin.[1]

The Hundred Acre Wood was, of course, a self-contained world. It was every bit as insulated from the realities of life in Britain in the decade before the Second World War as the literary worlds of Nancy Mitford or G. K. Chesterton, or the fondly imagined Merrie England of Stanley Baldwin. One might also add to these Meccanoland, a magical nursery floor scattered with expensive and beautiful playthings, and peopled with short-trousered schoolboys, their heads chock-full of batting averages and the names of favourite locomotives. Here was a 'Land of Happy Boys'. 'The sun never sets on Meccanoland,' trilled a 1925 promotional booklet, 'where there is always life and joy.'[2] In these warm places everyone was 'all right, really'.

Yet by the late 1920s these wonderful worlds were slipping away. In his paean to England, Conservative Prime Minister Stanley Baldwin famously eulogised a world being lost.

> The sounds of England, the tinkle of the hammer on the anvil in the country smithy, the corncrake on a dewy morning, the sound of the scythe against the whetstone, and the sight of a plow team coming over the hill, the sight that has been seen in England since England was a land, and may be seen in England long after the Empire has perished and every works in England has ceased to function, for centuries the one eternal sight of England. The wild anemones in the woods in April, the last load at night of hay being drawn down a lane as the twilight comes on, when you can scarcely distinguish the figures of the horses as they take it home to the farm, and above all, most subtle, most penetrating and most moving, the smell of wood smoke coming up in the autumn evening, or the smell of the scotch fires: that wood smoke that our ancestors, tens of thousands of years ago, must have caught on the air when they were coming home with the result of the day's forage when they were still nomads, and when they were still roaming the forests and the plains of the continent of Europe. These things strike down into the very depths of our nature, and touch chords that go back to the beginning of time, and the human race, but they are chords that with every year of our life sound a deeper note in our innermost being. These are the things that make England, and I grieve for

it that they are not the childish inheritance of the
majority of the people today in our country.[3]

No doubt the enduring popularity of these visions drew on the
very fact that with every passing month they became less and less
recognisable to the vast majority of the population. This turn of
events was not as recent as Baldwin imagined. More than a
generation had never known this 'childish inheritance'. They had
grown up instead battling against economic and social hardships
in a world where the tinkle of cowbells had long since been
drowned out by a human and mechanical cacophony. These
idyllic worlds with their smoky aroma and gentle sounds stood
apart from the world that Hornby had grown up in, and which –
even with his new fortune – he continued to inhabit. He was a
city-dweller and an industrialist. His decision to enter politics in
1931 was the culmination of a life devoted to industry, personal
and economic. While his imagination had conjured worlds that
were idyllic, he remained a steady and practical man. He was, in
his own words, a Liverpool Man. It was his experience of life in
Liverpool rather than a memory of a world lost, or a vision of one
to be won that drove him to embark on a political career in the
twilight of his life.

At the 1931 election the Conservatives swept past a rudderless
Labour Party to record a resounding victory. The supporters of
the victorious coalition government totaled 556 – of whom 472
were Conservatives. It was the largest parliamentary
Conservative Party the country has ever seen.[4] The Labour Party,
so jubilant just two years previous, had held just one in six of the
seats they had won at the 1929 election. One of the seats they had

lost was for Everton. The incumbent National Labour MP Derwent Hall – Caine saw his modest 1,567 majority obliterated as he was beaten into third place. The winner, who had fought with the slogan 'A Liverpool Man for a Liverpool Seat', was Frank Hornby.

Hornby had been interested in politics for some time. In 1912 he had been one of the founder members of his local Maghull  Conservative Party, but his decision to stand for election was probably not so much the determined act of a committed politician as a natural step for a successful businessman who had risen through the ranks to take his place in the local Liverpool establishment. For one thing, Frank was now 68 years of age – three years older than his party leader Stanley Baldwin, who was himself increasingly being derided as an 'old man'. Clearly this was not a career move for Everton's new MP, but a social one. Having made both his name and his fortune in business, and having illustrated the point ably by purchasing a grand family seat in the country, what could be a finer way to cement one's position as a member of the elite than to take a seat at Westminster as a Tory MP?

Yet Hornby did not regard his election as a sinecure and took both his duties and the status that accompanied them very seriously. Despite his age he regularly attended the late sittings of the House, and fitted his business commitments in around the business at Westminster. Though he rarely spoke, when he did it was with a solid and earnest commitment to the principles that had led him to Westminster in the first place: domestic industry, foreign trade, unemployment and the provision of social welfare. And yet it was clear that Hornby had come to the game late in life; while he took it seriously, he was no doubt aware that daemon lay elsewhere. He voted assiduously, but always with the government majority; he never held office, in government or opposition; he never served on a committee (or appeared before one); and seldom addressed the House. Indeed, on the sole occasion when he proposed some legislation one wag lamented that it was a shame to have to oppose Mr Hornby's Bill, since the Honourable Member for Everton so seldom interfered with anybody else's business in the House.

Frank Hornby took the decision to enter politics at a time when the worlds of trade and politics had become inextricably linked. Indeed, the overwhelming problem for amateur and professional politicians alike was to find a way to unravel the mess that had been brought about by the Great Depression of the early 1930s. The worldwide recession had led to a decline in international trade and a fall in the prices of internationally traded goods and services such as shipping. Naturally this meant a fall in British exports and consequently a fall in British income. This in turn led to a rise in unemployment – most particularly in those industries that had seen their markets abroad collapse. Prices fell and the public finances suffered. Hornby's interests demanded that he be involved in political attempts to resolve the situation. First, he was a manufacturer whose business was heavily orientated to the export market. He was a large-scale employer in a manufacturing industry, and one based in a city which found much of its employment in industries badly affected by the Depression – shipping, textiles, light engineering. Like other industrialists in his position he had been voicing his own ideas about the state of the domestic economy with increasing conviction throughout the 1920s, and had formulated coherent and definite views on the Depression and way to counter it.

The courses open to the Labour government were either to stimulate trade and production in order to reduce prices or to reduce prices and costs in order to increase profits in the hope that producers could then stimulate trade through entre-preneurialism and reinvestment. These two basic approaches boiled down to a handful of possible policies. The first was protectionism – the imposition of tariffs to protect domestic manufactures over foreign imports. The second was devaluation which would make British exports more competitive. The third option was to cut public spending so as to reduce inflation, thereby reducing prices and costs and making British goods cheaper. The fourth was to reduce unemployment through job-creation schemes funded from the public purse, and the last option was the perennial favourite – 'wait and see'.

Hornby was one of many Tories who fervently believed in tariffs to protect domestic markets and develop foreign ones. The Liberals, however, were staunch free-traders, and viewed tariffs with horror. Since Labour had a slim majority and relied on Liberal support in the Commons it tried to steer clear of tariffs. Devaluation was more universally unpopular, while deflation was seen on the government's benches as implying in its reduction of costs a reduction of wages, which was hardly compatible with Labour's policy aims. Job-creation schemes, on the other hand, raised awkward questions about how money would be spent, and by whom. These questions, coupled with the large sums involved, made such schemes as unpopular with the Treasury as with the City. Instead the government chose to wait and see, to 'unwittingly stand on the ancient ways'.[5]

Hornby was exasperated. As early as 1916 he had taken a protectionist stance. His suggestions were outlined in a letter to the *Liverpool Echo* dated 14 October 1916, prompted by the report of a Board of Trade committee charged with investigating the needs of British businesses after the war. Hornby humbly suggested that 'it [is] desirable that British manufacturers should be invited to express their opinions on these conclusions'. Speaking from his 'considerable experience in these matters' Hornby argued against 'speculative' ventures abroad, largely on the grounds of the unreliable nature of foreign laws and business practice. His experience of 'the meanest kind of patent infringement and colourable imitations' had been both tiring and costly, and he therefore stressed the preferable practice of concentrating on securing the domestic markets (from foreign imports), where companies were on safer ground. 'There are not the same risks in trading at home; our laws are just and understood by the trading community.'

He argued that 'controlled foreign trade' would be best secured by the careful development of domestic industry through a mix of protectionism and state intervention. At the height of the war he had noted the 'vigorous response' to the government's invitation to invest in new equipment and machinery in exchange for lucrative munitions contracts. By such investment in infrastructure the government could foster the development of 'factories big enough to supply Great Britain and her Colonies'. Lastly, he suggested the creation of a 'Government Department of Industries comprising trade sections headed by men competent to investigate the soundness of manufacturing concerns'. This department would have the authority to issue guarantees to lenders to enable companies to raise credit for expansion and investment in new equipment to increase their production capacity.[6] Fourteen years later, similar ideas were being advanced by Labour's young firebrand MP Oswald Mosley.

I am not suggesting that Hornby was a visionary – at least not in the way that Mosley promised to be before his hopes were dashed and his talents turned in on themselves. He was not an intellectual, neither was he a great wordsmith or orator. But he was a practical man; a thinker. His inventions were, after all, a demonstration of practical thought. None of this seems particularly novel now, but his thoughts on industrial development were revolutionary in comparison with the moribund ideas that held sway at the time. In the context of both British industry in general and the toy industry in particular Hornby was a man apart from so many of his contemporaries. His mind remained restless in its pursuit of success.

However, the feelings that impelled Hornby towards a political career in the 1930s were not simply those of exasperation at the lack of initiative in government. By 1930 the Depression was biting deep into Hornby's city and his industry. It was concentrated in those industries and regions that had suffered most in the 1920s. With its textiles, shipping and manufacturing Liverpool was suffering badly. Moreover, the recent gains by the British toy exports had also suffered a blow. Between 1929 and 1930 British toy exports fell by over £150,000 to just over £540,000 per annum, ending a period of steady growth that stretched back almost a decade. The journal of the British toy industry, *Toy Trader*, had long deplored the industry's concentration on the home market at the expense of overseas trade, and a lack of imagination with regard to marketing. This, as we have seen, was an accusation that could never be laid at Hornby's door. It therefore irritated him to see his company's profits almost halve between 1928 and 1930. This was  hardly a failing in either Meccano the product or Meccano the company. In 1930 Meccano's sales were worth nearly £275,000, of which almost half were exports. In addition to this were the equally impressive figures for Hornby Trains. Though a new line, they were already registering sales of just under £200,000 a year. To put this into perspective, over one-third of Meccano's annual sales were overseas during this period. At a time when annual exports for the whole of the British toy industry were averaging around £420,000 a year, Frank Hornby's products alone were accounting for over a third of them.[7]

By the beginning of the 1930s Hornby's life was entering a new phase. His company was leading the field, and with sales throughout the world could claim with some justification that Meccano was the world's greatest toy. Hornby's energy as well as his shrewd business acumen had propelled him to a position from which he began to feel increasingly able to see the direction in which the country – or at least its business affairs – should be driven. For twenty years he had been advocating a mix of protection for domestic industries coupled with a careful and planned development of foreign markets. His hard-won successes in the industry either side of the First World War had confirmed in his own mind the soundness of his approach. He had built up a company which was the embodiment of his economic principles, and which had been established in the teeth of difficult battles of competition and copyright. These successes had also cemented the fortune that accrued to him through the wartime munitions contracts. The result was that by the late 1920s Hornby was a self-made man with every reason to begin to think of himself as having the experience, the ideas and the position to consider a political career. Though his wealth and growing status remained tempered by his quiet and purposeful demeanour and a modesty that was so unshakeable as to be quite flinty, Hornby was of the view that he was ideally placed to play a part in solving the country's crisis. In 1930 Frank Hornby had the ideas to become a politician, he felt the need to become a politician, and the self-made industrialist was in a position to become a politician.

The company's success had moved Frank into the orbit of other successful local industrialists and businessmen, and he had taken his place among a class of men that were reshaping the landscape of national life as well as local politics. Once composed largely of Liberal members of the local aristocracy, the Liverpool establishment was changing as a result of the city's very success. Electoral reforms as well as social changes had eroded the power and influence of some of the old Liberal families. Increasingly the Liberal old guard were being challenged on all sides: from below by a working class swelled by more than a generation of Irish immigrants and in their own social world by successful industrialists, many of whom were more naturally inclined to Conservatism rather than Liberalism. New names from commerce, industry and manufacturing were emerging: Lyle (sugar), Brocklebank (Cunards), Sir Alfred Mond (later Lord Melchett) and Sir Max Muspratt both of ICI, the Pilkingtons (glass). These new powerful members of Liverpool's elites were taking their place alongside the likes of the Lords of Sefton and Derby. And among them was Frank Hornby. These individuals were amassing huge personal fortunes. That amassed by Hornby through Meccano compared favourably with those of Brocklebank, the Pilkingtons, Muspratt or Sir G. W. Paton of the Bryant & May match empire.

As the Liberal elite faded into the background of the city's political scene, the power of Tory and Labour influence grew. While Tory strength, centred on merchants, industrialists or white-collar workers, derived from the success of the port, Labour's early successes were in areas less connected to the trade off the Mersey. Together with Edge Hill and St Anne's, Everton was one of the districts in which Labour achieved some success prior to 1914. In addition to the large numbers of skilled and unionised workers, there was also a strong tradition of non-conformism and support for the co-operative movement. It was believed that the Everton seat had been lost to Labour in 1929 in part due to the growth of the Irish-Catholic vote in the constituency. The Labour Party under their Catholic leader Hogan had been very successful in winning the support of the city's Irish community. To a certain extent their support was inherited following the collapse of Irish nationalism with Irish independence. But there was also a sectarian element to Liverpudlian politics, and Labour's gains were achieved against a backdrop of hostility that ranged from irritation to racism. Richard Holt, the affluent leader of the Liberal Federal Council, was bemoaning 'the Irish-Labour efforts to exploit the ratepayer' in the 1920s, as Irish immigrants found themselves increasingly blamed for all of the city's woes. Sectarianism was becoming a feature of the landscape of Liverpudlian politics in areas like Everton, St Anne's or Edge Hill, despite the fact that in Everton the Irish community was largely 'respectable' skilled workers. An established Orange movement did little to diffuse racial and ethnic tensions, and the fears of religious leaders declaimed from the pulpit had led to a growth in violence between the Catholic and Protestant communities in the city. Canon Charles E. Raven wrote an inflammatory piece in the Church of England paper the *Liverpool Review* entitled 'The Irish Problem in Liverpool' in 1928. His conclusion was, 'that every form of public or private assistance is very seriously burdened by our Irish invaders' claims upon it', and that the Irish immigrant community was 'of the lowest class' and responsible for a great deal of the city's crime.

This message had found an audience, not least in Hornby's

would-be constituency of Everton. This was the base of the Liverpool Orange leader Pastor H. D. Longbottom, and the wards of St Domingo's and Netherfield returned a number of Conservative councillors who had successfully made a great deal of their Protestantism in the campaigns.[8] Already the Working Men's Conservative Association barred Catholics from membership, and the attempts to overturn Labour's 1929 gains in the city inevitably had a sectarian aspect, with a number of local Conservative MPs giving their support to calls for limits to (Irish) immigration to alleviate the city's economic problems. There is little evidence that Hornby shared any of the more extreme or intolerant views of some members of his party, and it is perhaps revealing that a Mr J. A. Kensit considered standing against Hornby as a Protestant candidate in the 1931 election.[9]

To recapture Everton the local Conservative Party had wasted no time in starting to rebuild the party's profile. They were keen to regain control of the constituency at the first opportunity and lost no time in looking for a new candidate. Mr Urding, Chairman of the Everton Conservative Division Council, discussed the opportunity with his friend and fellow Rotarian Frank Hornby in 1930, who agreed to allow his name to go forward. After meeting their prospective candidate the local association were delighted, and unanimously backed him as their official candidate at the next election – whenever that might be. The *Daily Post* reported that the Everton Conservatives were, 'pleased at Mr Urding's discovery of Mr Frank Hornby, who is not only an Evertonian by former residence, and a successful businessman, but also the soul of generosity and geniality'.

Yet while Frank enjoyed wholehearted Conservative support his position as Everton's next MP was far from guaranteed. Not only was there an election to be won, but it was far from clear that Hornby would have his nomination endorsed at a national level. Unknown to Hornby or the Conservative Association when he took up their offer of nomination was the fact that they were all about to be overtaken by events and the next general election would be different from any other. Even getting to the starting line would test both Hornby's own character and that of his supporters.

The mounting storm howling around the Labour government had led to the formation of a coalition, the National Government, in August 1931. It was agreed that the National Government would appeal to the electorate on a non-partisan platform at the general election to be held in October. Accordingly a gentleman's agreement between the main party leaders laid down that where the sitting MP declared his support for the coalition other parties supporting the National Government would not risk splitting the vote by contesting the seat. As a result over 150 MPs were returned unopposed, giving the National Government a healthy majority with which to try and steady the ship.

In Everton, however, the colourful and charismatic incumbent MP Derwent Hall-Caine was slow to declare his intentions. When the Labour government resigned on 24 August and a National Government was formed under the ex-Labour Prime Minister Ramsay MacDonald, the Conservatives under Stanley Baldwin and the Liberals under Sir Herbert Samuel instantly declared their support. While many – not least Baldwin – were unhappy with the arrangements, they fell into line behind MacDonald, singing a song of country before party with varying degrees of enthusiasm. Little more than a dozen Labour MPs did likewise, and these were mostly cabinet members.[10] It was initially unclear whether Everton's Hall-Caine would stand for re-election at all, and if so which party. Many Labour MPs opposed Ramsay MacDonald and the National Government, and the Labour Party announced it would contest every seat throughout Liverpool. It was a month before Hall-Caine came out as a supporter of the National Government. In doing so he lost the support of his local party, though by backing his leader and Prime Minister ensured he had his support. He hoped that with the imprimatur of the National Government's cause he could make up for this lack of local support through the support of local coalition supporters, particularly from the Conservative camp. He now waited for Hornby to withdraw from the contest.

Given the crisis, the state of the Parliamentary Labour Party and the fact that Everton was a traditional Tory stronghold, it was widely envisaged that the Labour candidate Samuel Treleaven had little or no chance of success. For one thing he was not even a local man but came from Birmingham, where his political record was far from illustrious. His experience was largely confined to a number of local elections which he had contested unsuccessfully. The Everton contest therefore showed every sign of developing into a two-way struggle between Hornby and Hall-Caine: two candidates professing to stand on the same National Government platform.

Under the agreement reached by the party leaders Hornby should have withdrawn from the contest in favour of the sitting MP. Yet Hornby refused, much to the anger of Hall-Caine and his leader Ramsay MacDonald. Hornby argued that there had been too much doubt and uncertainty surrounding Hall-Caine's candidature from the outset, and it had not been fully resolved. Within a few days of Hall-Caine's announcement that he would stand as a National Government candidate a newspaper report appeared intimating that he might not stand for re-election after all. The report was almost certainly mischievous, and unlikely to have come from the Hall-Caine camp, despite the difficult position he was in as a Labour MP reduced to trying to win the largely Conservative electorate from a Conservative candidate by professing much the same aims. Whatever the origins of the story, Hornby pounced on it as a

further justification of his decision not to stand down. In an election handbill entitled 'The "Agony" of Mr. Hall-Caine', Hornby criticised his opponent's vacillation:

His leader, Mr. Ramsay MacDonald was not thinking of the Labour Party, he was thinking of the country. HE DID NOT REQUIRE A MONTH TO MAKE UP HIS MIND.

Mr. HALL-CAINE PLEADED WITH THE EVERTON LABOUR PARTY TO SUPPORT HIM, BUT INSTEAD THEY DENOUNCED HIM.

Days pass and he gives no sign and in a well-known newspaper it is definitely announced Mr. Derwent Hall-Caine will not seek re-election. This announcement remained uncontradicted. Were the Conservatives to stand idly by, with a full-blooded Labour Socialist Candidate in the field and let the grass grow under their feet? Not likely![11]

However, Hornby was being a little unfair to Hall-Caine, and his account of the situation in Everton was not entirely accurate. For one thing Sam Treleaven, the 'full-blooded Labour Socialist candidate' who Hornby suggested was stealing a lead in the campaign, was not confirmed as the official Labour candidate until October, at least two weeks after Hall-Caine's declaration of intent. Until that point Labour had announced they would contest all of Liverpool's seats, but not with whom, while the Liberals were similarly undecided. 'We shall make no pact anywhere at the General Election,' declared the Liverpool Labour leader Alderman Hogan. 'We shall fight all opponents of the Labour Party, be they Conservatives, Liberals, ex-Labourites or anything else.'[12] It is questionable, therefore, whether the cause of the National Government was ever having to make up ground on that of Labour.

There was also a reason why Hall-Caine had taken his time. Hall-Caine's father, a celebrated novelist, had only recently died. It was a fact that cannot have escaped Hornby's attention since the funeral on the Isle of Man was a society affair, and widely reported in the local press. In a letter to Ramsay MacDonald announcing his decision to back his plea for coalition, Hall-Caine explained his delay in coming forward as being the result of the family tragedy:

> As you are aware, the recent sad bereavement in my own
> family has during the past few weeks removed me from
> politics, and up to the moment I have expressed no view
> on my personal position in relation to the situation,
> either inside or outside my constituency.

Of course, it would be naïve to think that Hall-Caine had been entirely disengaged from events inside or outside his constituency. He went on,

> But my enforced absence has at least given me the
> opportunity of examining the whole position from an
> angle uninfluenced by any personal or party pressure
> from any quarter, and prevented me from taking any
> action on the spur of the moment without full knowledge
> of the salient facts.

> Judged therefore in the light of these circumstances I have
> come very definitely to the conclusion that no-one who
> has the real interests of the workers of this country at
> heart could have taken any other step but the one you
> have taken, if all that the Labour Party has worked and

suffered for over so many years was not to be brought to naught.

> I shall therefore give my support to the present
> Government under your leadership, feeling sure that
> whatever may be said now in the heat of party
> disappointment, posterity will acclaim your wisdom.[13]

Clearly Hall-Caine had been canvassing opinion, and weighing the feelings of Labour Party colleagues against both his conscience and regard for posterity. Hornby's problem had been that Hall-Caine had not simply withdrawn from politics generally as he claimed, but had initially withdrawn from the election altogether. For a fervent protectionist and an employer with a vested interest in the protection of domestic industry, trade and employment Hornby did not want to give up his only chance of going to Westminster to fight for a cause that in one form or another he had been championing for almost two decades.

The question now, as the *Liverpool Echo* noted, was whether the local Conservative Association would accept his credentials as the National Government candidate and withdraw Frank Hornby. However, Hornby remained sceptical of Hall-Caine's motives, suggesting that his support for the coalition was largely spurious and born of a wish to hold his seat, rather than out of principle. Yet Hall-Caine had not chosen an easy path, for his declaration for the National Government meant he was very much in the minority in his own party (the support of the premier not withstanding), and could expect little help from that quarter. His announcement brought the number of declared 'National

Labour' MPs to just 14. When the party rejected him in due course he was forced to appeal to his traditional opponents for votes. The Conservative Association were not about to direct their constituents towards Hall-Caine, however. 'What does Mr. Hall-Caine care for the cause of Conservatism?' Hornby asked in his campaign literature.

> 'Nothing – BUT HE WOULD LIKE CONSERVATIVE
> VOTES NOW.
>
> HE IS ANNOYED BECAUSE CONSERVATIVES
> PREFER THEIR OWN CANDIDATE, MR. HORNBY.
> He thought his mere adhesion to the National
> Government would secure him an unchallenged return to
> Parliament. BUT EVERTON ELECTORS HAVE THEIR
> OWN OPINIONS.[14]

He was indeed annoyed, as was Ramsay MacDonald. Giving a talk in support of Liverpool candidates Ramsay MacDonald's son Alistair pointed out the Labour dissatisfaction with the situation in Everton, and also hinted that vote-splitting was an irritant to the leaders of all parties:

There is only one real National Candidate, and that is
Mr. Hall-Caine. It was agreed by the Prime Minister and
the other leaders where a sitting member supported the
National Government at this election, and where that
arrangement has not been adhered to it has been done
against the wishes of the leaders of the party.[15]

Hornby's own party *was* embarrassed by the situation. Baldwin
was committed to the agreement that National Government
candidates would not split the coalition vote by standing against
each other, and here was Hornby stubbornly refusing to stand
down. At the same time there remained suspicion of Hall-Caine's
commitment, and the length of time he had taken to reach a
decision had not gone unnoticed. The day after Hornby reiterated in the press that he would fight on, the chairman of the
Conservative Party Lord Stonehaven wrote to him to explain
Baldwin's dilemma.

21st October 1931

Dear Mr. Hornby,

I am very sorry that it has not been possible for the
Leader of the Party to send you the letter which he has
dispatched to those candidates who are contesting seats
in other constituencies. The matter had his most earnest
consideration, and he was forced to the conclusion that it
would be impossible for him to interfere in a Division
where a member of the Prime Minister's Party, who had
supported him since the formation of the National
Government, was standing again.

It is particularly unfortunate in your case, for, of course, Mr. Derwent Hall-Caine relinquished his candidature, and only came back at the last moment. Please do not be under any illusion, however, as to Mr. Baldwin's personal feelings towards you and your Association. It is only the exceptional nature of the contest that prevents him from sending you the same letter as he is sending to other members of the Party. We must all recognize the delicacy of his position, and I am sure that, notwithstanding your natural disappointment, you will be able to appreciate it.

Yours sincerely,

Stonehaven.

On the back of the letter in his own hand Hornby drafted a reply to Stonehaven in which he expressed his hope that when the full facts were available his work in Everton would be 'better understood and commended'. He also underlined that it would be 'a great joy to me to win a seat back to the fold', and closed by reiterating once more his commitment to the National Government cause. Whether Hornby felt that he was being undervalued or snubbed by the party leadership mattered little. The Conservative Party at the time was neither driven by its leadership, nor handicapped by its constituency parties. The local parties had little say in determining policy, while the leader could often do little when confronted by a candidate who was wilful, independent, affluent or well supported locally. Hornby was all of these.[16]

Both candidates fought on, almost exclusively with each other and for exactly the same ground. While Baldwin perforce kept quiet, Ramsay MacDonald sent a message of encouragement to Hall-Caine. As one of the few prospective Labour MPs in the National camp it fell to him 'to carry our colours'.[17] While Hall-Caine had the support of his leader, he did not have the support of his local party and was forced to appeal to Tory voters. Hornby, conversely, enjoyed a staunch backing from his local association, but had a leader who was unable to declare his support for him.

As the country settled down to campaigning the candidates began to outline their policies and state their cases. Hornby laid out his position in the local press, which over the coming weeks reprinted the manifestos of the three candidates side by side. Unsurprisingly both Hornby and Hall-Caine claimed to be the only 'real' National candidate. Hornby even claimed to be the first not simply in Everton, but in the country:

> Since my adoption two years ago I have continually
> advocated measures that give increased employment to
> British workers and increase the prosperity of the
> country. I have also emphasized the importance of a
> closer economic unity with our Empire, and have taken
> as my slogan 'Britain First! Empire Always!' This slogan
> expresses the views of the leading men in the National
> Government, and I claim therefore to be the first
> National Government candidate in the country.[18]

This was the line the Conservative Party activists sought to emphasise when Ramsay MacDonald attacked Hornby's refusal to stand down ('If Mr. Hornby insists on opposing then the responsibility for wounding the National cause will rest on his shoulders'). The response from the Everton Conservative Association was stubborn: 'This is not a coalition, and the Premier cannot dictate as to who is, and who is not a National Candidate. Mr. Hornby was the first National Candidate in England, and he is going on.'[19]

Aside from claiming to be first in the field under the National colours, the central plank of Frank's manifesto was economic. Naturally this meant tariffs, but more generally the typically dogged and prudent financial husbandry upon which the success of Meccano Ltd was built.

> As a supporter of the National Government I stand for
> economy, wise administration, and a reduction in the
> heavy burden of taxation that is crushing our industries.
> The extravagance of the late Socialist Government
> impaired our credit abroad and brought the country to
> the brink of disaster. The immediate danger has been
> averted by the prompt and decisive action of the National
> Government, and our Budget has been balanced. But we
> still have the task of getting our vast army of unemployed
> back to work, so that they may be able to earn a real
> living wage instead of having to exist on unemployment
> relief, and this can only be done by safeguarding our
> industries.

In mentioning unemployment Hornby was getting to the nub of the problem at a local level. While the National Government was rallied round the two tasks of balancing the budget and saving the pound, at a local level the crisis meant one thing above all else

– joblessness. Liverpool had been hit particularly hard. Again the solution was clear to Hornby – protectionism:

> Safeguarding has always been the central feature of my policy. In 1930 more than 1,000,000 British workers lost their employment, yet in the same year we purchased from foreign countries manufactured articles to the value of £280,000,000!

> I stand for the protection of our home market, therefore, in the interest of the wage earners of this country. This protection can only be given by imposing an effective tariff that on the one hand will stop indiscriminate dumping of foreign manufactured goods, and on the other will give us bargaining power to negotiate for better conditions of trading with foreign countries. I believe that safeguarding and . . . economic unity offer the only means by which we can restore prosperity to our country.

The election campaign also had a personal dimension. Hall-Caine accused Hornby of selfishness in refusing to stand down. In a speech given on 22 October he said, 'The posters being displayed by Mr Hornby's Conservative supporters read "Service Before Self!" They might very properly be changed to "Self Before Service!"'[20] Hall-Caine, whom Hornby described as a 'Socialist Pink' in his election materials, was criticised for his politics and his character. Hornby sought to make as much of his radicalism – citing the incident some years previous when Hall-Caine had carried a red flag through the streets of Everton, as evidence of this vice. Having once changed party Hornby labelled him 'semi-detached', and an election poster mocked him:

> 'FIRST HE SAID HE COULDN'T.
> THEN HE SAID HE WOULDN'T.
> NOW HE SAYS HE WILL.
> *And brazenly thrusts himself on us squealing for help*
> *'Please sir I won't do it again.'*
> CAN YOU TRUST HIM?

This was the rough and tumble of the local party agents, the bill-posters and the rallies. Throughout the campaign 'rowdies' from both Labour and Conservative associations sought to disrupt meetings – usually those of Hall-Caine or senior National Labour figures sent up to lend their support. Yet generally speaking this tone was typical neither of Hornby's character nor of the way in which the campaign was fought by the protagonists. Hornby and Hall-Caine (and to the extent that he managed to feature at all, Treleaven) maintained a dignified stance throughout. The colourful Manxman Hall-Caine had his hands full stressing his own National credentials, and at any rate Hornby provided little to work with for the would-be character assassin. For his part Hornby simply wasn't equipped for fire-and-brimstone politics. He relied on a personal authority that was by definition quiet. This was politics conducted by a staid Victorian bank manager or the local vicar, who in the words of Hornby's own handbills 'has the confidence of all who know him and work with him'. He was serious, and concerned, and conducted himself in a neat, soft-spoken and modest way. Confrontational politics was not a style that came easily to him, not least because, for all his apparent seriousness, Hornby was naturally generous.

On the eve of the election Sam Treleaven was admitted to the Royal Infirmary with appendicitis. Save for a rallying message to his party workers delivered from his sickbed, he was to play no further part in the campaign. On hearing of his opponent's ill-health Hornby was typically magnanimous. He called at the hospital to visit his adversary, whom he described as 'down but not out'. While the incident was reported in the *Liverpool Echo*, and cannot have done Hornby's reputation as a straightforward and considerate chap much harm, it probably was not a publicity stunt. Hornby had shown himself during the campaign to be earnest and honest rather than relaxed under the glare of the hustings' lights. He was engaging and trustworthy rather than charismatic, and had tended to shun the fiery public meetings and grandiloquent speech-making of some of the Liverpool candidates, Hall-Caine included. He was not a natural politician, but was naturally decent. 'I just wanted to see him,' Hornby explained, 'apart from politics altogether, to ask him how he was to-day.'[21]

He need not have bothered. How he was feeling was probably pretty clear to most people. Treleaven was exhausted. He had fought a sound campaign, and had appealed to the Labour supporters on a platform of full unemployment benefit, nationalisation of the financial sector and a rejection of tariffs that would raise the cost of living for the working man. But he had had to battle against the perceptions of the late Labour administration's 'extravagance', and in-fighting that had followed MacDonald's call for the coalition. Treleaven had to make the case that having presided over the crisis, Labour were the best placed to resolve it. In the end he preferred to concentrate on policies aimed at treating the symptoms rather than the cause, while Hornby continued to prescribe a stiff dose of prudence. In addition Treleaven had fought hard to win the attention that had been garnered by the head-to-head of the two National candidates. By the eve of the election it was becoming clear that despite healthy support he was not going to be able to repeat the success of 1929 and secure a Socialist victory in Everton.

There was little doubt that the most intriguing aspect of the

Everton battle was the competition between Hall-Caine and Hornby. Though they both fought for the same ground, their styles were very different. Hall-Caine, of course, was by far the most experienced of the Everton candidates. The son of the late novelist Sir Hall Caine, Derwent Hall-Caine was as colourful as his name suggests. He relished the public meetings and seemed to enjoy speaking, even to hostile gatherings. Ramsay MacDonald's son Alistair came to Everton to speak on behalf of Hall-Caine, and despite heckling from Socialist and Conservative members of the audience had fought hard to 'turn the jeers into cheers'. Hall-Caine met similar opposition, but was a charismatic and accomplished speaker. 'Support for Mr. Hall-Caine in Everton', noted the *Liverpool Echo*, 'is becoming more obvious. At every Conservative meeting he has a number of champions, and even at Labour gatherings questions have been asked on his behalf.'[22]He relished the theatrical, and made much of his reception in Everton, where nomination papers full of signatures on his behalf were flourished. 'All the women had come from neighbouring houses, and those that were unable to sign the paper showed their disappointment. So another paper was produced and that was soon filled too . . . I find the women are wholeheartedly for me.'[23]

Hornby's style was far quieter. He did not relish the large meetings in the same way as Hall-Caine, and was far happier on the streets, meeting housewives and chatting with dock workers or old sailors. He listened intently to these small groups like a country doctor in consultation, his head inclined to one side and a look of grave concentration his face ('I see, and when did you first notice the trouble?'). His election motto, 'Vote solidly for Frank Hornby, "The Man You Can Trust!"' was the statement of a steadfast High Tory, grave, reliable and paternalistic. He listened quietly and spoke plainly in his soft Liverpudlian accent, taking pains to spell out his commitment to tariffs as the cornerstone of his policy. This contrasted with Hall-Caine's vagueness. 'This election', he had stated, 'does not mean that tariffs will be applied, but that the question will be examined in relation to the questions that arise.' This was not the reassuring prescription that the crisis seemed to demand.[24]

After a slow start to polling the party agents began to predict a record turnout by the afternoon of Election Day. Last-minute attempts to woo voters by writing on the walls in whitewash 'Vote For—!' were largely sabotaged by children who had great fun scrawling 'Don't' in front of them with chalk. Bill stickers raced around the constituency pasting their own posters over those of their rivals, and the Conservative Association sent a van with a loudspeaker on a tour of the area exhorting everyone to 'vote at all costs'. Naturally, all the candidates declared themselves happy with proceedings, and predicted success to varying degrees, Treleaven from the confines of his hospital bed. When the results were announced Everton learned that it was to have a new MP, but it would not be Sam Treleaven. With a turnout of just under 35,000 Frank Hornby was returned as the MP for Everton. He polled nearly half of the votes, and beat Treleaven into second place with a majority of 4,400. Hall-Caine finished third, about 3,000 votes adrift.[25] On 4 November 1931 a small band of well-wishers gathered at Lime Street Station to wave off their new MP Frank Hornby, every inch the politician with his bow-tie, neatly waxed moustache and cigar as he set off for the final chapter in his remarkable career.

9

Frank Hornby, MP

Following the 1931 election the Conservative Party was in rude health, though the Honourable Frank Hornby, MP was not. He was ageing, suffering from diabetes and about to undertake the gruelling schedule of late-night sittings of the House and frantic commuting between Westminster and his provincial constituency that had ruined far younger men. Moreover, he was contending with a set of problems which, as both politician and businessman, were extremely challenging. The country was facing tremendous problems, and the ageing member for Everton had placed himself in the eye of the storm. Though he was deeply involved and interested in the problems that he was attempting to address, his interests were in many ways vested . . . He was not best placed to take advantage of the position his party was in, but he applied himself to the new work with the determination that had been the hallmark of his early Meccano days.

Hornby was now in a party that was extremely well placed.

Labour had been trounced and its leader 'imprisoned in Downing Street' thanks to an arrangement which had been foisted upon all sides and which left MacDonald the Labour leader of an overwhelmingly Conservative National Government. Baldwin had clipped the wings of the trade unions in 1926, banished the troublesome Churchill, and old Lloyd George had finally found himself on the outside looking in. Increasingly the government illustrated the strength of the Conservatives within it through the rejection of free trade and the adoption of protectionism. This was largely in the form of imperial preference: essentially, free trade within the Commonwealth and between its countries coupled with tariffs for imports from outside the happy gang. This was predicated on the hope that by trading largely with each other the Commonwealth countries would stimulate growth in their economies and protect their own markets from outside competition. By the time of the Ottawa Conference which underlined this policy, however, it had largely been overtaken by developments in the wider world. Britain could no longer absorb all the products of its Commonwealth partners, and they in turn were looking beyond the motherland for their imports.

Moreover, by denying European countries the opportunity to trade with Britain the Ottawa agreement compelled these countries to become ever more dependent on the likes of Germany. Germany's impressive economic growth throughout the 1930s mirrored that of the USA and contrasted with Britain's limp and limping condition. Though there was recovery, revival was a different matter. The British toy industry had managed a fairly impressive sustained recovery after the slump of the early twenties. Output rose from £1,468,000 in 1924 to £2,993,000 in 1935, while imports remained fairly static, hovering around the £2½ million mark. However, these figures disguised a more ominous development. Since 1920 Germany's share of imports into Britain had been rising steadily. They accounted for only 50 per cent of the imports in 1920, but 86 per cent by the end of the decade.[1]

The aloof attitude that many toy manufacturers adopted towards European markets was reflected in the fact that although British toy exports were rising, they were still modest in comparison with those of Germany. At their high point before the Second World War they amounted to just under £700,000 in 1929 – less than a third of total German exports to Britain alone. This reflected the fact that, while British toys were able to compete with German ones in terms of quality, internal currency crises in Weimar Germany meant that German manufacturers were trying to sell their goods abroad wherever possible, and European buyers preferred them on the basis of their relative cheapness.[2] Still, as we have seen, Hornby continued to regard the European markets as vital. The French factory had opened outside Paris at Boissy in 1921, initially the centre of distribution and warehousing (French versions of Hornby trains in local livery were prepared here). While Meccano did not attend many of the large international trade fairs such as Leipzig (unlike other manufacturers like Chad Valley), it was more because the international agencies were well established rather than through indifference, as was the case with other British manufacturers.

The British toy manufacturers were, however, no longer in the shadow of their continental competitors – at least in terms of quality. While Meccano set the standard in terms of metal and constructional toys there were a host of other British firms such as Brimtoy or A. Wells and Co. Britains' miniature soldiers towered over the nursery battlefields without peer and Chad Valley had even managed to make inroads into the German heartland of the soft-toy market and take on the legendary Stieff in their own backyard. Chad Valley even showed a grasp of marketing that Hornby might have approved of, producing their own comic (*Happyland*), which extolled the virtues of educational toys in general and their own in particular. Many of these companies were employing around two or three hundred workers (some on a seasonal basis), and some even had a number of sites. The largest, however, was Lines Brothers, makers of toy prams, pedal cars and other wheeled toys, which had a labour force of 1,000 in the 1920s. Seasonal redundancies allowed firms to maintain a certain flexibility that helped them to absorb fluctuations in the market more readily. Many companies hired a large number of juvenile workers (in Meccano's case usually 14-year-olds), subsequently laying them off out of the peak (Autumn–Christmas) season.

However, there was little that most could do when the tidal wave of the 1929 Wall Street crash broke on European shores. The effects reverberated throughout Europe, and businesses were buffeted by the inevitable consequences. By 1930–1 a number of companies were going out of business. *Toy Trader* recorded a dismal catalogue of wholesalers, importers, buyers and retailers driven over the edge. The global crisis, declining capital, balance of trade deficits, hastily imposed tariffs and general depression hit the toy industry hard. Advertising contracted, trade journals all but disappeared and even the government pulled its subsidy for the British Industries Fair. A host of household names from Gamages to Hamleys were impaired.

The manufacturers faired little better. Some companies were forced to make similar economies either by slashing wages (Basset Lowke), or else by prostituting themselves. The jigsaw manufacturers R. H. Journet survived by making advertising and promotional products for food companies like John West and Crosse & Blackwell. Others simply went bust. Out of over 1,300 companies involved in the toy business as wholesalers, manufacturers, importers and the like, fewer than half made it beyond 1930. Only 280 of these companies were to be found among the 1,330 companies in the business in 1940. Many of the rest were opportunists or entrepreneurs, innovators or chancers touting bold new products or jumping on bandwagons and following crazes. One such craze was miniature golf, which swept the country in 1930. Another was the yo-yo, which appeared in 1932.[3] Some survived by quitting the toy business altogether, and others thought about it. Walter Lines even approached Frank

Hornby to ask him if he would be interested in buying him out. Hornby refused. He had more than enough to contend with on his own account. Hornby was forced to hive off his American factory to one of his larger US competitors, A. C. Gilbert. Though Gilbert, manufacturer of the Erector Set, was not one of the companies against whom Hornby had brought a lawsuit, his view of most competitors as imitators generally extended to everyone in the field of metal mechanical constructional toys. It must have been particularly galling for Frank to have to let the American

wing go only a decade after his triumph in the courts protecting his US business, and given the huge investment in both time and money which he had made in developing his business there.

He was also now an MP, and attempting to commute from Westminster to his factory in Liverpool to oversee his business. Every weekend he left Westminster and caught the train to Lime Street. There he was met by his chauffeur, Tatler. Tatler had been with Hornby for some years, ever since the business had taken off and Frank had become sufficiently wealthy to run a Rolls-Royce or Daimler limousine, as befitted a wealthy self-made company director. From Lime Street Tatler would take Hornby direct to the factory so that he could catch the last hour or so of the week's business. The staff expected him, and late Friday afternoon was marked by a sudden increase in activity and sharpening of demeanour in preparation for the arrival of the boss. It was a gruelling schedule, and physically it began to take its toll on Hornby. Although he smoked (a pipe and more usually cigars), he did not drink, which probably helped. One employee recalled that occasionally he would drink a strange mixture of what appeared to be milk and soda, served to him with great pomp and formality by a uniformed silver-service waitress in his office at Binns Road. This restorative tonic was possibly medicinal, for in his later years his diabetes became exacerbated by his arduous schedule – and his age.

As the Depression bit into the industry Hornby was attempting to combat it on two fronts, as a businessman and a politician. Neither constituted a particularly restful way of spending one's dotage, but then Hornby had never been especially restful. The larger toy businesses were managing to weather the storm, but were battling against the economic elements which howled around them. This typhoon was posing more problems for the larger vessels, which caught the full force of the tempest broadside, than for the smaller companies who were able to ride the storm. These large companies had had to swiftly reposition themselves. They faced competition from newer, smaller, more agile opportunists in an industry which (as Hornby knew only too well) had always promised the chance of rich rewards for upstart entrepreneurs who showed boldness and imagination and who understood the modern world. As a result there were a number of new companies jostling for position in the market. Stimuli to the trade had come in the form of new materials such as plastic, or the interest in educational toys for younger children fostered by the kindergarten movement. Others had joined the trade as a sideline to other interests. Waddingtons, makers of Monopoly in 1935, were printers who had diversified into jigsaws and later board games. Palitoy, the giants behind Action Man in the 1960s and 1970s, had their roots in doll manufacture between the wars as a branch of early plastics and celluloid manufactures.

Hornby's response was typically combative. While smaller and/or newer companies made up the majority of the names listed in the trade magazines and journals in the early 1930s, it was the older, more experienced companies which were in the vanguard of the fightback. While neighbouring Liverpool toymakers such as Gray and Nicholls slipped under in 1930 this was the peak year for Meccano, with the company selling over a quarter of a million pounds' worth of kits worldwide. Train sets added almost £200,000 more. Though the company would never again sell as many Meccano sets (and the company's profits would never quite achieve the heights of the mid-1920s), Meccano undertook a further expansion. While others consolidated, merged and expanded throughout the early 1930s Meccano went public in 1932. They managed to raise £300,000 which was invested in new factory facilities, though increasingly it was not Meccano itself but the Hornby and Dinky lines which were accounting for the bulk of the company's sales. Lines Brothers followed suit, and they too expanded both their factory facilities and their stable.

While he attempted to secure his company's fortunes through

investment Frank was more reticent about using his position as an MP to argue on behalf of his industry. His deeply held belief in the protection of British industry through tariffs surfaced from time to time in newspaper articles or trade pieces, but he was not much of a lobbyist on behalf of his industry. In general he kept his head down and voted with the majority. While many accused the National Government of inactivity on a whole range of issues, Hornby was muted in his calls for action, and phlegmatic in his

acceptance of their justification of the status quo. The National Government had been formed to address two immediate questions: how to balance the budget and how to save the pound. After balancing the budget (but not saving the pound) the government had to turn its attention to the greatest problem arising from the Depression: unemployment. The overriding perception of the National Government's response to the problems was that it either did not understand them, did not know what it was doing, or did not really care. This is only partly true. Certainly the principal view of the problem of unemployment held by most people who were not unemployed, was that it was insoluble. That said it had to be ensured that any attempted solution at least did not waste money (by allowing abuse and dishonesty among claimants). The widely held belief was that these unfortunates were a breed apart. In a sense this was true since generally the blight of unemployment affected particular industries and areas disproportionately (shipbuilding, shipping, textiles, the coal industry). The view of the unemployed as some strange race of malingerers and scroungers did little to help overcome the commonly held view that unemployment relief was futile. Hornby was one of those who came from an area of industry badly affected by unemployment. He was a 'Liverpool Man', and Liverpool as a port and centre for the textile industry had been hit badly by unemployment.

He had taken his initial mandate as a National Government supporter seriously – indeed he clung to it long after the government had tried to slough it off as an inconvenient and unrealistic embarrassment. Unemployment, trade and the Empire, protectionism and poor relief were the only topics that Hornby spoke on as an MP. They were possibly the only ones he cared enough to speak about, for he was hardly tireless in his espousal of any particular viewpoint. Conservative National Government supporters were wary of adopting any programme of relief which might threaten to unbalance the books. Socialist supporters viewed any proposed solutions phlegmatically: in their view they amounted to fiddling around the edges of the problem, and a real solution necessitated a root-and-branch reform that was nothing less than the substitution of socialism for capitalism. In the meantime both sides agreed one had to be wary about wasting money, unbalancing the books or setting the wrong tone by indulging the indolent tendencies of the workshy and dishonest rump of unemployed by doling out money willy-nilly.

Whether it was inexperience or the straight-speaking of a northern businessman, Hornby pressed the case for improved unemployment relief. Though prudent in the conduct of his own business he had first-hand experience of the problems of unemployment in industrial areas like Liverpool. Possibly having once had to lay off workers after the boom-and-bust of the early 1920s Hornby was more sensitive to the plight of the unemployed than the average industrial employer. In particular Hornby was unimpressed by the current arrangements for disbursing unemployment relief. The scheme of transitional benefit was a product of the 1927 Unemployment Insurance Act. Before the First World War the unemployed were expected to survive through a mix of savings, reduced expenditure, the help of family and friends and any private charities or friendly societies they could avail themselves of. When these failed only the Poor Law remained to help the most desperate. Though an insurance scheme had been introduced in 1911 it was limited to those trades in which employment was expected to fluctuate fairly regularly – shipbuilding, the construction industry and engineering – and covered only about a sixth of the labour force. During the war insurance cover was extended to all those working in munitions. This included all of Frank Hornby's staff at Meccano. After the war insurance was widened to cover the bulk of the working population. The government's commitment, first embodied in the 'out of work donation' framed after the armistice, had been seen as a short-term measure. Enshrined in the Unemployment Act of 1920 it expanded cover to manual workers and others earning less than £250 a year. Yet there were many exceptions – teachers, nurses, farm or railway workers among them. The scheme was applied more liberally, and the effect (though most certainly never stated explicitly) was that the state had undertaken to support the unemployed rather than simply help the individual in his own efforts. During the postwar boom this probably did not seem to pose much of a problem. Unfortunately for the government, unprecedented levels of unemployment were just around the corner.

The scheme was based on a principle of insurance whereby employers, employees and the state built up a fund through weekly payments that could be set against any future periods of unemployment. The attraction of the scheme to the government was that, as with any other insurance scheme, unemployment insurance was supposed to be financed largely by the individuals concerned and their employers. However, as became increasingly clear throughout the 1920s there were a number of flaws in the scheme. First, the government did not correctly anticipate the levels of unemployment. Secondly, unlike any other insurance scheme, the groups least likely to have to make a claim, such as domestic servants, were excluded from it, and were therefore not paying into it for the benefit of others. Finally, the contributions that the insured were paying were not high enough to cover the increased payments that could be claimed, or the fact that claims could be made earlier than previously.

The scheme was something of a shambles. Yet any scheme would probably have struggled to cope with the unforeseen levels of unemployment in the Depression years. When they materialised there was a feeling that it was a little harsh not to extend the benefit of cover to all the unemployed – even if they had not paid for it. This 'uncovenanted' benefit could be ill-afforded by the government, but Hornby was one of a large number who shared the view that the need to balance the books had to be weighed against the impossibility of refusing benefits to families merely on the basis of accountancy. The revamp of the benefit system in 1927 was essentially a compromise between the

desire to continue to extend benefit cover to all unemployed (even if they had not paid enough contributions), and the desire to rein in such expense. It too was a failure, not because it was a compromise, but because it was clear that the government had not learned from the failure of its predecessors. For one thing, the 1927 scheme was predicated upon yet another optimistic forecast of unemployment rates. However, the law laid greater emphasis on applicants being examined to ascertain whether they were genuinely seeking work. By 1929 around two-thirds of all rejected claims were on the basis of applicants not demonstrating to the boards that they were genuine and active in their efforts to find work.

Those whom the courts rejected were forced to look elsewhere for support, and the first hope was public assistance from the local corporation. This involved appearing before a committee to plead one's case. This was often as daunting as it was unrewarding, since many local authorities did not allow claimants to appear before the public assistance committees with representatives. Since the most vulnerable members of society were not always the most self-assured or eloquent advocates, many were being failed by the system. Perhaps unsurprisingly, therefore, Hornby's maiden speech was as part of the Commons debate on unemployment in November 1932. He spoke as 'an employer of labour', arguing that 'every consideration should be given to the welfare of work-people, not only by the employers but also by the State'. These considerations should take three forms, all of which were fairly long-standing hobby-horses of Hornby's. The first was that increases in relief would only go so far, and instead 'steps should be taken to expedite our own prosperity'. This meant

> Exploring the possibilities of our own market, which for
> us is the finest in the world, and we should exploit it with
> all the energy and intelligence at our command, as it will
> be some time before international trade will revive and
> before we shall be able to receive any substantial benefits
> from the agreements with the Dominions [the Ottawa
> Agreements].[4]

This had been Hornby's belief since 1916 at least, and one of the principles upon which he had campaigned for parliament. His second point was that the maintenance of low prices and restrictions in working hours and wages should be forgotten. It was necessary to keep production costs low, but utility schemes should be encouraged to create jobs and stimulate the economy. His last point, which had also been a feature of his letter to the

Liverpool Echo in 1916, was that the government must develop credit facilities to enable businesses to invest in growth.

Yet the government was wary of attempting anything too creative or speculative to remedy the problem. It was, in the words of one MP, wedded to a 10-foot plank which it was determined to use to cross the 20-foot ditch. In the meantime the burden of unemployment continued to fall on the regions. Hornby had addressed the problems of local government having to bear the costs of insurance (unemployment) benefit in his first question from the floor of the House on 11 April 1932:

> Mr. Hornby asked the Labour Minister Sir Henry
> Betterton if he is aware that owing to the action of courts
> of referees in disqualifying persons in the transitional
> class from insurance benefit, many have had to seek
> public assistance, and that this number is increasing,
> causing a burden on the rates of many cities and towns;
> and whether he is prepared to promote legislation making
> poverty arising from unemployment a national charge?[5]

Sir Henry was not. He believed – or more probably desperately hoped in the face of mounting evidence to the contrary – that the current arrangements would do. As an employer and an industrialist as well as an inner-city MP, Hornby was well aware that the system was failing the unemployed in a quite dramatic fashion. Betterton for his part rejected Hornby's assertion that those who adjudicated claims for transitional insurance were failing, either in relation to the unfortunates who subsequently had to throw themselves on the mercy of the local corporations, or those local bodies that had to try and catch, then support them.

Hornby's question was prompted by a concern with the blight of unemployment as much as the plight of the unemployed. The burden accruing to the local governments charged with supporting the unemployed was mounting and threatened to become an enervating responsibility. Though Hornby suggested that the number of unemployed disqualified for transitional insurance and relying on public assistance was standing at 3,500 and rising, the government was wary of accepting liability on a grand scale for the support of that group of the country's unemployed, who were by definition least equipped to bounce back into work quickly.

Despite his government refusing to be drawn by questions on local poor relief, Hornby returned to the issue in 1933, demanding to know from the Minister of Health the exact amount levied by local authorities for the maintenance of the able-bodied unemployed. The minister refused to be tempted down that alley, suggesting that the figure could not readily be separated from the figure for public assistance as a whole. Later in the day, in another speech, Frank again tried to get the government to address the state's responsibility for unemployment relief. Would Sir Henry Betterton, the Minister of Labour 'give an estimate of the cost involved to the exchequer if it accepted the entire maintenance of unemployed able-bodied persons?' 'No, Sir,' replied Betterton.[6]

Over the next few years Hornby only spoke a handful of times, usually on issues of trade and employment. He spoke on the protection of trade within the Dominions (beet sugar factories, 14 March 1932); import tax and duties payable by British importers to Australia (New South Wales Taxation, 31 May 1932); the dissemination of information between the Ministry of Agriculture and agriculturalists (10 November 1932); and unemployment. His interventions were invariably brief and to the point, usually some technical question seeking clarification, probably at the behest of a constituent, though sometimes revealing the characteristic concerns of Hornby himself – international trade and exports, and the problems faced by manufacturers not unlike himself. Generally, though, he was not much of a representative of his industry. He never spoke out on behalf of the toy industry, for instance over the Anglo-German Pact or the steady rise in German or Japanese imports, despite the fact that they alarmed a number of manufacturers and commentators and had become the focus of much disagreement within the industry and between the trade press and retail and manufacturing interests. In fact, in comparison to the MP J. D. Kiley, who had been an advocate for toy retail interests in the House up until 1921, Hornby was a poor mouthpiece for the industry. In all he made only six contributions from the floor of the House, and none of them set the political landscape on fire.[7]

Hornby's most significant contribution as a member of parliament was, however, to do with toys in a roundabout way.

It neatly drew a line under his parliamentary career, and grew out of his twin interests of stimulating the economy and promoting toy buying. Having announced his intention of standing down from parliament and not seeking re-election in 1935 the Christmas (Facilities) Bill would have been a fitting end to his career as a politician. On 24 July 1934 Hornby moved to introduce his Bill. 'I beg to move', he began, 'that leave be given to bring in a bill to extend the facilities for shopping during the Christmas Season, and for other purposes connected therewith.'

Hornby was not the most imposing of public speakers, and needed extensive notes. Indeed, they were so extensive that one of his fellow MPs raised a point of order, accusing Hornby of breaking Commons rules by reading his speech rather than delivering it off the cuff, though the Speaker ruled in favour of Frank. The use of notes reflected the fact that Frank had seldom spoken from the floor (and never at any length) and was unused to it. He spoke steadily, but it was not fiery oratory, rather a quiet, sensible and pedestrian contribution. Here was a neat dovetailing of self-interest and political common sense. The object of the Bill was to amend existing legislation to enable an extension to shopping hours in the two-week run-up to Christmas so as to promote trade. This necessitated amendments not only to trading and by-laws, but also consideration of public transport provision and the payment of interest and dividends by savings banks and mutual societies in time for people to do their last-minute shopping. Hornby proposed to amend legislation so as to maximise trading in the fortnight (12 trading days) immediately preceding Christmas. This period usually accounted for the bulk of sales and business in a number of industries and therefore steps should be taken to make sure opportunities were not being missed. 'When this period comes about,' he explained,

> Serious congestion takes place. Some shops are overcrowded, and it is difficult for shopkeepers to cope with the enormous rush of buying. Passenger traffic facilities are overstrained, and the buying public are unable to move about with any comfort. Goods traffic is also constrained . . . The object of the Bill is to make this extra trade and employment possible, and so to confer on the country as a whole all the benefits which must arise from the very appreciable additions to its trade.[8]

These benefits were not for all the country, of course. In a move which perhaps strengthens Hornby's image as a friend of children everywhere, he also suggested that instead of beginning a couple of days before Christmas, school holidays be brought forward and schools break up two weeks before Christmas. This was not, however, a result of Hornby's concern and care for his myriad little friends. This was a shameless business ploy. The extended holidays would be of great benefit 'to the trade of the whole country but also for the educational value to the scholars, who could visit the shops and inspect the exhibited displays of British-made goods and materials of a scientific nature for after-school occupations'.

It does not take much to envisage exactly what 'British-made goods of a scientific nature for after-school occupations' Hornby had in mind, and one can only assume that even Hornby baulked at conjuring the image of the flower of the country being fleeced of their pocket money: instead, the extended holidays merely gave them greater opportunity for 'inspecting' displays. Curiously no one quizzed Hornby too closely on his own considerable interests, and exactly how he might benefit from the passage of the Bill. Possibly it was because no one knew who he was. Mr Rhys-Davies pointed out that 'The Hon. Member for Everton (Mr. Hornby) intervenes so seldom in our debates that I am reluctant to oppose his Bill, but I am going to do so', His arguments were largely based on the extension of working hours that the Bill implied for shop assistants and others in ancillary trades, and that this might be extended to other public holidays.

By a narrow majority of 115 to 101 votes Frank was given leave to introduce his Bill. He never did, there being for whatever reason insufficient time in the session. His diabetes was worsening. One of the characteristics of the illness was failing eyesight, which made reading difficult. This was obviously a problem in politics as much as in business. With his health deteriorating and with growing concerns over the state of his business Hornby had determined to stand down at the coming election, and in 1935 he duly withdrew from political life. In due course he found that he was unable to continue with Meccano, and with some reluctance he accepted the inevitable conclusion that at 72 he had to vacate the chair of the board in favour of his long-time colleague George Jones.

Throughout 1936 Frank's health worsened. His eyesight continued to deteriorate to the point at which he became virtually blind, and he had also developed a heart condition. The fact that he was so unwell did not deter him from continuing to be involved in Meccano, though he became increasingly unable to offer any real help to the company. The task of caring for him fell to Clara, but the strain was too much. After nursing him through several bouts of illness the strain began to affect her health too. Her doctor advised that she rest. She was a keen traveller, a stout and vivacious tourist, bustling through the piazzas and boulevards of Europe with her cloche hat pulled down over her grinning round face, a companion on one arm and her handbag on the other. It seemed natural, therefore, for Frank to suggest that she take a short trip with some companions to relax and enjoy a break from caring for him. It also seems that Frank intended to stay behind in order to make preparations for their golden wedding celebrations the following January. On 5 September 1936 Clara set off from Southampton aboard the *Arandora Star* on a Mediterranean cruise accompanied by a niece

and other companions. The *Arandora* was a modern, luxurious Blue Star liner which could accommodate some 400 well-heeled guests in its elegant staterooms and cabins.[9]

Shortly after her departure, however, Frank fell seriously ill. His heart condition had deteriorated. He was admitted to the David Lewis Northern Hospital in Great Howard Street, Liverpool on 18 September. He was immediately operated on, but died three days later. His death certificate recorded his death as caused by his heart condition, the diabetes and the operation.[10] Meanwhile Clara and her party were still at sea. It was decided not to tell her that Frank had died while she was still at sea. Somehow they managed to keep the news from her, despite the fact that it was posted on the ship's message board. Instead it fell to her son Roland to meet his mother off the boat seven days later. Not only did Roland have to tell Clara that Frank had died, he also had to pass on the grim news that the funeral had taken place, and her partner of almost 50 years had already been interred in the quiet graveyard in St Andrew's Anglican churchyard, Maghull. The church had been full to overflowing with local dignitaries, industrial and parliamentary colleagues, friends and well-wishers. Frank was laid to rest only a few yards from the ancient chapel of Maghull, built in the twelfth century, and nestling amid the churchyard trees in the shadow of the church itself. Now the enlarged A59 road runs hard by the graveyard.

10

The Toys that Made Engineering Famous

Jackie has read somewhere that architects and builders use Meccano parts for modelling out their structures in the first place, and that a big firm of makers of giant cranes build up special models of anything new they may be designing, with Meccano parts.

Jackie Coogan visits a Meccano Factory, 1926

Hollywood child star Jackie Coogan's apparent familiarity with the 'many commercial uses to which Meccano has been applied' would have impressed the Meccano marketing department, and it was duly recorded by them with coy satisfaction. Whether or not Coogan's intimate knowledge of the ways in which Meccano was being applied in the commercial sector were genuine, by the 1920s Meccano had established itself as a tool for grown-up engineers as much as growing ones. Indeed, by the time of Hornby's death in 1936 the story of Meccano had come full circle, from educational toys to tools of engineering. Sets featured in university departments, technical colleges and schools as well as children's toy boxes. It had become the chosen tool for the adult model-maker as both hobbyist and engineering-prototype builder. The fame it had earned as a toy was matched by the respect it was winning as a serious aid to research and development. According to Hornby, Meccano and Hornby trains were 'The Toys That Made Engineering Famous!'.

Having begun its life on the back of a testimonial from an eminent and influential engineer, Meccano's high point in the 1930s was accompanied by a glowing reference from one of the most celebrated firms of engineers, responsible for creating two of the icons of interwar engineering: the Tyne and Sydney Harbour bridges. Naturally Hornby was not shy about relating this in full in the pages of *Meccano Magazine*:

> The value of the magazine from an engineering point of view has been freely recognised by leading engineers, whose general attitude may be summed up in the following extract from a letter from Dorman Long & Co. Ltd., the famous engineering firm who undertook the colossal task of constructing the Sydney Harbour Bridge: 'We know your Magazine and appreciate its educational value to those who, as you rightly remark, will become the engineers of the next generation.'

A generation of engineers did grow up with the *Meccano Magazine* poking from their blazer pockets. Meccano had even brought out kits styled as 'Inventor's Accessory Outfits' in 1920. Between the wars other products and publications stressed the fact that Meccano was more than a toy. *The Meccano Engineer's Pocket Book* was a small sketchbook containing graph paper to encourage Meccano Boys 'to take a note of any engineering feature that strikes them as being of interest – possibly with a view to improving upon it, or perhaps reproducing it'. Sketching was only part of the engineering process and the Meccano Boy was not just a miniature engineer, but an engineer in miniature. It was important that he was true to the principles of the profession that he was following:

> The Meccano Boy is at once an inventor, consulting engineer, draughtsman and practical engineer. He is entirely responsible to himself for the successful completion of any models he decides to construct, and therefore should take care to base all his schemes on sound engineering principles.

The Meccano Book of Engineering was part of the overtly educational mission that Binns Road had embarked upon which was at all times underpinned by the liturgy of *Meccano Magazine*, occasionally supplemented by publications such as the *Meccano Standard Mechanisms* which elucidated in greater detail the general principles of levers, pulleys, gears, clutches and the like.[1]

Meccano was the first of a range of educational, constructional, engineering or scientific toys which the Binns Road factory brought out over the next few years. Indeed, it was one of the most successful and famous of technological toys. It was not alone, however. As we have seen it emerged at a time when toy makers, locksmiths, carpenters and architects all over the world were turning their hands and minds to the creation and patenting of constructional and mechanical toys. Not only that, but other educational toys that would inculcate all the values of modern technological advancement were springing up and capturing children's imaginations and their parents' aspirations. Across Europe and North America the huge success of toys like Meccano, Erector and train sets illustrated tremendous faith, optimism and pride in engineering and its great gift of modern convenience. Toys which paid tribute to these achievements while simultaneously schooling the next generation were of enormous appeal to parents earnestly hoping to raise white-collar engineers or scientists. At the very least, boys' toys would make men's men.

Construction toys were only part of the genre. Just as engineering and mechanical construction sets had become

extremely popular worldwide in the 1920s and 1930s so too chemistry and electrical sets, many of which had been around in one form or another for over a decade, became bestselling educational toys between the wars. They appealed to similar instincts in both scientifically minded children and their ambitious parents hoping for a chemist in the family. (Porter Chemicals, the American firm behind Chemcraft kits, encouraged children to form their own local Chemcraft Clubs.)

In 1920 Meccano had launched a range of electrical components which allowed the addition of an electric dimension to models, initially as separate kits, then as a standard feature of many sets. The introduction of electric motors into both Meccano and the train sets were hugely popular, as were electrical and scientific toys generally. By the end of the decade electrical and chemistry sets were hugely popular among children of a certain age. Meccano were well aware of this market (it should be remembered that their first advertisements had been carried in the *Model Engineer and Amateur Electrician*, and there had been a certain degree of interconnectivity among the hobbyist fraternity). Where once the world had been driven by steam and built with steel, it was increasingly powered by electricity and internal combustion too. Electricity and chemistry were everything that engineering was and had been. Toy manufacturers had naturally spotted a very lucrative market, and this was not lost on Meccano, since adverts for many such products were regularly carried in *Meccano Magazine*. Lotts chemistry sets were the most successful and were leading the way in Britain, so much so that Meccano attempted to join the field. In 1933 Meccano brought out the Elektron and the Kemex outfits. Different from and incompatible with Meccano, Elektron was basically a construction set with metal components. Its aim was to teach electricity in the way Meccano had made mechanics easy:

> In these days of radio, X-rays and electric trams and
> trains every boy should have a knowledge of electricity.
> The only way to gain this knowledge is by means of
> experiments, and the Elektron outfits have been produced
> specially for this pupose. They provide the necessary
> material for carrying out a series of fascinating

experiments in magnetism, frictional electricity, and current electricity.[2]

It was a natural step for Meccano to take, and their American rival A. C. Gilbert was to bring out his own electrical set, the Atomic Energy Set.

The Kemex sets were simply opportunistic. There was little to distinguish them from their rivals other than the respected Meccano imprimatur and some stylish packaging and artwork, and despite a range of three kits – the largest of which vaguely promised '350–400 Experiments' – the sets were not one of Meccano's best products.

The company was now diversifying, however, buoyed by extremely healthy sales of both Meccano and train sets. In 1934 yet another range was added – the Dinky Builder. It consisted of flat tinplate pieces with rolled edges forming interlocking tubular flanges connected by means of rods which slid through them. It billed itself as 'Fascinating-Instructive-Attractive-Indestructible' and was geared at a younger market than any of Meccano's other products. The parts were enamelled in jade green and salmon pink and the packaging featured girls as well as boys, underlining the company's desire to attract a female following as well as a younger one. To this end the range of models included bedroom furniture as well as trucks and, bizarrely, a meat safe.

More in keeping with the spirit of Meccano as a manufacturer of engineering and scientific toys for boys was the firm's entry into the radio market in the 1920s. Inspired by the advanced state of radio broadcasting in the USA, the American wing of Meccano had developed a crystal radio set using some Meccano parts. The radios, which used crystals – usually galena, but in Meccano's case 'Meccolite' – and a lengthy aerial to pick up radio signals from the ether captivated Frank. He was immediately enthusiastic about the possibilities for Meccano – probably because here was a product that was already established as a hobby, a science and an industry. He set the *Meccano Magazine* off to promote this new hobby and product:

> In future it is our intention to devote considerable space
> in the Meccano Magazine to Radio matters. News from
> all parts of the world relating to wireless will be collected
> and reported, and the latest developments and inventions
> in this new science will be featured and illustrated. With
> the aid of Meccano parts any boy can now build his own
> Radio Set and the Meccano Magazine will keep him right
> up to date on all Radio improvements.[3]

Despite some teething problems (including objections from the GPO over experimental receiving apparatus like Hornby's sets which necessitated a redesign in 1922) and an initially expensive 55-shilling price tag, Hornby pressed on.

Less expensive, and more neatly poised somewhere between the Meccano and the Dinky ranges, were the aeroplane and motor-car construction sets that the company brought out in 1931. Made from tinplate, these sets featured realistic fashioned parts including bumpers, headlamps, 'numberplates' and 'Dunlop' branded tyres. Typically the range also included a garage and Meccano aeroplane hangar (price 25s). The range also included nicely observed detailing that would please any fastidious child, such as pilots or drivers, and in 1932 speedboats and pleasure cruisers were added. The range grew to include an impressive array of models, but by 1932 Hornby's mind – or those of his model-makers, had turned in yet another direction. The X Series was a hastily put together and short-lived range of somewhat clumsy models for a junior market. They imitated, in fact, a rival range of models known as Trix and sold through high street retailers such as Woolworths. With a pathetic range of parts, flimsy instructions and an even flimsier rationale the X Series was lucky to last for the four years it did. Hornby does not seem to have been as ashamed of the X Series as he should have been, either for its near blatant imitation of a rival product, or for its ill-conceived manufacture. They, or parts like them, featured in Meccano literature at the time, such as Hubert Lansley's *Adventures in Meccanoland – The Strange Tale of Dick's Travels in a Wonderful New Country* (which told of a benevolent Meccano dictator made of X-Series parts who punished Meccano Boys for the ultimate transgression of falling asleep at their Meccano kits). Perhaps Hornby thought that Trix was an imitation of Meccano, though how he justified selling the inferior X-Series kits for only sixpence less than a proper Meccano set is unclear.

X Series was an attempt at diversification, perhaps intended for a junior audience. It was part of the feverish and frenzied diversification of the 1930s which seemed to throw up products at an alarming (and perhaps alarmed) rate in the hope of buoying up sales in the Depression years. Another new line was the Dolly Varden range. From the early models born out of Frank Hornby's playtimes with his sons, most of the classic toys which leapt from his fertile imagination or those of his model-makers at Binns Road were intended for boys. Inevitably some girls found them appealing, and the lists of prizewinners for the Meccano model-building competitions occasionally featured girls' names. Generally, though, Meccanoland was a boys' world.

Only one of Meccano's products was designed especially for girls – the Dolly Varden Doll's House. Essentially the Dolly Varden House was a standard doll's house, though it hinted at its illustrious parentage by being advertised as 'For Dinky Toys Furniture'. It was, of course, a beautifully observed piece of model-making, and like Meccano or the train sets was aimed firmly at the upper end of the market. Made of reinforced leather board, the house cost 9s 6d new (excluding Dinky Toys  Doll's House Furniture) and was a slice of 1930s suburban niceness. Made to the same scale as Dinky Toys, the house stood about 18 inches (45cm) high and came in a mock-Tudor style, complete with half-timbered detailing and leaded windows. It had no constructional elements but came ready assembled in a container that opened out to form a well-to-do suburban lawn with tennis court, gravel 'carriage drive', rockery and poplar trees. The house was styled in a consciously modern way, every inch the counterpoint and complement to the interwar celebration of space and suburban conveniences embodied in the electric train sets. The house could be furnished from the Dinky sets – dining room, kitchen, bathroom and bedroom. The garden lawn could even be adorned with 'Hornby Trees and Hedging', though the advertisements showed a tennis net, garden seat and couch hammock that looked perfect (but were never actually produced). Only the miniature pink gins were wanting.

So too were the customers. The Dolly Varden House only lasted three years from its launch in the summer of 1936. The Second World War was undoubtedly the final blow, but prices had already been slashed by almost half. In 1939 a Dolly Varden House sold for 4s 11d. Nowadays they are among the rarest and most sought after of all Meccano's products.

The company had spent the thirties diversifying for all it was worth in an attempt to replicate the successes of the trains and Dinky ranges, and capture still more model makers, collectors and hobbyists of every age and kind. Yet it was not to be. Dinky was not the last good idea to emerge from Meccano, but it was the last toy to achieve greatness. The death of the founder in 1936 brought to a close one of the greatest chapters in the history of the British toy business. It has often been suggested that Frank's legacy was never tended with the energy, determination and vigour that had been the hallmark of his time on the throne of Meccanoland, and the inevitable consequence was that the company slipped like sand through the hands of its subsequent hapless managers. The reality was less straightforward.

Frank left a sizeable personal fortune more than comparable with that of his industrial contemporaries in Liverpool. The gross value of the estate was £231,086 together with the sprawling house of Quarry Brook, and the smaller Old House in Maghull. There were cash settlements for his family members, and his 'indoors and outdoors' servants were generously provided for. In addition Frank left shares in the business as potentially very lucrative assets.[4] Though Frank had expressed the hope in his will that his sons would live on in the estate – Douglas in the Old House and Roland in Quarry Brook after his mother's death – the estate was sold in 1946. His widow Clara lived there until after the war, but it was too large a house for one elderly widow and it began to decay around her. Its draughty rooms were too full of memories, and Clara was happier in the trouble-free grandeur of a suite at the Liverpool Adelphi Hotel, finally retiring to the south coast where she died aged 92 in 1953.

No doubt there were other factors that prompted the sale of the Quarry Brook Estate. Having spent so much time working in their father's factory and his shadow, his sons had little desire to move into his former home. It has been suggested that was paralleled by a reluctance to take his place in the boardroom as well, preferring the golf course to the factory floor. At any rate, the decline of the company seems to have coincided with their stewardship. Yet while neither Roland nor, in particular, Douglas cut the same earnest figure as their father, and while it would have been difficult if not impossible for either to have cared as much about Meccano as Frank did, they were unfortunate in inheriting Meccano when they did.

Like Quarry Brook, Meccano's days of grandeur were already behind it when Frank had departed for Westminster. In 1933 *The Times* had reported Hornby's speech at Meccano's annual general meeting in which he confessed that 'the year's trading is not quite so satisfactory as I had hoped. The year under review has been one full of difficulties, which have had the effect of impairing results not only in the home market, but in the foreign markets as well.'[5] Hornby told the board that 'new and attractive lines' (Kemex, Electron and Dolly Varden) were 'meeting with a very satisfactory demand', a point he reiterated the following year, but the company was still feeling the effects of depression that were affecting the industry as a whole and which had led to a 'demand

for lower-priced articles to fit the pockets of the people'. Parsimony had never really featured as a characteristic in the profile of a Meccano customer, and even the 'intensive technological development' (i.e. efficiency measures) which Hornby spoke of could only go so far.[6]

In addition, despite Frank's bullishness none of the new products were to prove as popular as Meccano, Hornby trains or Dinky Toys, and none would stand the test of time. The following year's AGM was largely taken up by Frank using it as a political platform for a speech which was little more than his last hurrah as an MP. After paying tribute to the 'beneficial effects of the National Government' he then spoke on the subject of his proposed private member's bill on extended shop opening hours.[7] Dividends continued to be paid to the shareholders at a rate of

2½ per cent, giving a healthy return on investment, but little attention was paid to the fact that sales of Meccano kits at home had shown little recovery from the post-1931 slump and overseas sales were falling. Moreover, Hornby's charismatic and energetic advertising manager Ellison Hawks had left the company under a cloud in 1935, adding insult to injury by setting up in competition to Meccano in 1936 as a director of 'Construments Ltd – Manufacturers of Educational Pastimes', in Gray's Inn Road, High Holborn. The steady growth in train and Dinky Toy sales home and abroad disguised the fact that Meccano seemed to be struggling to adapt to new conditions. In 1936, the year of Frank's death, domestic sales of Meccano were only 44 per cent of what they had been in 1930 while exports amounted to only 36 per cent of the 1930 figure.

Within three years the country was at war. The manufacture and sale of toys were subjected to stringent controls which threatened the very existence of the smaller companies. Labour costs, materials and other overheads such as transport soared, and consequently so did toy prices. In January 1942 the manufacture and supply of metal toys was abruptly banned, and manufacturers like Meccano and Lines stumbled on using old stock while having to turn their attentions to munitions work (although some, such as Basset Lowke the model-train manufacturers, continued model-making – in their case mini-Mulberry harbours of military prototypes for the government).[8] Distribution centres in London were devastated by the Blitz. Despite a general feeling that the priorities of the nation at a time of total war did not really include children's toys, the successful proselytising of educationalists during the 1930s lauding toys that teach ensured that there remained a tension. There was a certain relaxation of restrictions for the purposes of morale, but British exports understandably all but ceased. Meccano complained that other Commonwealth manufacturers were taking advantage of this. Australia, for example, was not bound by the same requirements to undertake munitions work. As a result the production of metal toys rose there dramatically. Among them were a flurry of Meccanoesque construction toys such as Ezy Built, Buzz Builder and Technico, all 'Australian and Guaranteed'. As a result Meccano struggled to recover their sales and market share upon the cessation of hostilities. After the Blitz, evacuation and six years of total war it was not just childhood that would never be the same again. The industry that emerged on the other side was as different as the world which it catered for.

Perhaps the final nail in the coffin, however, was Lego. In an age of postwar austerity the advantages of newer materials over those that had always marked Meccano products out as of superior quality (and therefore more expensive) became magnified. Typifying this new generation was the plastic construction set that would eventually usurp Meccano's place in the toy cupboards of generations. Lego was the brainchild of Danish woodworker Kirk Christiansen, who had drifted into toy making via doll's furniture, simple construction toys and the craze of 1932 – the yo-yo. The enduring popularity of construction toys after the war had encouraged him to persevere with his modified building blocks. In 1955 he brought out Lego, a simple plastic shape which had all the attractions of the building block as well as a number of advantages over its humble forebear. It snapped together easily and, thanks to Christiansen's marketing nous, soon grew into a varied and ever-changing range of kits and toys. Devotees of 'grown-up' construction sets like Meccano and Erector pooh-poohed its babyish simplicity. It required the same grasp of hand–eye co-ordination, spatial awareness and creativity, but none of the skill, delicacy or patience. Its advantage over kits like Meccano was also its most

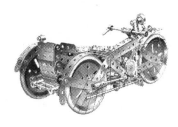

damning quality to enthusiasts of the 'world's greatest toy': Lego was easy. It did not require understanding or appreciation of mechanical principles; it did not build on an interest in engineering. To build with it required neither a screwdriver nor a love of engineering.

Meccano also fell foul of a number of factors which affected companies across Europe. The end of the protection so beloved by Hornby and afforded by the tariff quota system in the 1950s opened the toy market to unseen levels of competition. Not only was the domestic market under pressure, but the traditional overseas markets were targeted by the economic industrial superpowers whose presence in the toy industry was a reflection of their importance as players in the world of light engineering at large. By the 1950s American firms were beginning to look abroad to expand their markets. Disney had brought out Snow White dolls as a marketing tie-in in 1937 and soon American toy manufacturers like Fisher-Price, Ideal and Lionel were buoyed by their status as Disney licensees. The successful development of licensing in film and radio (fully established for Disney by the late 1930s), and the eventual creation of character toys (from Dick Tracy to Mickey Mouse) ran hand in hand with a gradual shift from construction toys which celebrated and taught the agreed virtues of the adult world to fantasy toys which merely aped them. From Little Orphan Annie to Buck Rogers American manufacturers led the way, ably abetted by a brilliant understanding of the new media. Educational play was under siege from an increasingly aggressive new kind of imaginative play – role play.

There were more general causes of Meccano's eventual demise, too. The oil crisis of the 1970s and the consequent international slump did little to help a company that was by that time already ailing, having failed to move on in thirty years. In 1963 *British Toys* had observed that 'Meccano has been made for over thirty-five years without any major change in its design or finish'. Their once progressive and successful franchise-selling technique was becoming increasingly outdated, limiting Meccano outlets to a relatively small number while rivals flooded the shops and town centres with their cheaper and often superior products. Lesney and Mettoy cars eclipsed Dinky, and by the 1950s Triang trains were carrying more child passengers to magical worlds of escape and imagination. Such escape was beyond Hornby's successors. By the early 1960s Meccano was recording trading losses, and in 1963 they amounted to £165,000. An offer of £781,000 was enough for Lines Group to take over the company. Roland and his sister-in-law Una were forced off the board, and after clearing debts and paying taxes were left with little of Hornby's legacy intact. The irony was made even greater by the fact that it had been Walter Lines who had approached Hornby during the Depression to ask if he was interested in buying out Lines Brothers, so dismal was his view of the economic prospects for his company.[9]

The cut-price Meccano was hardly a bargain, however, since the company had massive debts. It took Graeme Lines, the new managing director, four years to return a profit. His economies and attempts to turn the great vessel about were not aided by over sixty years of righteous self-confidence that the company and its products were the best in the world. With this mantra (and no sign of the corollaries of hard work, determination and imaginative and dogged marketing that Hornby had underpinned his company with) the company's management had sailed on blithely. Graeme Lines later described Meccano as an old auntie – friendly, but still firmly believing things should be done the way they were when she was a girl.[10]

Successive difficulties and takeovers kicked over the traces of much of Hornby's legacy. In 1964 the Hornby name was being phased out, and the tools for the Hornby Dublo train sets were sold to G. R. Wrenn Ltd, a subsidiary company within the Lines Group. In 1970 the company name was changed to Meccano-Triang. In 1971 Lines Group hit their own difficulties. After an American investor decided not to pour £5 million into the company the group went into liquidation. The break-up of the Hornby stable saw Meccano acquired by plastic-model specialist Airfix, while Hornby trains headed south to Dunbee-Combex (who themselves went into receivership in 1980). On Friday, 30 November 1979 the workforce were informed that the factory would close at the end of the day for good. A spirited sit-in protest ensued for three months and workers maintained a vigil outside the factory amid graffiti which began to appear on the once immaculate façade of Hornby's factory demanding that supporters 'Bomb Airfix'. It was the end of an era of British toy making. Hornby Hobbies emerged from the ashes, while Meccano, after yet more changes of ownership, was finally acquired by Japanese firm Nikko. Along the way much of Hornby's legacy had been washed away.

Yet despite the depredations which robbed the factory of much of its archives, papers, fixtures and fittings and finally flattened the building itself, there is still a monument to the former meat-importer's clerk from Everton. His were the toys that made engineering famous. Advertising material in the 1930s touted Meccano as 'An Apprenticeship to a Career', and Meccano Boys as 'Our Future Engineers'. And so it was. Generations of engineers – mechanical, electrical, electronic, marine and civil, architects, scientists and designers – were schooled by and with Meccano. And like all good students they did not forget their debt to their former tutor. By the 1920s Hornby had realised that Meccano was being used for prototype inventions in disparate fields, and typically had been quick to promote the kits as inventors' tools. But the inventors themselves had little need of such advertising. Having grown up learning, in Nasmyth's words, the importance of the fingertips as conduits of a scientific knowledge that was as practical as it was delicate and dextrous, inventors were comfortable with Meccano as a natural aid. Larger 'scaleable' sets were incorporated into laboratories working on everything from early computers to vehicle components, robots to buildings.

Differential analysers were a type of analogue computer which emerged in the 1930s and 1940s on both sides of the Atlantic at research institutes and universities such as MIT and Manchester University. They used motors to drive wheels on shafts with gears, and could solve simple mathematical equations. While later versions were incredibly sophisticated and could employ hundreds of motors, thousands of vacuum tubes, miles of wire and weigh as much as 100 tons, earlier models were simpler. Manchester University's differential analyser was built of Meccano. Other early computers (one reputedly used at Bletchley Park to crack German codes during the Second World War) were also made of Meccano. Early pioneers of electronic engineering recalled that it was the medium of choice for experiments in robotics and artificial intelligence, since it was adaptable and beautifully suited to accommodating all manner of mechanisms, motors and other components. By the 1960s the generation of Meccano Boys who had bought or been given the sets in the golden years of the 1930s had moved into laboratories and workshops of their own, and they had let a childhood friend in through the side door. Meccano Boys could be found in the British Aircraft Corporation, the Atomic Weapons Research

Establishment and the UK Atomic Energy Authority. Meccano had been used to prototype everything from the automatic transmission on Issigonis's classic and revolutionary Mini car to helicopter rotor blades for the US aeronautics firm Piaseki. Meccano was even involved in the development of the record-deck stylus. International architectural and design giants such as the Richard Rogers Partnership and Ove Arup have both used Meccano for modelling, and its influence has been felt in icons of modernity such as the London Eye.[11]

Hornby probably could not have wished for more. He always hankered after respectability – not so much as a businessman, a man of means or an MP, but more fundamentally as an engineer. Even though his business has been brought low, his fortune dissipated and his political career is remembered as little more than a footnote to the epic tale of politics between the wars, Hornby's credentials as an influential engineer are intact. Generations of industrialists, engineers and scientists – Nobel Laureates, fêted academics, knights and peers of the realm – openly acknowledge the impact that the little strips of tin developed by a humble clerk had upon them and the world they strove to change. More than that, despite everything, Meccano and Hornby trains are still going strong. The bestselling *Harry Potter* inspired *Hogwarts Express* locomotive has brought the whole story full circle: it is a story about a man, his inventions and their impact on thousands of children around the world, but mostly it is a story about toys[12]

Notes

Introduction

[1] Gary Cross, *Kids' Stuff*, 1997, pp. 6–10.

2 Total British toy exports in the same period amounted to £437,000 p.a. Kenneth D. Brown, 'Death of a Dinosaur: Meccano of Liverpool, 1908–1979', Business Archives Sources and History, 1993.

[3] National Museums and Galleries on Merseyside Archives Department, Business Records Centre, Meccano Archive (hereafter B/ME)/21, Leipziger Messeamt to Meccano, 15 June 1953.

[4] Selincourt's *Cricket Match* (1924) had also used the word in an allusion, but had not departed from the idea of Meccano as a physical mechanical construction: 'I shall make a prison cell of Meccano and pretend you're . . . locked inside it.'

[5] *Dick's Visit to Meccanoland*

Chapter 1

[1] Evelyn Waugh, *The Diaries of Evelyn Waugh*, 1976, p. 640.
[2] Quoted in Stephen Kline, *Out of the Garden*, 1995, p. 46.
[3] Phillipe Ariès, *Centuries of Childhood*, 1962.
[4] See Nicholas Orme, *Medieval Children*, 2001; 'The Culture of Children in Medieval England', *Past & Present*, August 1995.
[5] Peter and Iona Opie (eds), *The Dictionary of Nursery Rhymes*, 1951.
[6] Kline, *Out of the Garden*, pp. 78–9.
[7] *The Poetry and Prose of Geoffrey Chaucer*, ed. John H. Fisher, 1977, p. 908.
[8] Eric Quayle, *The Collector's Book of Children's Books*, 1971, p. 17.
[9] Roland Callois, *Man, Play and Games*, trans. Meyer Barash, 1962.
[10] Brian Sutton Smith, *Toys as Culture*, 1986, p. 138.
[11] Susan Stewart, *On Longing*, 1993, pp. 57–60.
[12] Gary Cross, *Kids' Stuff*, 1997, pp. 11–17.
[13] Jean Jacques Rousseau, *Emile*, cited in Cross, *Kids' Stuff*, p. 18.
[14] Kenneth Brown, *The British Toy Business: A History Since 1700*, 1996, p. 50.
[15] From 7,380,000 children in 1850 to 10,550,000 in 1900; ibid., p. 51.
[16] Quoted in Linda A. Pollock, *Forgotten Children: Parent-Child Relations from 1500–1900*, 1983, p. 236.
[17] Ibid., p. 237.
[18] John Locke, *Some Thoughts Concerning Education*, 1968 (1693), pp. 211–12.
[19] G. C. Bartley, 'Toys', in G. P. Bevan (ed.), *British Manufacturing Industries*, 1876, p. 154.
[20] *The Times*, 21 April 1908.
[21] Ibid., p. 245.
[22] W. H. Cremer, *The Toys of the Little Folks, of all Ages and Countries*; or, *The Toy Kingdom*, London, 1873, p. 52.
[23] Brown, *The British Toy Business*, quoted p. 53.
[24] *Athletic Sports, Games and Toys*, Jan. 1896, p. 6, quoted ibid., p. 56.

Chapter 2

[1] *The Hornby Pedigree*, 1968, Liverpool PRO.

[2] James Stonehouse, *The Streets of Liverpool*, 1879, p. 81.

[3] A. Sutcliffe, 'Working Class Housing in Nineteenth Century Britain: A Review of Recent Research', *Bulletin of Labour History*, 24 (1972).

[4] J. R. Kellet, *The Impact of Railways on Victorian Cities*, 1969.

[5] Other critics of the railways included the likes of Oxford University and Eton, the latter proposing a 10-ft high, four-mile long wall to screen themselves from the ghastliness of the new contraptions. Quoted in Sir Llewellyn Woodward, *The Age of Reform*, 1962, p. 46.

[6] 'The Improvements in Lime Street and Neighbourhood', *The Porcupine*, 11 (Apr. 1869–Mar. 1870), 28 August 1869, p. 208.

[7] Richard Perren, *The Meat Trade in Britain, 1840–1914*, 1978.

[8] Christening Roll for St Simon's St Church, Gloucester Rd, Liverpool. Liverpool PRO, microfilm no. 548.

[9] In 1861 infant deaths per 1,000 for males were 71.8 (aged 0–4), 6.7 (aged 5–9) and 4.3 (aged 10–14). Ten years later they were even higher, with 8.5% of children dying before adolescence. Girls fared a little better, with around 62 out of every 1,000 infants dying before their fifth birthdays.

[10] Scarletina 'the principal plague of this age' would ensure that only around 685,000 would survive past puberty.

Chapter 3

[1] Quoted in Sir Eric Ashby, 'Education for an Age of Technology', in Charles Singer, E. J. Holmyard, A. R. Hall and Trevor I. Williams (eds), *A History of Technology*, vol. V, 1958.

[2] Quoted in *James Nasmyth: An Autobiography*, ed. Samuel Smiles, London, 1883, p .97.

[3] Thomas Carlyle, 'Signs of the Times', *Edinburgh Review*, 49 (1829), p. 449.

[4] 'Improvements in Toy or Educational Devices for Children and Young People', Mechanics Made Easy, Patent no. 587, 9 Jan. 1901.

[5] Samuel Smiles, *Self Help*, 1859, p. 5.

[6] Smiles described the biographies in *Self Help* as 'busts rather than full-length portraits', though even this description is fairly flattering. For discussions on the style and format of Smiles's pen-portraits see Dennis Smith (ed.), *Perceptions of the Great Engineers*, 1994.

[7] Addressing the Manchester Mechanics' Institute in 1827 Benjamin Heywood explained the aims of the society: '. . . to teach the workman (be his trade what it may), those principles of science on which his work depends; to show him their practical application, and how he may make his knowledge of them profitable; to enable him thoroughly to understand his business, and to qualify him for making improvements in it; to teach him how he may advance himself in the world, and to give him an honourable and delightful employment for his leisure'. Quoted in Ashby, 'Age of Technology', p. 777.

[8] Hole argued that the institutes should become the colleges of a national industrial university. W. H. G. Armytage, *A Social History of Engineering*, 1961, p. 145.

[9] Smiles, *Self Help*, p. iv.

[10] Ibid., p. v.

[11] Frank Hornby, 'The Life Story of Meccano: Romance of the World's Greatest Toy', reproduced in ten instalments in *Meccano Magazine*, 17(1)

(January 1932) – 18(2) (February 1933)

[12] Smiles, *Self Help*, p. 257.

[13] Ibid., p. 75.

[14] Hornby, 'Life Story of Meccano', p. 6.

[15] Smiles, *Self Help*, p. 277.

[16] Hornby, 'Life Story of Meccano', p. 6.

[17] For a family on 18 shillings per week around a third would go on rent. Household expenses could account for a further 6s and food for about 8s. After the head of the household had been fed enough to allow him to do a day's work the rest of the family could be left with a daily food allowance of about tuppence a day. M. S. Pember-Reeves, *Round About a Pound a Week*, 1979, pp. 42–3, 94–6, 132–3.

[18] B. Love and J. Gamble, in *The Meccano System* (1985), suggest Hornby could have been on a salary of around £65 a year at Elliott's. This is surely too low since it amounts to only 25 shillings a week. F. G. D'Aeth, writing in the *Sociological Review* in October 1910 laid out seven social groupings. A Loafer earned around 18s per week and low-skilled labour about 25 – sufficient to afford 'some change of clothes and a collar in the evening'. Comfortably housed artisan earned around 45s, with smaller shopkeepers, clerks and elementary teachers on around £3 a week. Businessmen earned about £300 per annum, heads of companies about £600 and the rich about £2000.

[19] Quoted in Donald Read, *England 1868–1914*, 1979, pp. 26–7.

[20] Hubert Lansley, 'My Meccano Days', *Constructor's Quarterly*, 1994, p. 12.

[21] Hornby, 'Life Story of Meccano', p. 6.

[22] Ibid.

[23] Ibid., pp. 6–7.

[24] H. Gladston, *Report of the British Association for the Advancement of Science*, 1879, Section F, p. 475.

[25] Maurice Whitta, 'Meccano in 1819', *Model Engineer*, 13 Feb. 1998. The description of Farish's system appears in Gregory's *Mathematics for Practical Men*, 1848, chapter 2. The chapter in Gregory's *Mathematics* dealing with Farish was based on *Transactions of the Cambridge Philosophical Society*, 1820.

[26] Cross, *Kids' Stuff*, pp. 37–8.

[27] United States Patent Office, Patent no. 135,417, 4 Feb. 1873.

[28] United States Patent Office, Patent. no. 195,689, 30 Mar. 1877.

[29] Imperial German Patent Office, Patent no. 46312, Class 77; Sports, 8 April 1888.

[30] Her Majesty's Patent Office, Patent no. 14,442, 30 July 1895.

[31] The basic principle was that constructions were made of four types of member: *a*, *b*, *c* and *d* all bearing a mathematically fixed relationship to each other. Piece *a* could be of any size, then *b* would be equal in length to the diagonal of a square formed by *a*; *c* would be equal to the diagonal of a square formed by *b*; and *d* would be the diagonal of an oblong whose sides were *c* x *b*. The equation to work out the distance of the perforations relative to each other was a little more complicated.

[32] Her Majesty's Patent Office, Patent no. 10,040, 21 May 1895.

[33] United States Patent Office, Patent No. 570,688, 3 Nov. 1896.

[34] The largest blocks were rectangles, twice as long as they were broad, and twice as broad as they were wide. Other blocks were then half or a quarter this size, and so on. The holes on each face were then located according to a

simple scale relationship, rather than being a set distance apart on each piece. In other words, holes were located on each face at distances proportionate to the size of the block. Though they were regularly spaced on each block, different sized blocks had holes spaced at different intervals.
[35] United States Patent Office, Patent no. 731, 309, 16 June 1903.
[36] German Imperial Patent Office, Patent no. 153,854, 4 June 1903.
[37] United States Patent Office, Patent no. 916,243, 23 Mar. 1909.
[38] The metric equivalents are, approximately, 64, 140, 318 and 13mm, respectively.
[39] UK Patents Office Provisional Specification, 'Improvements in Toy or Educational Devices for Children and Young People', 9 Jan. 1901.
[40] When Mechanics Made Easy finally went on the market the kits included a steel key and a screwdriver in addition to the flat strips, grooved rods, angle-piece, crank, hook, pulley wheel and flanged wheel, bush for the wheel and a ball of string.
[41] Patent no. 587, 'Improvements in Toy or Educational Devices for Children and Young People', 30 Nov. 1901, pp. 2–4.
[42] In addition to being a keen motoring enthusiast and a founder member of the RAC, Hele-Shaw was one of the first people to be prosecuted under the 1865 Road Traffic Act for a motor-car offence. While testing his patented vehicle clutch in Liverpool it failed, and his car careered downhill, backwards, at more than the 4 mph allowed by law. W. H. G. Armytage, *The Social History of Engineering*, 1965, pp. 257–8.
[43] Hornby, 'Life Story of Meccano', p. 93.
[44] E. E. Williams, *Germany*, 1970, p. 112. Williams was describing the products of the model makers Britains. For more on Britains see Kenneth D. Brown, 'Models in History: a micro study of late nineteenth century British entrepreneurship', *Economic History Review*, 42 (1989).
[45] Hornby, 'Life Story of Meccano', p. 93.
[46] Lansley, 'My Meccano Days'.

Chapter 4

[1] 1841 Census (P.P. 1844, XXVII), pp. 31–41.
[2] William Lindop of Manchester (indoor games), J. & T. Thorp of Manchester (wooden toys) and Peacock & Co. of Islington (building blocks and models) are among the significant firms which date from this time.
[3] By 1891 the number of people working in the industry had risen to 6,776 individuals aged over 10 with 2,500 living in London; 1,000 worked for themselves, while the ratio of employers to employed was about 1:6.7. Many small toy manufacturers would have not shown up on the 1907 census of production, since it concerned itself only with larger-scale operations.
[4] Williams, *Germany*, p. 112.
[5] A number of German exports were shipped via Dutch ports. It was British Customs policy to classify imports according to the port of origin, rather than the country of origin, so the actual figure could be even greater with the inclusion of some of those imports listed as Dutch.
[6] Much of this paragraph is based on Brown, *British Toy Business*.
[7] Ibid.
[8] The 1907 census of production was probably unreliable for this reason: £265,000 was recorded for toys (£216,000 from toy manufacturers + £51,000 from other manufacturers who also made toys). Not counted were £437,000

of miscellaneous rubber goods which included toys, or the miniature versions of some other products which were often produced as marketing aids, spin-offs or play-versions.

9 William Barbour of waxed-jacket fame was one such manufacturer. To promote his linen thread the firm began making small dolls in the late 1890s. Bissells, the American makers of vacuum cleaners began making children's versions in 1897, principally to use up left-over parts from the adult ones and to help promote their wares in shop windows. They proved so successful, however, that they ended up making them as toys in their own right in five different sizes. Brown, *British Toy Business*, p. 61.

10 Henry Mayhew, *London Labour and the London Poor*, 1861.

11 Brown, *British Toy Business*, pp. 68–70.

12 Kenneth D. Brown, 'Models in History: a micro study of late 19th century British entrepreneurship', *Economic History Review*, 42 (1989), pp. 531–2.

13 B. S. Rowntree, *Poverty: A Study of Town Life*, 1901; B. S. Rowntree and M. Kendall, *How the Labourer Lives: A Study of the Rural Labour Problem*, 1913.

14 Hornby, 'Life Story of Meccano'.

15 *Meccano Magazine*, 21, Nov. 1936.

16 *Mechanics Made Easy: An Adaptable Mechanical Toy*, instruction booklet, 1901–2.

17 B/ME Accounts, 1901–1903. The accounts reproduced in Love and Gamble's *The Meccano System*, p. 19, record slightly different figures and show a trading loss of £18 4s 6d. They also reveal that Elliott and Hornby were also trading in toy boats at this time.

18 *Model Engineer and Amateur Electrician*, 6, 1 June 1902, p. 263.

19 Hornby, 'Life Story of Meccano', p. 93.

20 Love and Gamble, *The Meccano System*, p. 18.

21 *Hobbies*, 19 Oct. 1895.

22 Ferdinand Zweig, *The British Worker*, 1952, pp. 97–8.

23 Margaret Phillips, *The Young Industrial Worker*, 1922, pp. 18–19.

24 Ross McKibbin, 'Work and Hobbies in Britain, 1850–1950', in Jay Winter (ed.), *The Working Class in Modern British History: Essays in Honour of Henry Pelling*, 1983, p. 138.

25 Hornby, 'The Life Story of Meccano', p. 6.

26 Smiles, *Self Help*, p. 74.

27 George Carette was a French émigré working in Germany producing beautifully crafted clockwork cars, trains and boats, many of which were hand-painted. At the peak of his career he was supplying the larger firms such as Gebrüder Bing, but as the First World War dragged on he was forced to leave Germany. He later went on to make trains for the celebrated British toy train makers Basset Lowke.

Chapter 5

1 John Martin, 'Sleuthing Duke St', *Constructors' Quarterly*, 50, Dec. 2000, pp. 52–6.

2 Hornby, 'Life Story of Meccano', p. 93.

3 B/ME Accounts, 1907–8 The wage bill had risen from £29 6s in 1907 to £241 12s 11d in 1908.

4 Reka raised £2,000 in 1914, and Multum in Parvo the same amount in 1896. Brown, *British Toy Business*, pp. 70–1.

[5] Love and Gamble, *The Meccano System*, p. 34.
[6] Africa (Egypt, Kenya, South Africa, Rhodesia), North America (USA, Mexico), South America (Bolivia, Brazil, Chile, Colombia, Peru, Uruguay, Venezuela), Europe (Czechoslovakia, Finland, Greece, Hungary, Luxembourg, Ireland, Poland, Portugal, Romania, Yugoslavia), Asia (Ceylon, Japan, Turkey).
[7] B/ME/C Card Index.
[8] Hornby, 'Life Story of Meccano', p. 7.
[9] B/ME/22/1, 20/12/1944.
[10] B/ME/22/1.
[11] B/ME/22/1.
[12] *La Suisse*, 5 Sept. 1936.
[13] *The Hornby System of Mechanical Demonstration*, 1910.
[14] Hornby, 'Life Story of Meccano', p. 7.
[15] United States Circuit Court of Appeals, 6th Circuit, Francis A. Wagner (Trading as the American Mechanical Toy Company) and the Strobel and Wilken Co., Brief for the Plaintive Appellee, 1917, p. 15.
[16] Ibid., p. 12.
[17] Hornby, 'Life Story of Meccano', p. 16.
[18] District Court of the United States, South District of Ohio, Western Division, Meccano Ltd v Francis A. Wagner (Trading as the American Mechanical Toy Company) and the Strobel and Wilken Co., 1915.
[19] Ibid.
[20] Everard Wyrall, *The History of the King's Regiment (Liverpool)*, 14–19, vol. I, 1914–15, 1928, pp. 124–31; T. R. Threlfall, *Story of the King's Regiment*, p. 163. It is likely that Roland was with C Company under Captain Brocklehurst. C Company saw the heaviest of the action and made the actual assault on the hill, Brocklehurst dying in the process.
[21] The Board of Trade organised an exhibition of such toys, turned over its collection of German Trade catalogues to manufacturers and by 1916 it was claimed that 1,500 types of these toys were now being made in Britain. Brown, *British Toy Business*, pp. 82–3.
[22] Ibid., p. 95.

Chapter 6

[1] Frank Hornby, 'Our Future', *Meccano News*, 1, Nov. 1920, p. 1.
[2] Ibid., pp. 2–3.
[3] Brown, *British Toy Business*, p. 99.
[4] Hornby, 'Life Story of Meccano', p. 253.
[5] Ibid., p. 500.
[6] Ibid., p. 574.
[7] Ibid.
[8] Kirsten Drotner, *English Children and Their Magazines, 1751–1945*, 1988, p. 154.
[9] Ibid., p. 184.
[10] Ibid., pp. 183–201.
[11] Brown, *British Toy Business*, p. 112.
[12] Love and Gamble, *The Meccano System*, p. 67.
[13] Hornby, 'Life Story of Meccano', p. 575.
[14] B/ME.
[15] Hornby, 'Life Story of Meccano', p. 575.

[16] *Jackie Coogan Visits a Meccano Factory*, 1926, p. 8.
[17] *Dick's Visit to Meccanoland*, 1925.
[18] B/ME.
[19] Lansley, 'My Meccano Days', p. 11.
[20] *The Story of Meccano by the Meccano Boy*.
[21] Asa Briggs, *Mass Entertainment: The Origins of a Modern Industry*, 1960, p. 18.
[22] *How to Run a Meccano Club*, 1931, p. 9.
[23] Hornby, 'Life Story of Meccano', p. 501.
[24] All these activities were suspended in 1939, but restarted after the war, together with a rather less well supported Dinky Collectors' Club, and ceased with takeover of Meccano by Lines in 1964. Many of the local clubs continued under their own steam, many forming the basis of the current adult enthusiasts' clubs. (The Hornby Railway Collectors' Association was formed in 1969 by Bedfordshire enthusiasts.)
[25] B/ME/Misc.
[26] In 1925 sales of Meccano in Gateshead amounted to only £47 compared to £2,648 in Newcastle (and £7,928 in Glasgow). This amounted to sales of around 7s 6d for every thousand people in the town, as opposed to around £9 12s 7d per thousand across the river. In 1923 Meccano sold only £9 worth of toys in the town.

Chapter 7

[1] Hornby, 'Life Story of Meccano', p. 412.
[2] Ibid., p. 413.
[3] B/ME.
[4] Ibid.
[5] Betjeman, 'The Metropolitan Railway', *Collected Poems*, 2001, p. 169.
[6] Lansley, 'My Meccano Days', p. 12.
[7] 'Night Mail (Commentary for a G.P.O. film)', in W. H. Auden. *Collected Shorter Poems, 1927–1957*, 1977.
[8] 'Great Central Railway, Sheffield Victoria to Banbury', in *Collected Poems*, 1966, p. 256.
[9] Paul Oliver, Ian Davis and Ian Bentley, *Dunroamin': The Suburban Semi and Its Enemies*, 1994, pp. 79, 123–8.
[10] Quoted in Brown, *British Toy Business*, p. 132.

Chapter 8

[1] A.A. Milne, *The Complete Winnie the Pooh*, 1998, p. 255.
[2] *Dick's Visit to the Home of Meccano*, 1925, p. 2.
[3] Stanley Baldwin, *On England*, 1926, p. 7.
[4] The 472 Conservative MPs far outstripped the 338 members of the 1918 parliament, or even the 396 of Margaret Thatcher's 1983 landslide.
[5] A. J. P. Taylor, *English History, 1914–1945*, 1988, pp. 284–6.
[6] Letter to the *Liverpool Echo*, 'Trade After the War: Secure Home Markets First', 14 Oct. 1916.
[7] B/ME, Meccano Balance Sheet & Accounts, 1930–6.
[8] Socialist Research Group, *Genuinely Seeking Work: Mass Unemployment of Merseyside in the 1930s*, 1992, pp. 163–76. Longbottom stood as a Protestant candidate for Liverpool Kirkwood in 1931.

[9] 'Four Candidates for Everton?', *Liverpool Echo*, 14 Oct. 1931.

[10] The number of National Labour candidates eventually rose to 26.

[11] 'The "Agony" of Mr. Hall-Caine', election handbill.

[12] 'Liverpool Fights: Labour for all Divisions', *Liverpool Echo*, 6 Oct. 1931, p. 4.

[13] 'Everton M.P.'s Surprise: Mr. Hall-Caine to back Premier', *Liverpool Echo*, 23 Sept. 1931.

[14] 'The "Agony" of Mr. Hall-Caine'.

[15] *Liverpool Echo*, 21 Oct. 1931, p. 9.

[16] Taylor, *English History, 1914–1945*, pp. 263–4.

[17] *Liverpool Echo*, 15 Oct. 1931, p. 12.

[18] *Liverpool Echo*, 22 Oct. 1931, p. 4.

[19] *Liverpool Echo*, 15 Oct. 1931, p. 12.

[20] *Liverpool Echo*, 23 Oct. 1931, p. 5.

[21] *Liverpool Echo*, 27 Oct. 1931, p. 4.

[22] *Liverpool Echo*, 12 Oct. 1931, p. 10.

[23] *Liverpool Echo*, 14 Oct. 1931, p. 14.

[24] *Liverpool Echo*, 22 Oct. 1931, p. 10.

[25] Hornby polled 12,186 votes; Treleaven 7,786 and Hall-Caine 4,950.

Chapter 9

[1] Brown, *British Toy Business*, p. 116.

[2] Ibid., p. 118.

[3] Ibid., pp. 125–30.

[4] Hansard, 4 Nov. 1932, pp. 2155–8.

[5] Hansard, 11 Apr. 1932.

[6] Hansard, 23 Mar. 1933, p. 474.

[7] See Hansard, vol. 263 (1931–2), p. 35; vol. 264 (1931–2), pp. 551–2; vol. 266 (1931–2), pp. 990–1; vol. 269 (1931–2), pp. 2155–7; vol. 270 (1931–2), p. 501; vol. 276 (1932–3), pp. 474, 478; vol. 292 (1933–4), pp. 1656–62.

[8] Hansard, 24 July 1934, pp.1656–62.

[9] During the war the *Arandora* took part in the evacuation of British troops from Narvik in Norway, and from the French coast in 1940. However, it achieved some degree of infamy in July 1940. It sailed from Liverpool carrying passengers deemed to be enemy aliens and bound for Canada: 473 Germans (of which 123 were merchant seamen captured at sea), and 717 Italians, mostly from Italian communities in South Wales or Scotland. On 2 July it was struck by a torpedo 125 miles north-west of Ireland; 486 Italians and 175 Germans were lost at sea. Colin Hughes, *Lime, Lemon and Sarsparilla: The Italian Community in South Wales, 1881–1945*, 1991, pp. 97–103.

[10] Love and Gamble, *The Meccano System*, p. 163.

Chapter 10

[1] *Meccano Engineer's Pocket Book*, Liverpool, c.1925; *Meccano Standard Mechanisms* appeared as a series of articles in *Meccano Magazine*, and was published in a separate volume from 1925 onwards. See Roger Beardsley's *The Hornby Companion*, pp. 175–227.

[2] Meccano Elektron Outfit leaflet, 1933.

[3] *Meccano Magazine*, 26, 1922.

[4] Probate of Will of Frank Hornby, 16 September 1931 (codicil 27/8/35).

[5] *The Times*, 31 August 1933.

[6] *Financial Times*, 29 August 1934.
[7] B/ME, A.G.M., Mr. Hornby's Speech, 31 August 1935.
[8] Brown, *British Toy Business*, p. 146.
[9] Ibid., pp. 128, 183.
[10] Ibid., p. 184.
[11] *Guardian Society*, 30 May 2001, pp. 2–3.
[12] In the six months up to September 2001 Hornby's profits were up 52 per cent to £794,000 on a turnover of £10.6 million. This amounted to sales of over 70,000 train sets and 100,000 model locomotives.

Bibliography

Ariès, Phillipe, *Centuries of Childhood*, Paris, 1962

Armytage, W. H. G., *Social History of Engineering*, London, 1961

Ashby, Sir Eric, 'Education for an Age of Technology', in Charles Singer, E. J. Holmyard, A. R. Hall and Trevor I. Williams (eds), *A History of Technology*, vol. 5, Oxford, 1985, pp. 777–98

Auden, W. H., *Collected Shorter Poems, 1927–1957*, London, 1977

Baldwin, Stanley, *On England*, London, 1926

Balmer, Stan, 'Binns Road, 1938–1967: Reminiscences by Stan Balmer as Told to Lloyd Spackman', *New Zealand FMM Magazine*, August 1998

Bartholomew, Charles, *Mechanical Toys*, London, 1979

Bartley, G. C., 'Toys', in G. P. Bevan (ed.), *British Manufacturing Industries*, London, 1876

Beardsley, Roger, *The Hornby Companion*, London, 1992

Betjeman, John, *Collected Poems*, London, 2001

Bill of Complaint in the District Court of the United States for the Southern District of New York, Meccano & John Wanamaker, New York, 8 October 1917

Bridger, Francis, *A Charmed Life: The Spirituality of Potterworld*, London, 2001

Briggs, Asa, *Mass Entertainment*, Adelaide, 1960

Brown, Kenneth, 'Models in History: A Micro Study of Late Nineteenth-century British Entrepreneurship', *Economic History Review*, 42, 1989

— 'The Death of a Dinosaur: Meccano of Liverpool, 1908–1979', *Business Archives: Sources and History*, 1993

— *The British Toy Business: A History Since 1700*, London, 1997

Callois, Roland, *Man, Play & Games*, trans. Meyer Barash, New York, 1962

Carlson, Pierce, *Toy Trains: A History*, London, 1986

Carlyle, Thomas, 'Signs of the Times', *Edinburgh Review*, 49, 1829

Chaucer, Geoffrey, *The Poetry and Prose of Geoffrey Chaucer*, ed. John H. Fisher, London, 1977

Christening Roll for St Simon's St Church, Gloucester Rd, Liverpool, Liverpool PRO, microfilm no. 548

Cremer, W. H., *The Toys of The Little Folks, of all Ages and Countries; or, The Toy Kingdom*, London, 1873

Cross, Gary, *Kids' Stuff*, Cambridge, 1997

Culff, Robert, *The World of Toys*, Feltham, 1969

Dick's Visit to the Home of Meccano, Liverpool, 1925

Dick's Visit to Meccanoland, Liverpool, 1925

District Court of the United States, South District of Ohio, Western Division, Meccano Ltd. & Francis A. Wagner (Trading as the American Mechanical Toy Co.) and the Strobel & Wilken Co., Brief for the Complainant on Final Hearing, Ohio, 1915

Drotner, Kirsten, *English Children and Their Magazines, 1751–1945*, New York, 1988

Fraser, Antonia, *A History of Toys*, New York, 1966

Gladston, H., *Report of the British Association for the Advancement of Science*, London, 1879

Gould, M. P., *Frank Hornby: The Boy Who Made $1,000,000 with a Toy*, London, 1915; reprinted London, 1975

Hornby, Frank, 'Our Future', *Meccano News*, no. 1, November 1920

— 'The Life Story of Meccano: Romance of the World's Greatest Toy', *Meccano Magazine*, 17(1)–18(2) (January 1932–February 1933)

The Hornby Book of Trains, various editions, Liverpool, 1925–1939

How to Run a Meccano Club, Liverpool, 1931

Hughes, Colin, *Lime, Lemon & Sarsparilla: The Italian Community in South Wales, 1881–1945*, Bridgend, 1991

Huntingdon, Bernard, *Along Hornby Lines*, Oxford, 1976

Ikin, Bruce, 'Happiness Unlimited', *Liverpool '68*, no. 15, Liverpool, 1968

Improvements in Toy or Educational Devices for Children and Young People, Mechanics Made Easy Patent, no. 587, 9 Jan. 1901

Jackie Coogan Visits a Meccano Factory, New York, 1926

Jarvis, Adrian, *Samuel Smiles and the Construction of Victorian Values*, Stroud, 1997

Jenkins, Roy, *Baldwin*, London, 1987

Kellet, J. R., *The Impact of Railways on Victorian Cities*, **Place?**, 1969

Kline, Stephen, *Out of the Garden: Toys and Children's Culture in the Age of TV Marketing*, London, 1995

Lansley, Hubert, 'My Meccano Days', *Constructor Quarterly*, Centenary Special Edition, January 1994

Locke, John, *Some Thoughts on Education*, Cambridge, 1968

London Museum, *Toys in the London Museum*, London, 1969

Love, Bert and Jim Gamble, *The Meccano System and The Special Purpose Meccano Sets*, London, 1986

The Magic Carpet, Liverpool, 1925

Martin, John, 'Sleuthing Duke Street', *Constructor Quarterly*, no. 50, December 2000

Mayhew, Henry, *London Labour and the London Poor*, London, 1851

McCrindle, Ron, *The Collector's Guide to Toy Trains: An International Survey of Trains and Railway Accessories from 1880 to the Present Day*, London, 1985

McKibbin, Ross, 'Work and Hobbies in Britain', in Jay Winter (ed.), *The Working Class in Modern British History: Essays in Honour of Henry Pelling*, Cambridge, 1983, pp. 127–46

Meccano, Liverpool, four editions, 1929–1933

The Meccano Book, Liverpool, 1934

The Meccano Book of Engineering, Liverpool, 1928

Meccano News, no. 1, November 1920, Liverpool, 1920

Meccano Products [catalogue], Liverpool, 1920

'Meccano – The Toy that Made Engineering Famous', trade bulletin, Liverpool, 1928

Milne, A. A., *The Complete Winnie the Pooh*, London, 1998

Nasmyth, James, *James Nasmyth: An Autobiography*, ed. Samuel Smiles, London, 1883

Oliver, Paul, Ian Davis and Ian Bentley, *Dunroamin': The Suburban Semi and Its Enemies*, London, 1994

O'Neill, Richard, *Collector's Encyclopaedia of Metal Toys: A Pictorial Guide to Over 2500, from 1850 to the Present Day*, London, 1988

Opie, Iona and Peter Opie (eds), *The Oxford Dictionary of Nursery Rhymes*, Oxford, 1951

Orme, Nicholas, 'The Culture of Children in Medieval England', *Past & Present*, August 1995

— *Medieval Children*, London, 2001

Ottenheimer, Peter, *Toy Autos, 1890–1939: The Peter Ottenheimer Collection*, London, 1987

Our Selling Service: Meccano, Hornby Trains and Accessories, Liverpool, 1928

Pember-Reeves M. S., *Round About a Pound a Week*, **Place?**, 1979

Perren, Richard, *The Meat Trade in Britain, 1840–1914*, Aberdeen, 1978

Phillips, Marion, *The Young Industrial Worker*, Oxford, 1922

Plumb, J. H., 'The New World of the Child in Eighteenth Century England', *Past & Present*, 67, May 1975

Pollock, Linda A., *Forgotten Children: Parent–Child Relations from 1500–1900*, Cambridge, 1983

Quayle, Eric, *The Collector's Book of Children's Books*, London, 1971

Randall, Peter Edward, *The Products of Binns Road: A General Survey*, London, 1977

Read, Donald, *England 1868–1914*, New York, 1979

Rowntree, B. S., *Poverty: A Study of Town Life*, London, 1988

Rowntree, B. S. with M. Kendall, *How the Labourer Lives: A Study of the Rural Labour Problem*, London, 1918

Smiles, Samuel, *Self Help*, London, 1859

Smith, Dennis (ed.), *Perceptions of the Great Engineers*, National Galleries and Museums on Merseyside & Science Museum, Liverpool, 1991

Socialist Research Group, *Genuinely Seeking Work: Mass Unemployment of Merseyside in the 1930s*, Liverpool, 1992

Stewart, Susan, *On Longing: Narratives of the Miniature, the Gigantic, the Souvenir, the Collection*, Baltimore, 1984

Stonehouse, James, *The Streets of Liverpool*, Liverpool, 1879

The Story of Meccano by the Meccano Boy, Liverpool, c.1916

Sutcliffe, A., 'Working Class Housing in Nineteenth Century Britain: A Review of Recent Research', *Bulletin of Labour History*, no. 24, 1972

Sutton-Smith, Brian, *Toys as Culture*, New York, 1986

Taylor, A. J. P., *English History, 1914–1945*, 8th edn, Oxford, 1988

United States Circuit Court of Appeals, 6th Circuit, *Francis A. Wagner (Trading as the American Mechanical Toy Co.)* v *Meccano Ltd.*, Brief for the Plaintive Appellee, 1917

Waugh, Evelyn, *The Diaries of Evelyn Waugh*, ed. Michael Davie, London, 1976

Whitta, Maurice, 'Meccano in 1819', *Model Engineer*, 1998

Williams, E. E., *Germany*, Brighton, 1970

Woodward, Sir Llewellyn, *The Age of Reform*, Oxford, 1962

Wyrall, Everard, *The History of the King's Regiment (Liverpool), 1914–1919*, Vol. 1, *1914–1915*, London, 1928

Zweig, Ferdynand, *The British Worker*, Harmondsworth, 1952